SOCIALIST THOUGHT IN IMAGINATIVE LITERATURE

SOCIALIST THOUGHT IN IMAGINATIVE LITERATURE

Stephen Ingle

ROWMAN AND LITTLEFIELD
TOTOWA, NEW JERSEY

© STEPHEN INGLE 1979

First Published in the United States 1979
By Rowman and Littlefield, Totowa, N.J.

Library of Congress Cataloging in Publication Data

Ingle, Stephen.
  Socialist thought in imaginative literature.

  Includes bibliographical references and index.
  1. English literature—19th century—History and criticism. 2. English
literature—20th century—History and criticism. 3. Socialism and literature.
4. Authors, English—Political and social views.
5. Socialism in Great Britain. I. Title.
PR468.S63I58 1979   820'.9'31   78-23801
ISBN 0-8476-6129-6

Printed in Great Britain

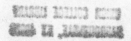

For my parents

Acknowledgements

The author and publishers wish to thank the following who have kindly given permission for the use of copyright material.

Chatto & Windus Ltd and Harper & Row Publishers Inc., on behalf of the Estate of Aldous Huxley and Mrs Laura Huxley, for the extracts from *Brave New World*; A. M. Heath & Co. Ltd on behalf of the George Orwell Estate and Mrs Sonia Brownwell Orwell for the extracts from *Nineteen Eighty-Four* and *Homage to Catalonia*; Lawrence & Wishart Ltd for the extracts from *News from Nowhere*, by William Morris; A. D. Peters & Co. Ltd, on behalf of Arthur Koestler, for the extracts from *Darkness at Noon*, published by Jonathan Cape Ltd; and A. P. Watt Ltd, on behalf of the Estate of H. G. Wells, for the extracts from *A Modern Utopia*.

Contents

1 Introduction: 'The Most Effective Means of Propaganda'

The importance of literature in the study of politics, especially in the development and propagation of political ideas, has not been investigated in any depth in Britain; at least, not by students of politics. Several recent studies indicate a growing interest in the relationship between politics and literature, but none was written by or principally for students of politics. One such study was written by a sociologist, Alan Swingewood. Indeed, there has been a considerable upsurge in interest in the sociology of literature over the last few years, prompted by a growing awareness of the influence of imaginative literature upon Marx himself.[1] As its title, *The Novel and Revolution*,[2] suggests, Swingewood's book deals almost exclusively with the theories and practices of revolution. Naturally enough, its emphasis is sociological and, more specifically, Marxist, though it contains much to interest and inform the student of politics. The second study is part of an older and, from the point of view of the student of politics, less fruitful tradition. It is called *Writers and Politics in Modern Britain*[3] and is written by an English specialist, J. A. Morris. The book is organised thematically but not, from the point of view of the student of politics (for whom it was not written), systematically. Neither book sets out to examine the contribution of creative writers to political thought, though the first more nearly does so, and so neither fills the gap. A third work, *Politics and Literature in Modern Britain*,[4] is a collection of essays by George Watson which, by its nature, would not claim to provide a systematic treatment of the relationship. All the same, these essays probably provide the best example to date of an exploration of the connections between imaginative literature and political thought.

In a collection entitled *Literature and Politics in the Nineteenth Century*,[5] John Lucas begins by admitting that his subject is a daunting one. The relationship between literature and politics is 'problematic, elusive and uncertain', he says, yet these very difficulties make the subject fascinating. Not merely fascinating but important! To the student of literature it is important because—as Lucas says *a propos* of the great nineteenth-century writers—so many chose, at some time or another, to confront political issues in their work. To the student of politics, however, the relationship is more important because of one simple fact: major writers have always been widely read. If any group of men deserve to enjoy the status of opinion-formers, then imaginative writers surely do. Bernard Shaw, an active figure in politics as well as literature, was equally confident of the opinion-forming function of the imaginative writer. He claimed that 'fine art is the subtlest, the most effective means of propaganda in the world except only the example of personal conduct.'[6] Imaginative writers, after all, are highly intelligent men concerned with human affairs and relationships; many of them, as Lucas's book shows, write with the conviction that they can influence men and events. Moreover, though they have received little attention from students of politics in Britain, writers—and intellectuals generally—are certainly considered to be politically important in some societies, notably in France. How then are we to account for this omission in Britain?

I

Richard Hoggart illuminated an important problem when he pointed out that British social scientists are prone to 'mistake the technical boundaries between academic disciplines for divisions within human experience'.[7] This lapse tends to result in students of politics, for example, ignoring material in disciplines not immediately related to their own. Yet as far as politics is concerned, the problem goes deeper than Hoggart indicated. First of all, the study of politics is usually divided into two quite separate categories: political theory and political institutions. Although in principle this represents more a distinction of approach than of subject matter, in practice it distinguishes what is actually being studied. Despite its clear advantages for the organisation of the study of politics in academic institutions, such a division has very little to do with the real world. Its artificiality is potentially misleading to the student and its rigour creates the possibility that important aspects of politics will be insufficiently studied because they fail to fit neatly into either category. This, it can be argued, partially accounts for the fate that has overtaken imaginative literature. Because it does not fall squarely into either camp it is frequently ignored by academic institutions.

But there is more at work here than the sin of omission. That influential group of scholars associated with the behaviourist movement, which has tried to make a science of the study of politics, tends to be highly suspicious of those who, unsympathetic to scientific enquiry, mix opinion with 'knowledge', intuition with 'objectivity'. And quite rightly suspicious, as the words of W. H. Auden clearly show: 'In grasping the character of a society, as in judging the character of an individual, no documents, statistics, "objective" measurements can ever compete with the single intuitive glance.'[8] To behaviourists the 'intuitive glance' is anathema; it strikes at the very basis of their expertise. As Hoggart points out, 'like the early natural scientists, they fear a relapse into alchemy.'[9] For those who wish to approach the study of politics scientifically, imaginative literature does not fit happily into the scheme of things. The possibility that Greenwood's *Love on the Dole* might give a deeper insight into the social attitudes of the working class in Lancashire than any number of sociological surveys, or that Orwell's *Animal Farm* might lead to a fuller understanding of the nature of revolution than any 'scientific' analysis, is not to be countenanced readily. We need not attempt to register so ambitious a claim for imaginative literature, but should certainly maintain that works such as the above add substantially to an understanding of the topics with which they deal; topics, it need hardly be said, of great interest to students of politics.

The natural opposition of the behaviourists to the study of literature's 'intuitive glances' is strengthened by the fact that literary critics have scarcely held out a welcoming hand to the student of politics. F. R. Leavis, for example, although

willing to emphasise that literary studies have significant claims
on the attention of the student of politics as examples of 'important thinking about political and social matters',[10] nevertheless
goes on to warn that literature will only yield what it has
to offer if it is approached as literature. He expands his argument: 'No use of literature is any use unless it is a real use;
literature isn't so much material lying there to be turned over
from the outside, and drawn on, for reference and exemplifica-
tion, by the critically inept.'[11] Of course, Leavis is right to
say that literature should not be used out of context by critics
who are unfamiliar with its subtleties. But the same is equally
true of any discipline, and to make the point as belligerently
as Leavis does is surely to make a 'special case' for literature,
and this is difficult to accept.

Another factor which tends to limit the attention paid by
students of politics (and by politicians) to imaginative writers
is the fact that writers are an inextricable part of 'the intelligentsia', and in Britain at least this is likely to proscribe their
influence upon politics. The British intelligentsia, it would be
generally agreed, has seldom if ever enjoyed the political
eminence or prestige of its continental counterparts.[12]

We can easily recognise the difficulties that Leavis raises
concerning the use, or misuse, of literature out of its context;
we can understand the misgivings of political scientists concerning the 'accuracy' and 'objectivity' of the subject matter of
literature, and we can take note of the limited influence of
the British intelligentsia. But it must be remembered that in
the 'real' world, literature and politics are continually overlap-
ping, as history so amply illustrates. We have only to consider
the example of late eighteenth-century England and of writers
such as Jonathan Swift to appreciate the closeness of the connection. In the nineteenth century, too, the novels of Dickens,
Kingsley, as well as Disraeli and Trollope and the work of
Ruskin, Carlyle and William Morris clearly indicate that 'political passions are often nourished by literature and that literary
taste is much affected by politics.'[13] In the present century
the tradition has been maintained by writers like Shaw, Wells,
Orwell, Huxley, Koestler, and many others.

2

All this is strong evidence of the importance of imaginative literature to the study of politics. But in a sense the evidence may also be slightly misleading, because it might be taken to suggest that it is the degree of political commitment of writers such as Orwell, Wells, Disraeli or Trollope which makes them influential and therefore the most fruitful for study. It is worth considering this proposition in detail, because if it is accepted that imaginative literature is politically important we ought to know which kind is the most important, so let us begin at the beginning: what do we mean by political commitment?

Some critics have gone so far as to suggest that all writers are committed in a specifically political sense, which is vague enough to deprive the phrase of any utility whatsoever. Naturally, if a political stance is adopted explicitly in any work we recognise the fact and attempt to put a label on the stance. If, on the other hand, overtly political themes are not present, have we the right to conclude that, for whatever reason, the writer must be generally content with the existing pattern of social-political arrangements and may be so labelled accordingly? Charques puts the case for doing so in the following terms: 'Those . . . who appear to be politically indifferent or who *make a show* of detachment are . . . the tacit supporters of the prevailing system.'[14] He calls them the servants of the propertied class. At first sight, this might seem an unreasonable conclusion to draw but in fact the argument is not as suspect as the terminology. After all, it is just about impossible to make any criticism of life that is totally devoid of political implications. If a man devotes his life to communicating to his fellows and if he refrains from communicating anything at all about contemporary political events or arrangements, then it is fair to conclude that, for whatever reason, he has come to terms with the existing social-political structure. On the other hand, Charques's argument completely fails to distinguish between the varying intensities of attitudes held by writers about politics and society. It makes sense to label a writer 'committed' if he introduces overtly political themes; it makes no sense at all to call one who doesn't do so 'committed', in the same sense, to the status quo! The first is far more deeply committed than the second, and thus merits the description 'politically committed'. Charques may well be right to point out that political commitment is universal and necessary, but his point is not of great substance. What matters is the *intensity*, not the ubiquity, of political commitment.

Having thus clarified what we mean by commitment, is it now safe to assume that writers with a high 'commitment score' will necessarily prove the most fruitful for the student of politics? I think we need to explore this assumption more closely. I believe it to be only partly true, and where false, dangerous.

George Orwell, who would score as high on commitment as any recent British writer, was one who analysed his own attitude to writing and to commitment in depth.[15] He elucidated four motives for writing which, he thought, were to be found in every author, though mixed in different proportions. They were: sheer egoism, the desire to be remembered after one's death and to be talked about during one's life; aesthetic enthusiasm, a perception of beauty, a pleasure taken in the impact produced by the juxtaposition of sounds, a sense of rhythm, a desire to share important aesthetic experiences; historical impulse which, since it has heavy Orwellian connotations, is best described in his own words as a 'desire to see things as they are, to find out true facts and to store them up for the use of posterity'; political purpose, the desire to push the world in a certain direction, to 'alter other people's ideas of the kind of society that they should strive after'.

Orwell goes on to tell us that these impulses may be at war with each other, each struggling for the ascendancy. He himself felt that had it not been for his own involvement in the Spanish Civil War, the strength of the first three would have outweighed decisively that of the fourth.

All the same, Orwell did not imagine that commitment need dominate the work of other writers. He did believe, however, that the 1930s were unique and that in such a politically charged atmosphere (but only then!) 'a novelist who simply disregards the major public events of the moment is generally either a footler or a plain idiot.' Even so it is interesting to note that Henry Miller, whose meeting with Orwell had stimulated this particular essay, was readily acknowledged by him to be neither a footler nor an idiot. Miller was thought to be a writer of considerable value because he had managed to maintain some genuine contact with the life of the 'ordinary man'. Although Orwell maintained his criticism that Miller and those like him 'always take care to stay inside bourgeois-democratic society, making use of its protection while disclaiming responsibility for it',[16] it is quite apparent that Orwell recognised artistic and social merit in Miller's work and believed that Miller had something important to say about politics.

In another celebrated essay, Orwell criticised the apparent absence of political commitment in the writing of Charles Dickens. He found an 'utter lack of any constructive suggestion anywhere in his work'.[17] Yet in the final analysis Orwell was prepared to acknowledge the value of Dickens's own brand of social commitment and to conclude with a far more sympathetic appraisal of Dickens's position than that with which he had begun: 'I said earlier that Dickens is not *in the accepted sense* a revolutionary writer. But it is not at all certain that a merely formal criticism of society may not be just as "revolutionary" . . . as the politico-economic criticism which is fashionable at this moment.'[18] In fact, Orwell comes round to accept as perfectly viable Dickens's view on the primacy of reforming human nature in the revolutionary agenda. So although himself politically committed, Orwell accepted the value of writers with different commitments, and different levels of commitment, indicating the measure of their worth by his own standards—that is, their contribution to 'revolution'. In other words, Orwell thought these works to be *politically important despite their lack of clear political commitment*.

If Orwell's notion of commitment is taken more seriously than he apparently took it, it would rule out certain kinds of book from consideration by the serious reader, especially in a 'political' age. Yet how much more restrictive are the ideas of Jean-Paul Sartre. Sartre believed the very nature of literature—or anyway prose writing—was one of total political commitment; of a *littérature engagée*. For Sartre the notion of commitment was quite specific—it meant commitment to his particular idea of freedom. The task of literature then, is to accompany or indeed to stimulate the process of permanent revolution in the classless society.[19] For Sartre, the immediate task is obviously to work towards the creation of such a society, to be a catalyst energising men to change the world they live in by 'anticipating the view of the potentially free reader'.

It is not difficult to see where Sartre's theories lead us. His theory of commitment, like Orwell's, provides criteria for assessing the 'revolutionary' merit of a work, which is held to be more or less synonymous with its literary merit. But Sartre holds to the theory much more tenaciously than Orwell. He is more open to the charge that his 'commitment' is detrimental to the 'true' aims of literature, more open to the charge, to use Julien Benda's celebrated phrase, of the '*trahison des clercs*'.[20]

Benda argued that modern intellectuals, especially writers, occupied a role in society similar to that of the medieval clerks: they transmitted values. By accusing the modern clerks of treason, Benda implied that they were defecting from their long-term responsibilities. In being politically committed to the extent of becoming the mouthpiece of a particular ideology, a writer was abandoning his independent judgement, hence his literary integrity. Benda had in mind the pre-1939 neo-fascist writers but after the war he made the same indictment of the pro-communist writers in a Preface to a new edition of his book and more recently in his critique of Sartre's existentialism; others have laid the charge at the door of pro-American liberal writers.

Conor Cruise O'Brien, whose active and prominent career as both politician and writer adds weight to his views, has argued along similar lines to Benda. The theme of O'Brien's argument[21] though, is to distinguish between various kinds of political commitment. So much political commitment, he argues, is assumed for the sake of fashion. As such it is 'treasonable'.[22] He argues, also, that a writer may, in his early career, strike up a mood evoking such a response from the public that he is forced into a pattern which soon ceases to represent his true feelings.[23] But of all, the most serious treason is the shedding of what Camus describes as 'the reserve which befits a good witness'; the taking on of the mantle of preacher. This must inevitably cause the writer to express thoughts which he does not necessarily think, because he must strive to be politically consistent. In short, for O'Brien the great treason of the clerk is to be in a false relation to politics. He makes the point that some sort of political perspective is a natural consequence of the exceptionally acute consciousness of the writer, as we have already observed, but it must be founded upon what O'Brien terms a 'true' consciousness.

O'Brien's argument can be seen to rest squarely upon the canons of 'objective truth'; this he freely admits. Orwell, too, was dedicated to the notion of objective truth. Much of his reputation as a writer is founded upon his integrity, upon his 'prose like a windowpane' which looked out upon the truth. But as one critic points out with reference to a major work: '*Homage to Catalonia* is about as unbiased a piece of history as an account of the English Civil War written by one of John Lilburne's Levellers.'[24] The reason Orwell is regarded as a writer of integrity is that he wrote *what he thought was the truth*; as Trilling said, he *was* what he wrote. It is in precisely this sense surely that a writer may be in a true or false relation to politics, to use O'Brien's phrase. A writer is not obliged to search out canons of objective truth as O'Brien would have him do, but to state accurately his own beliefs in order to fulfil the clerical function with integrity.

Few would deny the proposition that literature, if it becomes subservient to propaganda, ceases to have any literary value. As Orwell remarked, '. . . any writer who accepts the discipline of a political party is sooner or later faced with the alternative: toe the line or shut up.'[25] But the borderline between propaganda and literature is not calculated upon the *degree* of political commitment, rather upon the extent to which that commitment accurately reflects the beliefs and values of the writer. Where it does not, the exercise ceases to be a literary one in any strict sense. A writer who 'turns his back from a train of thought because it may lead to a heresy'[26] is no longer engaged in literature. He may still provide valuable material for the student of politics but ought to be considered as a propagandist not as an imaginative writer.

Sartre notwithstanding, political commitment is not a sufficient reason for the student of politics to study a particular writer: neither is it reasonable to assume that the quality of his writing will necessarily be diminished as a result of his commitment, however strong. If the status of a work is measured by its impact upon thinking people, its creative and stylistic qualities and the range of its philosophy, then the student of politics is likely to concern himself with authors and works whose status is beyond doubt and whose philosophical focus is mainly social-political: *but this, and not the reverse, must be his order of priorities.*[27]

3

In this book we shall be dealing only with writers who considered themselves to be socialists or who wrote about themes important to socialism. It may well be true that as a motive for writing, political commitment is more prominent, in Britain anyway, among writers who considered themselves to be 'of the left'. Perhaps dissatisfaction with the existing condition of society tends generally to be a stronger passion than satisfaction. All the same, it would not be difficult to conduct a similar kind of study, if one chose, into the political influences of 'right-wing' imaginative writers. Let there be no illusion, though, that we have restricted ourselves to a neat, easily managed set of inte-grated themes, for socialism is no such thing. This is not the place to undertake a detailed investigation of the nature and history of socialism; in any case this has been done before and done frequently.[28] All the same it is worth re-emphasising the breadth and richness of the socialist tradition. In a recent book R. N. Berki[29] describes socialism as 'not a single thing, but a range, an area, an open texture, a self-contradiction'. Berki's thesis is that major tendencies within socialism might not always pull in the same direction—might indeed pull in opposite directions—and that any analysis needs to take full account of socialism's contradictions. Of the contradictions which Berki's analysis suggests, one seems to be of fundamental importance to the development of socialism in Britain: it is that between a tradition of thought which seeks to give wider scope to individuals to play a part in the decisions which affect their lives, holding, almost invariably, that this can only be achieved in an egalitarian society; and one which believes that although government must be carried out in the interests of the many, it can only be managed *on their behalf* by their superiors. The first tradition we shall call the 'moralistic' and the second the 'scientific'.[30] The moralistic tradition, then, seeks social justice, an end to exploitation and alienation, and the creation of a classless society. It emphasises the individual's right to a full, unalienated life. The scientific, on the other hand, looks for the application of scientific knowledge and techniques to social and political organisations; it attacks the waste and inefficiency of capitalist society and believes that a centrally controlled socialist state run by a scientifically trained élite would be capable of maximising welfare for all. It empha-sises the collective rather than the individual good. Divided in their aims for reconstituting society the moralist and the scientific traditions also suggest different means to achieve their aims. The moralistic tradition is likely to favour large-scale and rapid, maybe revolutionary change, whereas the scientific is more likely to support a slower process of change, which is capable of being controlled. Divided, then, as to means and ends, the two traditions nevertheless have much in common, indeed complement each other, in their criticisms of capitalist society. What they share is an unwillingness to tolerate a society in which the majority of the citizens appear to be doomed to a life of poverty and frustration.

This study comprises three separate sections. The first deals with criticisms of capitalist society, the second with the means of changing that society and the third with the conflicting views of the socialist future. It is worth emphasising that the book's main objective is not to substantiate and demarcate the differences between two autonomous versions or traditions of socialism. Berki argues that socialism as a whole is the richer for containing these and other sometimes conflicting tendencies: it is just as true to say that the contradictions we shall be discussing (and no doubt others) may be found in many individual socialist thinkers. Perhaps their contribution to the development of socialist thought is also the richer.[31] Our main objective is simply to see what light imaginative literature throws on the nature of one of British socialism's central contradictions, and thus on the nature of British socialism itself.

The perspective of the creative writer encompasses much in the way of political, philosophical, cultural, social and economic history. It would be an invidious task to provide even the most rudimentary background to contemporary developments in these areas by way of introduction; so no such thing is going to be attempted. In any case this has already been done by many authors.[32] Other short-cuts, too, will be necessary. In terminology, for example, we shall be using the words which socialists have tended to use, without subjecting them to close scrutiny; in a sense words like 'capitalism' and 'working class' are a kind of shorthand which, so long as the imprecision is understood and not taken advantage of, have a meaning and an obvious value in communication.

Having resisted the claims of an historical and political introduction, and having restricted ourselves not merely to creative literature but to that section of it which deals with socialist themes, further restrictions might seem uncalled for: not so; the field remains vast. Which books ought we to discuss? The first problem here is one of time-scale, the second of author and material selection. In a way both are partly solved by common sense. Since the book is about British socialism and those writers who concerned themselves with themes central to it, a sensible time-scale would extend from the 'rebirth' of British socialism up to the establishment in power of the first socialist government with a parliamentary majority: that is, from the early 1880s to the late 1940s. Selecting a time-scale helps considerably with selecting authors. It is clear not only from critical acclaim, but also from the results of surveys of Labour MPs which will be discussed later, who the most influential writers were likely to have been. As for selection of material, common sense, the chief criterion for selection, is admittedly a Humpty Dumpty phrase, meaning pretty well what the user wishes. The material we shall be considering in the coming pages will contain extracts, books, or even authors, not considered especially important by some, and others, no doubt, will consider that vital material has been omitted. This must be accepted as inevitable, but there will be general agreement about the importance and interest of most of the material. (The case has already been argued at length for studying material which is not overtly 'political', even at the expense of some which is!)

This is not primarily intended to be an 'inter-disciplinary' study. It is a study about certain hitherto neglected dimensions of the development of socialist thought in Britain, and is intended primarily to broaden the outlook of students of politics (in the widest sense of the phrase) and to indicate the nature and importance of the influence of imaginative writers upon the development of politics through the example of socialism.

A CRITIQUE OF
CAPITALIST SOCIETY

There are basically three methods by which the writers we shall be looking at criticised the social system in which they lived. The first, associated in some measure with the 'realist' school, was basically descriptive. That is to say, writers tried to gain the sympathy of their largely middle-class readership by descriptions of the lives of the poor. In some cases such descriptions provided a basis for later social and political analysis, but not always so; in any case, this kind of formal description, as a means of attempting to influence one's readers, can be allowed to stand on its own. The second and third methods concentrate on two different schemes of analysis. The second method (associated with what we have called the 'moralistic' tradition) emphasises the moral implications of the social divisions within capitalism; it emphasises the moral effects of social division on the lives of the poor and the wealthy. It suggests that only in an equal society may the inevitably immoral social foundation of capitalism be dug up and replaced. The third method (associated with the 'scientific' tradition), on the other hand, suggests that the evils of capitalism are chiefly managerial, so to say. We are to be persuaded that misery is chiefly a consequence of a failure of leadership; that what is needed is not an equal society at all, but a better-run society in which the most able will look after the interests of society as a whole.

Although different, these methods of criticism are quite clearly related and draw sustenance from each other. In a sense the distinction between the two forms of analysis only becomes important when their propagators deal with what is to be done rather than what is wrong; when they become prescriptive and not just descriptive. All the same, each of the three methods of criticism provides a different perspective on capitalist society and therefore merits separate consideration, though works by H. G. Wells appear in both the chapter dealing with moralistic and that dealing with scientific critiques, illustrating the overlap. This first section, then, will deal in turn with descriptive, moralistic and scientific critiques of capitalist society.

2 The Poverty of the Many

There can be little doubt that of all the many and sometimes conflicting strands of socialist thought, a basic belief in equality (normally economic) is one of the most prominent and most enduring. Equally, the manifest and undenied economic inequalities of capitalist society have been a potent source of motivation for socialists. Moreover, it has always seemed unarguable to socialists that abundant misery was, in fact, an unavoidable consequence of any economic system based upon inequality, for inequality left the many poor and miserable and only a few wealthy and comfortable. None of its defenders sought to refute the charge of inequality and misery levelled at capitalist society. What they did claim, though, was that inequality was man's natural condition, and not the consequence of this or that social system; that misery was, to put it bluntly, man's lot. Naturally enough, those who said this usually had other men in mind, and not themselves, when they accepted the inevitability and abundance of misery. All the same, to admit that their argument was a selfish one is not to say it was erroneous. Indeed, those who argued that inequality was a natural condition could cite history as their chief defence. Where was the society of equals? When were the many not poor? They could also, if they were more selective, lean upon the teachings of the Church[1] (though so, with equal justice, could their opponents): had not John XII condemned over one hundred Franciscans to the stake because they had put their

egalitarian beliefs into practice? But above all, experience and
common sense indicated to its defenders that inequality provided
a basis for enduring social stability. It provided, that is to
say, a society in which everyone knew his place; his estate,
high or lowly, was numbered—and he knew it. 'You are to
consider', Johnson told Boswell, 'that it is our duty to maintain
the subordination of civilised society; and where there is gross
or shameful deviation from rank, it should be punished so
as to deter others from the same perversion.'[2]

It would be unfair to those defenders of economic inequality
though, were we to believe that their fatalistic acceptance of
superior status rendered them incapable of generosity to their
inferiors; the reverse would be nearer the truth. The British
aristocracy traditionally thought of itself as the guardian of
the interests of all citizens, a theory expounded by many, and
by none more clearly than Benjamin Disraeli. The Tory Democrats, fired by compassion, could indeed contemplate any social
reform so long as it did not destroy their privileged position.
The middle class, too, was willing to champion the cause of
social reform, though always with a careful eye on the interests
of industry.

For many socialists, though, paternalism and reformism were
so much cant. Bernard Shaw claimed that the ruling classes
were 'willing to sacrifice almost anything for the poor except
the power and practice of robbing them'.[3] Nothing less than
an end to poverty and inequality would satisfy the moralist
socialist, and what above all else raised his passion was the
belief that the misery of the masses could be avoided altogether.
They sought to move the reader by the power of their descriptions of the conditions of the poor. As we shall see, they sought
to break down the barrier of ignorance which they believed
prevented the wealthy from grasping the realities of poverty
and from understanding that it was not necessarily the result
of idleness and drunkenness.

I

George Gissing (1857–1902),[4] though he probably would not
have intended or desired it, fulfilled just such a task. He wrote
five novels of working-class life in the 1880s, *Workers in the
Dawn*; *The Unclassed*; *Demos, A Story of English Socialism*; *Thyrza*;

and *The Nether World*. Gissing was not interested in furthering
the cause of socialism, of helping to awaken class consciousness,
just the opposite in fact.[5] In *Demos*, the book's 'hero', a young
landowner named Eldon, despite some sympathy for the revolutionary movements of continental Europe, reviles their English
counterpart as being 'stamped commonplace, like everything
originating with the English lower classes'.[6] The intelligent
young working-class socialist, Richard Mutimer, whose sudden
acquisition of wealth and subsequent adventures form the plot
of the book, like Gissing's other radical or socialist characters,
is crushed by faults within his own personality and by events
outside his control. Similarly, John Pether, a revolutionary figure
in *Workers in the Dawn*, dies the death of an idiot, in total
isolation. John Hewett in *The Nether World*, whilst a more
sympathetic figure, is shown to be his own and his family's
worst enemy; a man whose socialism accompanies a native
streak of cantankerous idleness.

Gissing, like many British intellectuals was greatly influenced
by August Comte's positivist philosophy, especially during the
first years of the 1880s, and the idea of an immutable social
order never left him; the one central theme which emerges
from his novels is that life tends to be miserable and there
is little man can do about it. Swingewood points out the Gissing
novel contains 'no hint of the great events of the 1880s, the
rapid development of miltant trade unionism and escalation
of industrial conflict',[7] which is quite true. But then, Gissing
was a fatalist and, as he makes abundantly clear, could not
conceive of any working class movement being successful. This
seems to be the whole point of *Demos*, for Mutimer puts his
new wealth in to an Owenite rural industrial community which
fails; its failure appears to us inevitable. What Gissing wants
to say (whether he is right is another matter) is that the working
class is incapable of self-improvement. 'Our opportunities', says
Eldon's mother, 'lead us to see truths to which the eyes of
the poor and ignorant are blind.'[8] Gissing's fatalism leads him
to conclude that the poor must remain blind and ignorant.[9]

Despite his own bleak philosophy, Gissing's many descriptive
passages of the lives of the urban poor are so powerful, so
unremittingly cheerless, that the reader is forced to conclusions
quite different from the author's. We are not convinced by
Eldon's Tory Democracy: 'To the individual poor man or

woman I would give my last penny. It is when they rise against
me as a class that I become pitiless.' Still less are we convinced
by the reasoning of the vicar, Wyvern, the soul of common
sense, when he declares that happiness is fairly evenly spread
irrespective of material benefits and social position. 'Go along
the poorest street in the East End of London', he tells Eldon,
'and you will hear as much laughter, witness as much gaiety,
as in any thoroughfare of the West.'

The message to the poor, then, is to recognise their blindness
and ignorance and accept the life to which they have been
born. But this fatalism is not served by Gissing's harrowing
descriptions of the lives of the poor, especially since the spiritual
consolations of accepting one's social fate appear to be minimal.
The conditions under which Mutimer's jilted sweetheart, Emma
Vine, and her sisters live are so appalling as to make fatalistic
passivity an almost impossible response.

By the time he wrote *The Nether World* in 1889 Gissing's
anti-socialist views had moderated and from the beginning the
reader is brought to a much more realistic appreciation of
the rigours of working-class life than the Reverend Wyvern
appears to have had. Speaking about one of the streets in
which the poor live, Gissing tells us: 'At this corner the east
wind blew with malice such as it never puts forth save where
there are poorly clad people to be pierced . . .'[10] Certainly those
who lived in that street, like young Jane Snowdon, abandoned
by her father, and the Hewett family, expended little energy
on laughter and gaiety. 'Who was John Hewett that he should
look for pleasant things in his course through the world? "We
are the lower orders; we are the working classes", he said
bitterly to his friends, and that seemed the final answer to
all his aspirations.' But there are many worse off than John
Hewett. His son's 'honeymoon' constitutes one day's outing
to the Crystal Palace and even here the reality of poverty
does not allow them to escape. As they sit waiting for the
fireworks, Gissing describes the 'great review of the People'
which passes them.

On the whole how respectable they are, how sober, how
deadly dull! See how worn-out the poor girls are becoming,
how they gape, what listless eyes most of them have! The
stoop in the shoulders so universal among them merely means

over-toil in the workroom. Not one in a thousand shows the elements of taste in dress; vulgarity and worse glares in all but every costume. Observe the middle-aged women; it would be small surprise that their good looks had vanished, but whence comes it they are animal, repulsive, absolutely vicious in ugliness? Mark the men in their turn: four in every six have visages so deformed by ill-health that they excite disgust; their hair is cut down to within half an inch of their scalp; their legs are twisted out of shape by evil conditions of life from birth upwards.

Young Hewett's wife, unlike her drunken husband, was never able to abandon herself to the pleasures of the day. 'She was thinking all the time that on the morrow it would be necessary to pawn her wedding ring.'

Sidney Kirkwood, the working-class hero of the story, is by no means a revolutionary, but neither does he accept the existing social structure. With the ripening of his intellect, we are told, he saw 'only more and more reason to condemn and execrate those social disorders of which his own wretched experience was but an illustration'. Those with whom he discusses such matters, like John Hewett and Michael Snowdon, Jane's grandfather, are both socialist sympathisers. Moreover there can be no denying the vehemence with which Gissing criticises a social system which permits the kind of misery he so remorselessly portrays, and if he does not offer an analysis of the social system leading to the possibility of socialist alternatives, he does not leave us with the same note of condescension as in *Demos*. When Kirkwood meets Jane Snowdon at her grandfather's grave on his anniversary they appear as individuals broken by the social system, thwarted in all their ambitions, stunted intellectually and spiritually.

For all his sympathy with the inhabitants of the nether world Gissing cannot offer them hope: they are doomed. If there is any choice left them it is to act honourably, as do Jane Snowdon and Kirkwood, or dishonourably, like Bob Hewett and the vicious, sadistic Clem Peckover. Joseph Snowdon, a fairly likeable rogue, dies alone and penniless in the United States, having lost his fortune. Even Clara Hewett, self-willed and ruthless, who strikes out from the nether world to become an actress—indeed *especially* Clara Hewett—cannot escape. Acid

thrown in her face brings her back to a life without hope,
brings her back to hell. Gissing's intention is not to motivate
us into social action; his view of human nature seems to be
too pessimistic to permit hope for improvement.[11] His disparage-
ment of what Goode, in his introduction to the Harvester edition,
calls 'the destructive futility of philanthropy' may be taken
as epitomising his attitude to social reform. All the same, *The
Nether World* was, as Goode points out, considered to be a
'valuable document in the cause of reform', and it would
be difficult for the reader not to extend sympathy towards
Gissing's characters.[12]

2

George Bernard Shaw was a contemporary of Gissing's, an
avowed socialist, and a man with equally outspoken views on
the nature and effects of poverty.[13]

> The crying need of the nation is not for better morals, cheaper
> bread, temperance, liberty, culture, redemption of fallen sis-
> ters and erring brothers, nor the grace, love and fellowship
> of the Trinity, but simply for enough money.

Shaw believed that 'the greatest of our evils and the worst
of our crimes is poverty' and this was the theme of his most
active political campaigning. The most enduring pictures which
Shaw paints of poverty, accompanied by an analysis of its
causes, are to be found in his early plays,[14] *Widowers' Houses*
(produced in London 1892), *Mrs Warren's Profession* (first performed privately in London in 1902 and not publicly until
1925 in Birmingham, though it was produced in America in
1905) and *Major Barbara* (first produced in 1905). *Widowers'
Houses* provoked a major reaction when it was produced. In
the author's words: 'The newspapers discussed the play for
a whole fortnight not only in the ordinary theatrical notices
and criticisms, but in leading articles and letters.'[15] Shaw sought
to bring to the attention of the English middle class the horrors
of urban squalor

> which arise from the fact that the average homebred English-
> man, however honourable and goodnatured he may be in
> his private capacity, is, as a citizen, a wretched creature

who, whilst clamoring for a gratuitous millenium, will shut his eyes to the most villainous abuses if the remedy threatens to add another penny in the pound to the rates and taxes which he has to be half cheated, half coerced into paying. In *Widowers' Houses* I have shown middle class respectability and younger son gentility fattening on the poverty of the slum as flies fatten on filth.

The story concerns Sartorius, a self-made wealthy man, whose self-willed daughter Blanche is engaged to Trench, an exceedingly well connected young man of modest means. We learn that Sartorius's money comes from slum landlordism and that, by virtue of his position on the local council (vestry) he is able to ignore most of the sanitary and safety regulations, thereby maximising his profits. Lickcheese is his rent collector, well aware of the odium of his trade but caught in a trap of social necessity.

Why, see here gentlemen. Look at that bag of money on the table. Hardly a penny of that but there was a hungry child crying for the bread it would have bought. But I got it for him—screwed and worried and bullied it out of them. I—look here, gentlemen: I'm pretty seasoned to the work; but there's money there I couldn't have taken if it hadn't been for the thought of my own children depending on me for giving him satisfaction.

This information Lickcheese discloses to Trench who decides, on the spot, that marriage with Blanche is impossible unless they live entirely on his own meagre income. Sartorius, trying to save his daughter's happiness, defends his position.

My young friend: these poor people do not know how to live in proper dwellings: they would wreck them in a week. You doubt me: try it for yourself. You are welcome to replace all the missing banisters, handrails, cistern lids and dusthole stops at your own expense; and you will find them missing again in less than three days: burnt, sir, every stick of them.

Sartorius's most crushing argument, however, is to point out to Trench that his own income derives from property managed by Sartorius. Shattered, Trench asks if he is just as bad as Sartorius. 'If, when you say you are just as bad as I am, you mean that you are just as powerless to alter the state of society, then you are unfortunately quite right.' Trench is eventually won over and marries Blanche. The financial future of all is secured when, on Lickcheese's advice, Sartorius and Trench decide to improve their properties so as to secure the maximum compensation when the properties are to be demolished as part of an urban renewal programme. The emphasis in the play is on the living conditions of the poor; social analysis is rarely explicit and we are made aware that Shaw's principal intention is simply to inform us of the wretched lives of the majority of our fellow citizens.

The theme of *Mrs Warren's Profession* revolves around a mother-daughter relationship. Vivie Warren, just down from Newnham College where she has attained considerable academic distinction, is on the point of deciding her future. She anticipates trouble from her mother, whom she has met infrequently and knows little of, and is not to be disappointed. In the ensuing struggle Mrs Warren allows it to be known that her wealth is the result of prostitution, and Vivie, true to the standards of the *fin-de-siècle* new woman, extends her full sympathy and understanding. Mrs Warren's story is of two sets of half-sisters who travelled different paths. One set opted for 'respectable' work, the first half-sister dying of lead poisoning working twelve hours a day in a white-lead factory. 'She only expected to get her hands a little paralysed; but she died.'[16] The second half-sister did better. She married a labourer and 'kept his room neat and tidy on eighteen shillings a week—until he took to drink.' But Mrs Warren's full sister Lizzie took to the streets, and made herself comfortable; Mrs Warren followed her example. 'My dear mother', says Vivie at the end of the story, 'you are a wonderful woman: you are stronger than all England.' The *détente*, however, does not endure; for Vivie discovers that her mother is the manageress of a chain of top-class European brothels! Having raised herself from the misery imposed by capitalist society Mrs Warren is now profiting from 'the system'. She does not, like the wealthy heroine of one of H. G. Well's novels, use her money to build hostels for working-class girls to live in cheaply;[17] instead she builds more brothels. Vivie leaves her mother, sets up as an accountant, and makes her own way in the world without the help of her mother's tainted money. Shaw's major concern is to force

his middle-class readers to understand that poverty is so unacceptable a condition that any step towards avoiding it must be
taken—even prostitution!

Major Barbara continues this analysis of the nature and effects
of poverty. Andrew Undershaft, armaments manufacturer and
millionaire, dominates the play. He is described by Shaw in
the Preface as one who has become aware that 'our first duty,
to which every other consideration should be sacrificed, is not
to be poor.'[18] Shaw is quite clear as to his meaning; even
if men would choose to be poor they must not be permitted
the privilege, for:

> ... what does this Let Him Be Poor mean? It means let
> him be weak. Let him be ignorant. Let him become a nucleus
> of disease. Let him be a standing exhibition and example
> of ugliness and dirt. Let him have rickety children. Let him
> be cheap, and drag his fellows down to his own price by
> selling himself to do their work. Let his habitations turn
> our cities into poisonous congeries of slums. Let his daughters
> infect our young men with the diseases of the streets, and
> his sons revenge him by turning the nation's manhood into
> scrofula, cowardice, cruelty, hypocrisy, political imbecility,
> and all the other fruits of oppression and malnutrition ...

Undershaft's daughter, Barbara, is a major in the Salvation
Army, working in the East End of London with her fiancé
Cusins, a professor of Greek. Undershaft is separated from his
wife and family but the forthcoming marriage of his son necessit-
ates a temporary reunion. His philosophy, already expounded
in the play's Preface, is clearly at odds with Barbara's pacific
Christianity. She invites her father to come down to the West
Ham shelter to see what the Army is doing for the poor.
He accepts on the understanding that she will go with him
to his munitions works.

Shaw uses Undershaft's visit to paint for the audience a
vivid picture of the evils of poverty, through 'representational'
working-class characters. Peter Shirley is one. He is a skilled
worker who cannot find a job because he has become too
old; 'sent to the knackers like an old horse'. 'You'd pass still',
says Barbara, surprised, 'why didn't you dye your hair?'[19]
If Shirley is 'the victim', Snobby Price is 'the survivor'. He
stands by his class, doing as little as possible so as to leave

half the job for his 'fellow workers'. Also he is 'fly enough to know wot's inside the law and wot's outside it; and inside it I do as the capitalists do: pinch wot I can lay me 'ands on'. More important though, Shaw attacks the role of charity organisations like the Salvation Army, indeed he attacks the very virtue of compassion. Does he realise, Cusins asks, what the Army does for the poor. Certainly he does: it draws their teeth! By keeping their thoughts on 'heavenly things' it keeps them off trade unionism and socialism. Indeed, as a good businessman Undershaft writes out a cheque to the Army for £5,000. Barbara comes to realise that she is nothing but an administrator of conscience money for the rich when Bill Walker cynically asks her: 'Wot prawce selvytion nah?'

3

Around about the time that Shaw's Mrs Warren was making her first appearance before an invited London audience, a young American author, a committed socialist, came to Britain as a war correspondent. He arrived in London in the summer of 1902 only to discover that his contract had been cancelled. He decided to undertake a sociological investigation of the life of the poor in the East End of London. It is to this accident we owe the existence of Jack London's *The People of the Abyss*, an account of the life of the poor as gripping as anything written by George Orwell. London describes the Abyss as a 'huge man-killing machine', showing that it entices men in from the countryside who are physically healthy and within two or at most three generations, renders them unsuitable for strenuous employment. Like Orwell after him, London backs up general statements of this nature with factual evidence. In this case he cites the composition of the Metropolitan Police; approximately 12,000 country-born as against 3,000 London-born. These observations remind us that 60 per cent of volunteers for military service in the South African War were rejected on medical grounds. Indeed, in 1902 the government felt the need to establish an interdepartmental committee on physical deterioration,[20] whose report suggested that the deterioration was consequent upon man's adapting himself to an urban environment. London mixes this sociological approach with powerful descriptive passages, for example that of Frying Pan Alley:[21]

We went up the narrow gravelled walk. On the benches on either side arrayed a mass of miserable and distorted humanity . . . It was a welter of rags and filth, of all manner of loathsome skin diseases, open sores, bruises, grossness, indecency, leering monstrosities and bestial faces.

He describes his travels to the Poplar workhouse with two tramps, an ex-carter and an ex-carpenter, who pick up and eat any piece of food, whatever its condition—apple cores, orange peel, greengage stones (for the kernels), and so on—and casually asks: 'O dear, soft people, full of meat and blood, how can you ever understand?' And this state of affairs exists, as he points out, 'in the heart of the greatest, wealthiest, and most powerful empire the world has ever seen'. It is worth remembering that 1902 was the year of Edward VII's abortive coronation (as well as the actual ceremony), when, because the festivities were postponed, some of the prepared food was distributed among the poor. Robert Cecil writes: 'It was the poor of Whitechapel and not the sovereign kings, princes and diplomats who had the consommé de faisan aux quenelles, côtelettes de bécassines à la Souvaroff'; but not, however, the 2,500 quails, which were put on ice![22]

Another source of material which London uses quite extensively is documentation, usually with harrowing effect. The following is a doctor's report to an inquest at the coroner's office on the death of an elderly woman. The doctor

found the deceased lying across the fender on her back. She had one garment and her stockings on. The body was quite alive with vermin, and all the clothes in the room were absolutely grey with insects. Deceased was very badly nourished and was very emaciated. She had extensive sores on her legs, and her stockings were adherent to those sores. The sores were the result of vermin.

But London is not a sociologist, he is a novelist, and provides a more effective conclusion than dispassionate analysis would allow. 'If it is not good for your mother and my mother so to die, then it is not good for this woman, whosoever's mother she might be, so to die.' He treats white-lead poisoning (as an example of industrial illness) at much greater length, giving a detailed official description of 'the typical dissolution of a young, healthy, well-developed girl' who works in a white-lead factory. He goes on to quote several documented cases of young girls dying under the most painful circumstances, reminding us perhaps of the death of Mrs Warren's half-sister, who 'only expected to get her hands a little paralysed'. London completes this section by telling us about one Frank Cavilla who, after eighteen months without work, during which time his family slowly starved, cut the throats of his wife and four children with a pocket knife. London concludes:

> The unfit and the unneeded! The miserable and despised and forgotten, dying in the social shambles. The progeny of prostitution—of the prostitution of men and women and children, of flesh and blood, and sparkle and spirit; in brief, the prostitution of labour. If this is the best that civilisation can do for the human, then give us howling and naked savagery. Far better to be a people of the wilderness and desert, of the cave and the squatting place, than to be a people of the machine and the Abyss.

Frank Cavilla's death finds an echo in that classic novel of working-class life, *The Ragged Trousered Philanthropists* by Robert Tressell, written between 1906 and the author's death in 1911. On his way home from work one night the novel's hero, Owen, sees a placard outside a newsagent's:

TERRIBLE DOMESTIC TRAGEDY
Double Murder and Suicide

The details of the incident, very similar to that which overtook the Cavillas, are not disclosed immediately; but it is referred to on several occasions, as if weighing on Owen's mind. Over one hundred and fifty pages later he is still ruminating on the incident:[23]

> He thought of the man who had killed his wife and children. The jury had returned the usual verdict, 'Temporary Insanity'. It never seemed to occur to these people that the truth was that to continue to suffer hopelessly like this was evidence of permanent insanity.

Owen believes that capitalism, not this miserable husband-and-father, is to blame. Indeed, before he died the man had scrawled:

'This is not *my* crime but society's'. The condition of permanent suffering and permanent hopelessness in which families like this one were having to live provides the background to the book, the theme of which is Owen's attempt to convert his workmates to a 'true consciousness' of their situation. He works for a firm of painters and decorators and describes in detail the numerous ruses which the firm employs to 'bodge' and save money, so as to increase its profit, including paying its workers a Ricardian wage. The workers accept their pittance and the many humiliations which accompany it. After all, in the words of one, 'it can't never be altered . . . There's always been rich and poor in the world, and there always will be.' It is this attitude which Owen strives to change. Tressell makes it plain that he does not see the owners or their hangers-on as the real enemies of socialism. Owen acknowledges that most people in their position would act as the owners do. No, the real enemy was the majority of his fellow workmen.

> Those who not only quietly submitted like so many cattle to the existing state of things, but defended it, and opposed and ridiculed any suggestion to alter it.
> *They were the real oppressors*—the men who spoke of themselves as 'The likes of us', who having lived in poverty and degradation all their lives considered that what had been good enough for them was good enough for the children they had been the cause of bringing into existence.

Owen admitted to hating and despising them. *They* were the philanthropists of the title, because they gave away their due to their bosses! The intensely competitive nature of the trade in which they are engaged ensures that all the workers are taught to 'bodge', and consequently have no pride whatever in workmanship. When they arrive in the mornings they think only of breakfast time; after breakfast only of dinner time; after dinner they wish it were one o'clock on Saturday! If the job is not done quickly and cheaply the next will go to one of their competitors, Pushem and Sloggem, Bluffum and Doemdown, Dodger and Scampit, Snatcham and Graball, Smeeriton and Leavit, or Makehaste and Sloggit.

It remains only to add that Tressell's novel is autobiographical.[24] In the Preface he says: 'I have invented nothing. There are no scenes or incidents in the story that I have not either witnessed myself or had conclusive evidence of.' It is the story of lives lived on the edge of the Abyss, and its great strength lies in the images it creates symbolic of the life-style of the poor, and in Tressell's eye for detail which makes his descriptive passages, for example of the Easton's home, so vivid. Moreover, through Owen's and later Barrington's lectures to their work-mates we have set out before us the prospect of an alternative scheme of social arrangements, socialism. It was Tressell's inten-tion, no doubt, that those from the working class who read the book would sympathise with Owen and react strongly against the conservatism of his fellow workers; if society cannot be better organised than it is in Mugsborough then Jack London's ironic comment is apt; it would be better to live in the wilderness or the desert.

<h2 style="text-align:center">4</h2>

So far we have considered writers who wrote before the First World War, though Shaw, of course, continued to write until much later. Wars are supposed to be great levellers, and there is little doubt that a number of men who entered public life after the Great War had distinctly different social attitudes as a result of their war-time experiences.[25] In addition, whilst the land the politicians built after 1918 could only be said to be fit for heroes in the sense that survival for the majority of citizens demanded heroism, reformist legislation had been finding its way on to the statute book ever since 1906. The state, for example, provided old age pensions, free school meals for the needy, and unemployment benefits. Nevertheless, for the majority of the working class poverty, often grinding poverty, continued to be the normal condition of life during the inter-war years. Indeed J. B. Priestley argues that the working class was generally 'gloomier' after 1918. It had lost its 'innocence' during the war years—and anyway, too many faces were miss-ing.[26]

One novel which depicts working-class life during this period, and which achieved great acclaim almost immediately was Walter Greenwood's *Love on the Dole* (1933). Significantly the book opens with a quotation from James Russell Lowell on its inner cover: 'The time is ripe, and rotten ripe, for change;/

Then let it come . . .' The story concerns the people of Hanky Park, a working-class suburb of Manchester, and especially the Hardcastle family. Harry Hardcastle, just out of school, is working part time as a clerk to the local pawnbroker, but decides, against his parents' wishes, to go for an apprenticeship at Marlowe's, a big engineering works, because he thinks it more manly than book-keeping. He is taken on and so secures his manhood in this harsh world.[27]

> Such a row. As though a million boys were running stakes along iron railings, simultaneously. Every man stone deaf after a six months' spell of work there. Phew! But they *were* men.

With Harry and his older sister at work, the Hardcastle family has enough money to live a reasonably comfortable existence, and the picture Greenwood gives us of these times of sufficiency conjures up an atmosphere of wholesomeness rather like that which Orwell found in some working-class homes during his journey north, and wrote about so approvingly.

But Harry grows up. When his apprenticeship finishes Marlowe's give him his cards, just as he knew they would, and he suffers the indignity of unemployment. Immediately his relationship with the family changes, for he has now become a liability rather than an asset. But unemployment also strikes at his plans for marriage with Helen.

> 'No we don't want anybody.' Harry thanked him and withdrew, hurrying towards the next engineering works. Of course, he assured himself, of course, one couldn't expect success at the first time of asking. He was *certain* to find a berth with persistence. Why, he'd be running home before noon, running to meet Helen full of good news. Even at the next place, and the next, hope failed to die.
>
> Then gloomy forebodings insinuated themselves, forebodings that soon transformed themselves into scaring haunting dread. Billy Higgs and his generation—three years, now. That such a fate might be his . . .
>
> Gosh! And Helen to be told yet.

Unemployment grips Harry more and more firmly, like a debilitating illness, turning sour his old pleasures, weakening his spirit. Greenwood contrives to make us aware not only of the

physical hardships of poverty and unemployment but of the
state of mind of these men who are, after all, trained, and
accustomed to earning their keep:

> You fell into the habit of slouching, of putting your hands
> into your pockets and keeping them there; of glancing at
> people, furtively, ashamed of your secret, until you fancied
> that everybody eyed you with suspicion. You knew that your
> shabbiness betrayed you; it was apparent for all to see. You
> prayed for the winter evenings and the kindly darkness. Dark-
> ness, poverty's cloak. Breeches backside patched and
> repatched; patches on knees, on elbows. Jesus! All bloody
> patches.

Among the many others unemployed is Larry Meath, a self-edu-
cated artisan with strong left-wing views. He is to marry Harry's
sister Sally, but refuses to go ahead with the marriage when
he, too, becomes unemployed. Larry muses that planning to
marry was 'love's young dream', but the dream was shattered
by the lack of money. For Harry Hardcastle, too, love's young
dream turns into a nightmare when Helen becomes pregnant
and they have to get married. His father refuses to let them
live in the parental home—too many mouths to feed! Larry
Meath is a sick man and in fact his death follows shortly after
a demonstration by the unemployed which the police deal
with ruthlessly. Sally is left alone and decides to take her
fate into her own hands. She takes up the offer of an old
suitor, Sam Grundy the local bookmaker, a man with money
and influence, to become his mistress. Naturally enough her
father is mortified.

> 'So y'd go whorin' an' mek respectable folk like me an'
> y' ma the talk o' the neighbourhood, eh? Damn y'! Y'ain't
> fit t'be me dowter.'
>   'Yaa, who cares what folk say? There's none Ah know
> as wouldn't swap places wi' me if they'd chance. Y'd have
> me wed, wouldn't y'? Then tell where's feller around here
> as can afford it? Them as is workin' ain't able t' keep them-
> selves, ne'er heed a wife. Luk at y'self ... An luk at our
> Harry. On workhouse relief an' ain't even got a bed as
> he can call his own. Ah suppose Ah'd be fit t'call y'daughter
> if Ah was like that, an' a tribe o' kids like Mrs Cranford's

at me skirts . . . Well, can y' get our Harry a job? *I* can
an' Ah'm not respectable . . .'

In many respects Sally has taken charge of her destiny much
as Clara Hewett did, but Sally escapes the nether world of
Hanky Park, and her immoral liaison provides Harry with
a job, and one for her father, which he reluctantly accepts.

Greenwood indicates that if one is prepared to act immorally,
there is a way out of the squalor of the nether world, and
in this sense Sally resembles Mrs Warren more closely than
Gissing's unfortunate Clara Hewett. But we are left under no
illusions that Sally's actions are to be deplored and that Harry's
sense of guilt at obtaining work in such a backhand way is
justified. On his way back from work, with money in his pocket
for the first time, a smile on his lips at the prospect of handing
his wage packet to Helen, he saw

> a solitary figure standing on the corner of North Street.
> The smile died on his lips.
>   Jack Lindsay.
>   He was standing there as motionless as a statue, cap neb
> pulled over his eyes, gaze fixed on pavement, hands in pockets,
> shoulders hunched, the bitter wind blowing his thin trousers
> tightly against his legs. Waste paper and dust blew about
> him as they slid on the pavement.
>   No influential person to pull strings on his behalf; no
> wages for him tonight; no planning for the morrow. He
> was an anonymous unit of an army of three millions for
> whom there was no tomorrow.
>   Harry faltered, licked his lips then stole away, guiltily,
> down a back entry unable to summon the nerve to face
> his friend.

The success of *Love on the Dole* notwithstanding, the most
widely-read work on the conditions of the poor written in
the inter-war period has been George Orwell's *The Road to
Wigan Pier* (1937). In fact no writer concerned himself more
with poverty than did Orwell. We shall deal only with *Wigan
Pier* in this chapter, and that briefly, but will be discussing
Orwell himself in more detail in Chapter 3. In *Wigan Pier*,
as in *Down and Out in Paris and London* (1933), Orwell often
allows his descriptive passages to speak for themselves. For

example:[28]

> I remember a winter afternoon in the dreadful environs of
> Wigan. All round was the lunar landscape of slag-heaps,
> and to the north, through the passes, as it were, between
> the mountains of slag, you could see the factory chimneys
> sending out their plumes of smoke. The canal path was
> a mixture of cinders and frozen mud, criss-crossed by the
> imprints of innumerable clogs, and all round, as far as the
> slag-heaps in the distance, stretched the 'flashes'—pools of
> stagnant water that had seeped into the hollows caused by
> the subsidence of ancient pits. It was horribly cold. The
> 'flashes' were covered with ice the colour of raw umber,
> the bargemen were muffled to the eyes in sacks, the lock
> gates were beards of ice. It seemed a world from which
> vegetation had been banished; nothing existed except smoke,
> shale, ice, mud, ashes, and foul water. But even Wigan is
> beautiful compared with Sheffield.

Having set the confines of the world of the poor, we can
turn Orwell's focus a little closer:

> . . . the majority of these houses are old, fifty or sixty years
> old at least, and great numbers of them are by any ordinary
> standard not fit for human habitation. They go on being
> tenanted simply because there are no others to be had. And
> that is the central fact about housing in the industrial areas:
> not that the houses are poky and ugly, and insanitary and
> comfortless, or that they are distributed in incredibly filthy
> slums round belching foundries and stinking canals and slag-
> heaps that deluge them with sulphurous smoke—though all
> this is perfectly true—but simply that there are not enough
> houses to go round.

Finally, an example of Orwell's lens in close-up:

> At the back of one of the houses a young woman was kneeling
> on the stones, poking a stick up the leaden waste-pipe which
> ran from the sink inside and which I suppose was blocked.
> I had time to see everything about her—her sacking apron,
> her clumsy clogs, her arms reddened by the cold. She looked
> up as the train passed, and I was almost near enough to
> catch her eye. She had a round pale face, the usual exhausted

face of the slum girl who is twenty-five and looks forty, thanks to miscarriages and drudgery; and it wore, for the second in which I saw it, the most desolate, hopeless expression I have ever seen.

There are many such descriptive passages within the book, but the above will suffice to indicate the sympathy which Orwell is capable of arousing in his readers partly because his own feelings are so transparent. Orwell, an 'ordinary middle-class Englishman' (at least, that was his pose!) was shocked beyond measure by what he found in the north of England; it is to his credit as a writer that he managed to convey that shock so effectively.

5

It is impossible to assess how accurately these works reflect the reality of working-class life. We have tended to assume that misery *was* widespread and that the picture the writers have given was not out of focus. J. B. Priestley, though, says: 'It would be wrong to create the impression that the working class of these years was altogether downtrodden, dispirited, wretched',[29] and we have to balance this view against the evidence of documents such as Booth's *Life and Labour of the People of London*, Rowntree's *Poverty: A Study of Town Life* and the 1908 Minority Report of the Poor Law Commission. The evidence, surely, is too strong to be denied; as Samuel Hynes writes: 'the poor were more wretched and more numerous than at any other time in English history'; the rich, he goes on, were richer 'and more conspicuous in their luxuries'.[30] Perhaps Tressell provides a clue which helps to reconcile these apparently conflicting views. He describes not only the struggles of the workers but also the manner in which they take their pleasures. He indicates, though, that the pleasures are few and seized by the workers with enormous vigour, as for example, on the boisterous occasion of Owen's firm's annual outing.

At the beginning of the chapter, it was suggested that inequality might, after all, be a natural condition and that poverty might, as a consequence, be the unavoidable lot of the many. It could be argued that nothing these writers have said makes that any more unlikely a proposition. To show how debilitating a social sickness poverty is, is not to suggest that it is curable, and no doubt it is easier, anyway, to hate inequality than to love or even believe in equality. Yet what brought the socialists together (and excluded Gissing) was the belief that life could and should be better for the poor. It is not necessary, after all, even to consider the possibility of natural 'winners' and 'losers', like John Betjeman in his poem 'Slough' (1937), who speaks of: '. . . that man with double chin / Who'll always cheat and always win', nor indeed of the social distribution of winners and losers. What is of fundamental importance is to concentrate on describing the conditions in which the poor live: public sympathy is the most serviceable platform for state intervention. G. D. H. Cole once described socialism as a 'broad movement on behalf of the underdog'. It may well be a lot more but it *is* certainly *that*, and by the chillingly faithful and emotive pictures which they drew, these writers, Gissing included, did much to foster a general atmosphere favourable to the growth of socialist ideas. The importance of their task is emphasised by Orwell when he writes '. . . before you can be sure whether you are genuinely in favour of Socialism, you have got to decide whether things at present are tolerable or not tolerable, and you have got to take up a definite attitude on the terribly difficult issue of class.'[31] Priestley's comment on the middle class in Edwardian times is relevant to the whole of our period and beyond:[32] 'When it wined and dined, laughed and made love, it had not yet caught a glimpse of the terrible stone face this world can wear.'[33]

3 A Charge of Immorality

Two basic lines of argument concerning the nature of the alleged immorality of capitalist societies are common to socialist thought. The first and most obvious argues that in any system in which wealth is shared unequally, greed and envy will inevitably be fostered. If they wish to preserve the social and economic system under which they achieved their status, the wealthy may not deny the poor the opportunity to emulate them (indeed, like Undershaft, they will need to encourage the poor to do so); yet by the same token they will need to have recourse to strictly enforced legal sanctions to defend their property against those who might think to take short-cuts and 'expropriate the expropriators' in a strictly private and *ad hoc* manner. In such a society the social relationships between people will tend to be dominated by Carlyle's 'cash nexus' and the entire legal and constitutional framework governing that relationship will be based upon greed and envy. The second line of argument, which draws much of its inspiration from Marx's earlier writing, suggests that the division of labour necessitated by the capitalist industrial state, serving the interests of the property-owning class, destroys man's ability to derive any satisfaction from his work. Hence, since work is his most crucial activity, man will be unable to fulfil himself, unable to be fully human. To sum up both lines of argument, the unequal society inevitably alienates man from his fellows and from himself.[1]

I

Among the creative writers of the period we are studying, none addressed himself to these arguments more squarely than William Morris.

Before he became a socialist, Morris was a bohemian and Romantic; he was steeped in an intellectual tradition which encompassed writers like Ruskin (and, to a lesser extent, Carlyle and Arnold) whose inspiration, like his own, was frequently drawn from medieval civilisation.[2] It was a tradition which despised the culture and artistic achievements of its own age and which sought to revitalise, to 'purify', what it considered to be a decadent civilisation. His passion for medieval architecture led Morris to found a Society for the Protection of Ancient Buildings, whose operations enabled him gradually to appreciate that the state of the arts and the well-being of society were inextricably linked in a causal relationship. This was not a conclusion he reached with any joy, for it implied that the would-be reformer of artistic standards must interest himself in political reform. As he himself said, 'Both my historical studies and my practical conflict with the philistinism of modern society have *forced* on me the conviction that art cannot have a real life and growth under the present system of commercialism and profit-mongering.'[3]

Although he played a prominent part in socialist politics in the 1880s, Morris's political activities would scarcely have guaranteed him much of a place in the annals of British socialism. His writing, however, was another matter, for in a series of brilliant essays and speeches, in his 'socialist songs' and poems, and in his two major politically-motivated works, *A Dream of John Ball* (1887) and *News from Nowhere* (1890), Morris provided great inspiration for the socialist movement in Britain. As E. P. Thompson writes[4]:

The best and most honest of the literature at the end of the nineteenth century is marked by a profound disillusion, a searching for private reassurance, limited personal objectives, in the midst of a hostile social environment . . . Against this tide, Morris stood alone with full assurance, with conscious confidence in life. The rock he stood upon was his socialist convictions.

Morris's confidence in the socialist future was to prove to be contagious and the strength of his convictions unbridled.

Morris himself was first and last an artist. He believed that the fulfilled man, socialist man, was also an artist, and that man's basic instinct was creative and not political. Morris decided to become a socialist because the people he saw about him were stunted and incomplete and in no way compared to his vision of the creative man. They were the victims of inequality. Inequality, the natural product of the capitalist system, was guilty of the most heinous crime, said Morris: it had destroyed art. The capitalist system (or 'commercial' system as Morris usually calls it) had produced an inequality so intense that in England 'the terrible spectacle is exhibited of two people living street by street, and door by door—people of the same blood, the same tongue, and at least nominally living under the same laws—but yet one civilised and the other uncivilised.'[5] The result of this division was that art had been 'trampled down' and commerce 'exalted' into a sacred religion. The growth of commercialism, Morris went on, had destroyed the craft system of labour, in which the unit of labour had been the intelligent artisan, and had supplanted it with the 'workshop' system, 'wherein . . . division of labour in handiwork is carried to the highest point possible, and the unit of manufacture is no longer a man but a group of men, each member of which is dependent upon his fellows'.[6] Now, the aim of capitalist production was to increase profit, not to produce only what was needed, and as a result there was no necessary limit to labour. That was the 'superstition of commerce': that man was made for commerce rather than commerce being made for man, and its implications for the life of the individual were clear enough.

The economic system produced social stratification, with a small class of wealthy owners of capital (i.e. 'dead men's labour') who 'consume a great deal while they produce nothing'. So they had to be kept at the expense of those who did work. As to the middle class, the bulk of them worked but did not produce. Even where they did produce—usually wastefully— they consumed far more than they produced. 'It is their ambition and the end of their whole lives to gain, if not for themselves yet at least for their children, the proud position of being obvious burdens on the community.'[7] Next came the working class, employed in making 'all those articles of folly and luxury, the demand for which is the outcome of the existence of the rich non-producing classes; things which people leading a manly and uncorrupted life would not ask for or dream of.' Morris said of the working class that they were forced to produce either luxuries for the wealthy or shoddy goods for themselves, and hence by his definition were alienated. On all counts the demand which the capitalist supplied was a false demand. 'The market in which he sells is "rigged" by the miserable inequalities produced by the robbery of the system of Capital and Wages.' Every social class, then, was a slave to luxury, that 'invention of competitive commerce', and in such a system, the natural consequences of which were effeminacy and brutality, art, as defined by Morris was impossible, thus unhappiness—alienation—was inevitable.

2

One of those who attended the meetings of Morris's Hammersmith socialist group as a student, and who later became a Fabian was H. G. Wells. Like his fellow Fabian, Bernard Shaw (and unlike his close friend Gissing) he consciously attempted to use his creative writing ability to serve socialism and social reform.

Wells was a self-made man. His early life was totally devoid of the cultural inspiration from which Shaw and Morris so benefited. Wells made his way by dint of hard work and independence of mind to the Normal School (later Royal College) of Science at South Kensington. It was here that he joined the socialist society and made the journey to Hammersmith to listen to William Morris. But Wells's inspiration, in contrast to Morris's, was drawn from the future and not the past. He saw socialism as the application of scientific principles to social arrangements. The *fin-de-siècle* movement in literature sought to establish that, in the struggle between the individual and his circumstances, the chief good was not reconciliation of self to transcending morality (that is, to custom), but the realisation of self at almost any expense: in a phrase social rebellion. Wells's characters tended to struggle; what they struggled *against* was an unequal and unfair society which, by design, prevented their fulfilling themselves. If they did sublimate their desires and ambitions, then it was to a freshly formulated 'greater good': that of mankind in general, the 'good of the species' (for example, for more rational economic planning on a multi-national and eventually world-wide scale).

The setting for these struggles, especially in Wells's earlier works, was frequently scientific or futuristic, or both; for example, *The Time Machine* (1895), *The Island of Dr Moreau* (1896), *The Invisible Man* (1897), *War of the Worlds* (1898) and *First Men in the Moon* (1901). Only occasionally in these works does Wells attack the immoralities of capitalist society, most notably—or at least most unforgettably—in *The Time Machine*. This short story tells of a scientist who can travel in time. One of his journeys takes him to a world-state of complete equality (or apparently so) peopled by the Eloi, who are physically beautiful and obviously contented. They have won the struggle for existence, though at a cost which we shall be examining later. The time traveller's early enchantment with these people soon wears thin, but even so, he is ill-prepared for the discovery of another branch of the human race who cast a sinister shadow over this Pre-Raphaelite paradise. Beneath the surface of the earth live the Morlocks, a brutish ape-like people who tend huge machines. The time traveller concludes with some disgust that the nineteenth-century class struggle has been fought to this extreme conclusion, with the idle and degenerate aristocracy living off the labours of an animalized proletariat. But further discoveries throw some doubt upon the Marxian interpretations: the Eloi go in terror of the Morlocks. Before long the 'faint halitus of freshly shed blood' explains the nature of the relationship: not only are the Morlocks the masters but they eat the Eloi. The Eloi are in fact fattened and fed by their underground masters; probably their very beauty is the result of the selective breeding! The traveller reappraises the life of his aristocracy: 'Very pleasant was their day, as pleasant as the day of the cattle in the field.'

There are a number of skilfully drawn contrasts here, between aestheticism and utilitarianism, pastoralism and technology, leisure and action, hedonism and social purpose, beauty and ugliness. But there can be no doubt that above all Wells was attempting to show that the life of ease enjoyed by the British upper class was based upon the subjection of the mass of their fellows to the most appalling living and working conditions.

Wells took this division to its logical conclusion and showed where the inequalities could eventually lead. Inequality leads to a growing desire for luxuries and a life of ease on the part of one class and to a dehumanisation on the part of the other. The abdication of responsibility by the upper classes for the good government and welfare of the people seems to be an almost inevitable consequence of their desire for a life of ease.

First Men in the Moon is another celebrated work in which Wells projects social inequality (in this case more specifically the division of labour) to its extreme. Some brief examples will suffice to show the contours of Selenite Society. There are flea-like artists who draw incessantly but rarely eat or drink; mathematicians physically incapable of laughter except at the discovery of some mathematical paradox; machine minders with highly distended arms; profound scholars carried about in sedan chairs, attended by disseminators of their thoughts, with trumpet-like faces. At the head of this weird society stands (or rather sits, since he hasn't any legs), the Grand Lunar, who is simply an immense brain sitting on a velvet throne, whose acolytes frequently have to douse him in lime water to stop him from overheating. What Wells is saying is that social divisions based upon the division of labour prevent any man of whatever social position from being fully human. Indeed we all recognise the basic inhumanity upon which Selenite society is founded, but Wells will not let matters rest there. His parting thrust is deadly: 'It really is in the end a far more humane proceeding than our earthly method of leaving children to grow into human beings, *and then making machines of them.*'[8]

Another vivid story which acts as a vehicle for the author's criticism of the immorality of social division is *The Island of Dr Moreau*. In this case the upper class, in the shape of the scientist Moreau and his assistant, have not, like the Eloi, abdicated responsibility for the masses, but they use that responsibility in the most inhuman way for purely selfish ends. These ends have little to do with ease of life, but with rehabilitating the prestige of Moreau through biological discoveries of a terrifying nature. Moreau and his assistant have set themselves the task of 'humanising' animals by vivisection, muscle grafting, the reordering of certain basic nerve and brain functions—all performed at length and without any anaesthetic. The animals, then, are brainwashed in the most comprehensive manner by a process known as 'the bath of pain'. They are then taught to speak, walk erect and behave in a 'lawful' manner. Breaches of the law are punished with great brutality, and more regular reinforcement is provided through the chanting of a set of commandments praising the power and justice of the vivisectionist. Eventually Moreau and his assistant are killed and the traveller presides over the progressive dehumanisation of the beast men, who finally lose their power of speech and move on all fours—who, in short, revert completely. Fortunately, the traveller manages to escape, but forever after is haunted by the bestial characteristics he recognises in the human faces of a city.

If the principle theme here is similar to that of *The Time Machine*, namely the immorality of inequality, Wells has shifted his ground slightly. He does not charge the ruling classes with irresponsibility so much as inhumanity.[9] Moreau, for example, describes his work with chilling euphemism as being in the 'plasticity of form'. It is the fearful consequences of the attempt to mould men which Wells is criticising. He often wrote of the dehumanising aspects of the caste system of education in Britain, and the enforced rate of learning of unintelligible chants was something which he especially abhorred. We find it on Moreau's island, too.

But Wells did not restrict his attacks on the nature of capitalist inequality to allegorical tales. In his many social novels Wells turned again and again to the immorality of inequality. Nowhere was he more successful than in his early comedies, such as *The History of Mr Polly* (1910) and *Kipps* (1905). The former tells the story of an alienated man. Alfred Polly has, to use his own phrase, 'passed through the valley of the shadow of education', has become unhappily married, keeps a shop that does not pay in a small town which he loathes, and sees life in general as a concerted attempt to knock the stuffing out of people. His alienation is objectified by his digestive system. Had he been transparent, or even passably translucent, then 'perhaps he might have realised that he was not so much a human being as a civil war'. Polly's case is not so much against the confines of the human condition as against the procrustean social system which crushed the majority of men into inadequate lives of which his is symbolic. Because he feels too oppressed to countenance anything more positive, Polly finally decides to quit the human condition altogether. But his suicide attempt fails—though with much glory—and he then decides to run away. In other words, he decides to rebel against his enforced bourgeois life-style. Eventually he comes to accept social responsibilities again, though this time on his own terms and in a situation of his own choosing.

Polly's act is essentially that of a man who sets his individual fulfilment as the highest goal. 'If the world does not please you, you can change it. Determine to alter it at any price and you can change it altogether.' You can and by implication you should because 'the world' is grossly unfair to those in the lower strata. It can be argued that Alfred Polly is a good example of Wells's bourgeois background and habits getting in the way of his socialist intentions, for Polly is in many respects a bourgeois who, when pushed to it, reacts with true Samuel Smilesean vigour and ingenuity. He thinks and acts like a bourgeois. But really Polly is much more than this; through Alfred Polly, Wells is telling us that life for the majority is dehumanising but that it need not be. Polly's solution may be seen as individualist; it may also be seen as symbolic.

Kipps is another story of the individual at grips with society. It tells of an apprentice at a draper's emporium who unexpectedly comes into money and tries to enter South Coast 'society'. Abject failure and humiliation follow the attempt but a forgotten investment restores him to wealth. This time Kipps remains within his own class and survives. The book is another example of the successful use of comedy as a vehicle for social criticism. Wells wrote:[10]

> I have laughed at these two people . . . but I see through the darkness the souls of my Kippses as they are . . . little, ill-nourished, ailing, ignorant children, children who feel pain . . . and suffer and do not understand why. And the claw of the beast rests upon them. [The beast, of course, was the social system—not original sin.]

In *Kipps*, the realities of social division are criticised with great forcefulness. The moral shallowness and selfishness of the upper classes is contrasted with the warmth and compassion of Kipps's own class.[11] Wells nowhere raises intellectual issues concerning the nature of social division, as he does in *The Time Machine*, but concentrates upon what *actually happens* to an individual who tries to change classes. He does so in a humorous fashion, but as the last quotation indicates, he is in earnest.

It would be an unfortunate delusion to imagine Wells as simply a champion of the underdog. It is true that he recognises the overriding, if not always conclusive, importance of the unequal social system in determining the patterns of men's lives. But it is also true that, insofar as it affects adversely the lives of some, indirectly inequality affects the lives of all, for: 'The fact is, Society is one body, and it is either well or ill. The society we live in is ill. It's factious, feverish, invalid, gouty, greedy, ill-nourished. You can't have a happy left leg with neuralgia, or a happy throat with a broken leg.'[12]

3

A writer whose scientific background often leads to comparisons with Wells is Aldous Huxley. Although he described himself as a Fabian, Huxley's interest as far as we are concerned here is not so much the consequence of his vague socialism as his bitingly ironic descriptions of the life of his own class, the upper class. Better than any other writer he clothes in reality the theoretical explanation of the alienation of the wealthy. William Morris's analysis, it will be remembered, showed that the necessity to maintain the superiority of its status prompted the upper class into the ceaseless acquisition of luxury goods which had little or no practical use. Huxley was to show how aimless and shiftless was the life-style imposed by the naked pursuit of wealth and status, and to provide us, in Anthony Beavis, in *Eyeless in Gaza* (1936), with an equivalent to Orwell-the-Imperial Policeman; one who became disgusted by the life he and those around him led, and who found a new sense of purpose through personal and political commitment.

In his earlier work Huxley managed to capture the superficiality of the 1920s the decadence and abandonment to pleasure of the period. Yet the author himself always seemed to remain aloof. There is an air of detachment about books such as *Antic Hay* (1923) which gives the reader to understand that the author would scarcely be happy in the company of his characters. The pursuit of pleasure is shown to be aimless and doomed to failure. Like the story of the snowman who steals articles of clothing in order to keep warm and so eventually melts, the ability of Huxley's wealthy characters to do more or less as they please amounts to a kind of spiritual suicide:[13]

> 'Tomorrow', said Gumbril at last meditatively. 'Tomorrow', Mrs Viveash interrupted him, 'will be as awful as today.' She breathed it like a truth from beyond the grave prematurely revealed, expiringly from her death-bed within.

What has gone wrong? Huxley, like Orwell, was aware of the apparent breakdown of established morality, rooted in the Judaeo-Christian tradition. Orwell spoke of Western man's sawing away a branch on which he was sitting as he cut away the myths of the Christian system of beliefs, unaware that underneath him was a cesspool. Huxley, too, thought that scientific discovery impelled man to the belief that he was, in Russell's phrase, nothing more than the outcome of an accidental collation of atoms. Huxley's early work depicts a human landscape from which values have vanished and over which the philosophy of meaninglessness dominates.

But Huxley himself remained detached from the philosophy he depicted and sought to challenge the supremacy of the scientific explanations of causation. 'Our conviction that the world is meaningless is due', he writes, '. . . in part to a genuine intellectual error—the error of identifying the world of science, a world from which all meaning and value has been deliberately excluded, with ultimate reality.'[14] For Huxley, then, human values are of the highest importance and it is from this position that he develops his criticism of his own class, the upper class.

Point Counter Point (1928) is, among other things, a savage indictment of the selfish futility of upper-class life. Huxley does not identify and indict the class as a sociologist might; he simply introduces us to every member of that class and shows us the futility of their lives. They are, each one, alienated against their own natures and against their fellows. There is an almost total absence of love, compassion, indeed of any emotion except self-interest among this class, and we are given two points of reference, so to say, from which to judge the class.[15] They are the characters of Illidge, a working-class communist, and Rampion, based upon Huxley's friend and mentor at this time, D. H. Lawrence. Illidge says:[16]

There's something peculiarly base and ignoble and diseased about the rich. Money breeds a kind of gangrened insensitiveness. It's inevitable. Jesus understood. That bit about the camel and the needle's eye is a mere statement of fact. And remember the other bit about loving your neighbours . . . Neighbourliness is the touchstone that shows up the rich. The rich haven't got any neighbours . . . in the sense that the poor have neighbours . . . When you live on less than four pounds a week you've damned well got to behave like a Christian and love your neighbour . . . But you rich . . . never perform a neighbourly action or expect your neighbours to do you a kindness in return. It's unnecessary. You can pay people to look after you.

Rampion says much the same thing, in a suitably Lawrentian manner:

You people aren't stupider than anyone else. Not naturally stupider. You're victims of your way of living. It's put a shell round you and blinkers over your eyes.

It is not just that there is no individual at Lady Tantamount's party who could possibly command our respect, not just that the one character in the book who attains the goals he seeks (Burlap) is a target for the author's unremitting contempt, but that we get a glimpse through Illidge and more especially through the redemptive figure of Rampion of a far superior way of living not based upon alienated bondage to the ego but upon full membership of a community based upon human values.

In *Eyeless in Gaza* (1936) Huxley makes his philosophy of redemption much more central and his redemptive character, the anthropologist Dr Miller, plays a much more important part in the novel than does Rampion in *Point Counter Point*. The chief character, however, is Anthony Beavis, who can be taken to personify the alienated intellectual, a member of the upper class held as firmly as any in bondage to the ego. Beavis tries to avoid commitment of any kind. For example, he has an affair with Helen Amberley-Lethridge in which he simply pursues pleasure for its own sake, though Helen wishes for a fuller relationship. Their affair is brought to an end, and with it Beavis's life-style, in a rather dramatic fashion.

Whilst they are attempting to make love on the roof of their villa in Mexico, a dog is dropped on them from an aeroplane.[17] This none-too-subtle symbolism, perhaps, indicates Heaven's displeasure at Beavis's way of life. It certainly denotes an awareness on his part of the superficiality of his existence and the slow beginnings of a growing determination to commit himself to something or someone outside himself, to escape his bondage to the ego. Finally Beavis does commit himself, to Helen, and also to pacifism; not simply to pacifism in the strictly anti-military sense but in the wider sense of a life based on what we might call today non-violence. It is from this point of reference, the individual seeking self-fulfilment in a non-violent, non-competitive society, that Huxley criticises contemporary society. As always, he does this not through sweeping generalisations about this or that social class but simply by character analysis on a scale so extensive as to leave us in no doubt as to his intentions. The immorality of inequality, we learn from Huxley, stunts the rich and alienates them not only from the poor but from each other and from themselves.

4

If Huxley's concern was to depict the superficiality of a class alienated by its wealth and life of ease, George Orwell's was to examine the immorality of inequality from the other end of the sociological spectrum. Born in 1902 Orwell was one of the generation most influenced by the work of Shaw and Wells, in Orwell's case particularly the latter. But whereas Wells used his ability as a writer to take him out of poverty and towards a more distanced appraisal of the problems of poverty, Orwell's career took him in precisely the opposite direction. Though by no means wealthy, Orwell's family was comfortably off, but Orwell fled to a form of poverty which, though it may have been essentially contrived, became real enough all the same.

It was his recognition of the immorality of inequality which changed Orwell's whole life and took him out of 'the establishment'. It was one of the reasons for his giving up his post with the Imperial Police in Burma and it infused much of his early writing, *Burmese Days* (1935) being an obvious example. For present purposes, though, perhaps a better example, written in 1936, is a short essay entitled *Shooting An Elephant*.[18] The essay is autobiographical and it concerns the author as a young police officer in Burma having to cope with an elephant on the rampage. Orwell's feeling of alienation (and its cause) is made plain to us from the beginning. 'I was hated by a large number of people—the only time in my life I have been important enough for this to happen to me.' Those who hated him were, of course, the native Burmese. 'As for the job I was doing, I hated it more bitterly than I can perhaps make clear.' He was an oppressor and felt himself to be one; moreover, he hated those whom he oppressed, part of him believing that 'the greatest joy in the world would be to drive a bayonet into a Bhuddist priest's guts.' But the incident with the elephant brought these vague and often blurred sentiments into clear focus, giving him 'a better glimpse . . . of the real nature of imperialism—the real motives for which despotic governments act'.

The elephant's going on the rampage had been reported to him and Orwell had felt obliged to see what could be done. Although it turned out that the elephant had caused a considerable amount of damage and had, in fact, killed an Indian coolie, it had not gone wild but had simply gone 'must', a kind of sexual frenzy which would pass off. Orwell followed the trail to find the elephant in a paddy field looking 'no more dangerous than a cow'. He knew with perfect certainty that the elphant's frenzy was already passing and that he ought not to shoot it. But at the same time he became aware of the large crowd that had followed him and who expected him to shoot.

They were watching me as they would watch a conjurer about to perform a trick. They did not like me, but with the magical rifle in my hands I was momentarily worth watching. And suddenly I realised that I should have to shoot the elephant after all. The people expected it of me and I had got to do it; I could feel their two thousand wills pressing me forward, irresistibly. And it was at this moment, as I stood there with the rifle in my hands, that I first grasped the hollowness, the futility of the white man's dominion in the East. Here was I, the white man with his gun, standing in front of the unarmed native crowd—seemingly the leading actor of the piece; but in reality I was only an absurd puppet pushed to and fro by the will of those yellow faces behind. I perceived in this moment that when the white man turns tyrant it is his own freedom that he destroys. He becomes a sort of hollow, posing dummy, the conventionalised figure of the sahib. For it is the condition of his rule that he shall spend his life in trying to impress the 'natives', and so in every crisis he has got to do what the 'natives' expect of him. He wears a mask, and his face grows to fit it.

Supporters of empire had long acknowledged that the task of 'civilising' subject races would be a lonely and at times unpleasant one, but they did not question that the white man's burden was worth bearing, for all concerned. Orwell argues precisely the opposite, that both parties lose freedom of action and find themselves obliged to adopt policies which may disgust them. In a word, both parties are alienated from each other and from their roles (i.e. from themselves). What is true of imperial government is, Orwell says, true of all despotic governments—governments which exist to preserve the superior status of certain citizens at the expense of others.

Just as the relationship between imperialists and subject races alienated both, so did social division alienate both classes in Britain. When he visited the north of England, Orwell began to appreciate that the experiences which he shared with the very poor and destitute, and which he writes about in *Down and Out in Paris and London* (1933), were common to a whole class, though in a less severe form. As we see in *Wigan Pier*, he also came to understand the profound consequences for society of this inequality. Orwell takes for granted that everyone 'barring fools and scoundrels' would like to see an end to economic inequality, but questions whether it is generally realised what would be entailed in the abolition of class distinctions.[19]

Here I am, a typical member of the middle class. It is easy for me to say that I want to get rid of class distinctions, but nearly everything I think and do is a result of class distinctions. All my notions—notions of good and evil, of pleasant and unpleasant, of funny and serious, of ugly and beautiful—are essentially *middle class* notions ... When I grasp this fact I grasp that it is no use clapping a proletarian on the back and telling him that he is as good a man as I am; if I want real contact with him, I have got to make an effort for which very likely I am unprepared. For to get outside the class racket I have got to suppress not merely my private snobbishness, but most of my other tastes and prejudices as well ... What is involved is not merely the amelioration of working-class conditions, nor an avoidance of the more stupid forms of snobbery, but a complete abandonment of the upper-class and middle-class attitude to life. And whether I say Yes or No probably depends upon the extent to which I grasp what is demanded of me.

In other words the social barriers which alienate one class from another go much deeper than economics, and cannot be removed except by what Orwell recognises to be a supreme act of will.[20] But we may notice that this act of will is to be undertaken by the middle and upper classes unilaterally. Orwell does not speak of a dialectical process with some synthesising cross-class culture as its end product. To suggest, as Orwell does, that these classes have 'nothing to lose but their "aitches"' is palpably absurd. In a real sense the impracticability, and possible undesirability, of Orwell's solution serves to underline the gravity of the problem of social alienation, class against class.

Three of Orwell's novels deal directly with the theme of alienation, *Burmese Days*, *Keep the Aspidistra Flying* (1936), and *Coming Up For Air* (1939). Since we have already discussed the author's experiences in Burma, we shall focus attention on the other two.

Gordon Comstock, a young man trying to establish a reputation and career as a poet, is the hero of *Keep the Aspidistra Flying*. He has turned his back on a career in advertising and caused great consternation to his family, who made considerable financial sacrifices to secure a 'good' education for him in the expectation that he would take his place in the bourgeois scheme of things: 'get married, settle down, prosper moderately, push a pram, have a villa and a radio and an aspidistra. [Become] a law-abiding little cit like any other law-abiding little cit—a soldier in the strap-hanging army.'[21] Eventually Gordon is indeed conscripted into that army, but not before two years of bitter rebellion against 'bourgeois' values.

Comstock's thesis is a simple one. It is that all human relationships are governed by the 'cash nexus' and that in such a
society a poor man is *ipso facto* an incomplete man.

All human relationships must be purchased with money.
If you have no money, men won't care for you, women
won't love you; won't, that is, care for you or love you
the least little bit that matters. And how right they are,
after all! For moneyless, you are unlovable.

When his friend Ravelston asks him who his enemies are, he
callously replies (knowing Ravelston to be wealthy) 'Oh, anyone
with over five hundred a year.' Ravelston, a socialist himself,
acknowledges the sincerity of Comstock's position, and agrees
with him that every ideology is, as Marx said, a reflection
of economic circumstance. To this Comstock replies:

Ah, but you only understand it out of Marx! You don't
know what it means to have to crawl along on two quid
a week. It isn't a question of hardship—it's nothing so decent
as hardship. It's the bloody, sneaking meanness of it. Living
alone for weeks on end because when you've no money you've
no friends. Calling yourself a writer and never even producing
anything because you're always too washed out to write.
It's a sort of filthy sub-world one lives in. A sort of spiritual
sewer.

It is unnecessary to recount Comstock's experiences in any
detail. It is sufficient to reiterate his total alienation in a world
whose standards are regulated by money. 'Money is what God
used to be. Good and evil have no meaning any more except
failure and success. Hence the profoundly significant phrase,
to *make good*.' He is divided against himself in that he clearly
desires not to be a failure and yet cannot bring himself to
accept the criteria which society uses to measure success. On
the other hand he is not strong-willed enough to succeed even
by his own criteria. Hats off, says Comstock, to every factory
lad 'who with fourpence in the world puts his girl in the
family way. At least he's got blood and not money in his
veins.' In a similar situation, though, when his girlfriend Rosemary offers herself to him, Comstock finds he is incapable
of making love to her because he has only got eightpence
in his pocket and cannot afford the bus fare home! Finally,

though, he does make love to Rosemary and she becomes pregnant. Comstock forsakes his poverty to become a success in advertising and settles down with Rosemary into suburban life. Comstock accepts bourgeois life on its own terms; he becomes anti-Polly.[22]

That successful social rebel, Alfred Polly, provided Orwell with a theme for the second novel we consider here, *Coming Up For Air*. George Bowling is a man much like Polly, living a joyless life in suburbia and seething with revolt. Like Polly, too, Bowling steps out of his situation, so to say, and looks at it from the outside.[23]

> When you've time to look about you, and when you happen to be in the right mood it's a thing that makes you laugh inside to walk down these streets in the inner-outer suburbs and to think of the lives that go on there. Because, after all, what *is* a road like Ellesmere Road? Just a prison with the cells all in a row. A line of semi-detached torture chambers where the poor little five-to-ten-pounds-a-weekers quake and shiver, every one of them with the boss twisting his tail and the wife riding him like a nightmare and the kids sucking his blood like leeches.

Unlike Polly, though, Bowling's notions of a wholesome life are based on memories of the past, not hopes for the future. The book represents an indictment of urban and suburban life presented by means of a contrast—with pre-war life in a rural community. Bowling's disenchantment stems from the fact that he is not part of a community, that he is not a real man at all, but an actor playing several roles of husband, father and salesman, none of which he likes. Like Comstock, Bowling stands very low in his own esteem; he is a model of an alienated man, an idea which Orwell puts across succinctly and effectively by describing Bowling as a fat man with a thin man inside him. Bowling contrasts his life-style with that of the rural community to which he belonged as a boy.[24] The picture of the pre-1914 England is not a fanciful one. Bowling admits that people were probably worse off then, in material terms, yet their lives were infinitely richer. The image Bowling retains of that past age is of fishing in a quiet pond at Binfield House. In his modern world, fish continue to provide a symbol, but of a somewhat different nature. Bowling buys a frankfurter and found it necessary

to do a kind of sawing movement before I could get my
teeth through the skin. And then suddenly—pop! The thing
burst in my mouth like a rotten pear. A sort of horrible
soft stuff was oozing all over my tongue. But the taste!
. . . It was fish! . . . It gave me the feeling that I'd bitten
into the modern world and discovered what it was really
made of. . . . Bombs of filth bursting in your mouth.

Although Bowling's alienation is exacerbated by the proximity
of war and the very real dread of a totalitarian future, and
although these fears for the future allow another powerful contrast to be made with pre-1914 England, we can see that
his alienation has deeper roots, in the nature of capitalist society
itself. It is as if Comstock's worst fears about what fate holds
for him are realised in Bowling's drab, forlorn, suburban existence.[25]

For Orwell and William Morris the immorality of capitalism
resides primarily in the effect that social division has on the
lives of the vast majority who do not live at their ease; this
includes virtually the whole of the lower working class, and
also the lower middle class who inhabit the suburban prison
cells. The well-to-do can live unalienated lives only through
ignorance; if they became aware of what their life of luxury
costs the majority of their fellow citizens their peace of mind,
their 'wholeness', would be destroyed—barring fools and scoundrels—for as Orwell says:[26]

You and I and the editor of the *Times Lit. Supp.*, and the
Nancy poets and the Archbishop of Canterbury and Comrade
X, author of *Marxism for Infants*—all of us *really* owe the
comparative decency of our lives to poor drudges underground, blackened to the eyes, with their throats full of
coal dust, driving their shovels forward with arms and belly
muscles of steel.

For Huxley, however, even ignorance will not save the well-
to-do from alienation. Their social position obliges them to
lead shallow, selfish lives which leave them alienated in much
the way that Morris predicted. In short, the social divisions
of capitalism spare no class from alienation. This, we are told,
is the immorality of capitalist inequality.

4 Muddle and Inefficiency

A major dimension of the socialist argument against inequality in capitalist society is that it is inefficient. That is to say, so much of the misery which attends social divisions within capitalism could be avoided by putting social institutions and arrangements upon a more scientific footing. The word scientific is not plucked out of the air: it has a special interest and importance. The discipline of science seemed to offer new prospects to many socialist thinkers, especially in Britain, towards the end of the last century. After all, Darwin, by applying scientific methods, had made enormous advances in the study of evolution and appeared to have created a totally new perspective upon man's place in the world. Darwinism seemed to emphasise the importance of material factors such as environment upon man's development, and this fitted well with what Marx had argued: that it was the nature of the social system which determined man's consciousness and not *vice versa*. By better ordering his environment, therefore, man could alter the relationship between himself and others and even influence his subsequent evolution as a species! H. G. Wells wrote:[1]

The fundamental idea on which Socialism rests is the same fundamental idea as that upon which all real scientific work is carried out. It is the denial that chance impulse and individual will and happening constitute the only possible methods by which things may be done in the world. It is an assertion that things are in their nature orderly, that things may be computed, may be calculated upon and foreseen.

Among creative writers those clearly most influenced, though by no means in the same way, by the idea of applying scientific reasoning to social and political arrangements, were Bernard Shaw and H. G. Wells. Both were members of the Fabian Society, a group which, perhaps above anything else, believed in the efficacy of political science. Indeed, it is hardly accidental that two of the most influential of the early Fabian leaders, Beatrice and Sidney Webb, endowed a new university, the London School of Economics and Political Science, in order to provide the nation with the kind of scientists it would need to manage its affairs efficiently.

What is the connection between a morally based criticism of capitalist society and a scientifically based one? For the moralist the immorality of the capitalist system stems directly from unequal social division; for the scientist capitalism's inefficiencies stem from the inappropriateness or inefficiencies of its particular social division. Put political scientists in control and there will be no need to remove all social divisions; indeed, equality in any fundamental sense (as envisaged by Morris for example) could be positively injurious to the prospect of wise rule by a scientific élite. We shall be dealing with the more positive suggestions of these 'political scientists' in a later chapter but it is important to bear in mind the fact that their goal was not necessarily a classless society and that their criticisms of capitalist society were made from a different perspective to that of the moralists, as Wells's comment illustrates. 'If Socialism is only a conflict with poverty, Socialism is nothing. But I hold that Socialism is and must be a battle against human stupidity and egotism and disorder, a battle fought through all the forests and jungles of the soul of man.'[2]

I

The greatest single indictment of the capitalist system, according to Bernard Shaw, was that it was responsible for creating the proletariat and then, to make matters worse, for giving proletarians the vote. In his savage indictment of the workings of

parliamentary democracy, *On the Rocks* (1933), which we shall
be examining later, Shaw writes: 'As to building Communism
with such trash as the Capitalist system produces it is out
of the question. For a Communist Utopia we need a population
of Utopians; and Utopians do not grow wild on the bushes
nor are they to be picked up in the slums; they have to be
cultivated very carefully and very expensively.'[3] It was part
of Shaw's method of propaganda to highlight the shortcomings
of the working class and to attempt to dissociate socialism
from other working-class movements.[4]

> In nothing [he once wrote] is the middle class origins of
> the Socialist movement so apparent as in the persistent delu-
> sions of Socialists as to an ideal proletariat, forced by the
> brutalities of the capitalist into an unwilling acquiescence
> in war, penal codes and other cruelties of civilisation. They
> still see the social problem, not sanely and objectively, but
> imaginatively, as the plot of a melodrama, with its villain
> and its heroine, its innocent beginning, troubled middle and
> happy ending. They are still the children and romancers
> of politics.

Shaw had learned his own lessons, or so he believed, concerning
the revolutionary potential of the workers. 'You can buy any
revolution off for thirty bob a week', he once said.[5] His experience
of the failure of the demonstration in Trafalgar Square on
7 November 1877, Bloody Sunday, and his own conspicuous
part in that failure, inspired him to lend his full weight to
Sidney Webb's theoretical justification of Fabian gradualism
committing the group wholly to parliamentary socialism with,
if we are to believe Leonard Woolf, considerable consequences
for the development of British socialism.[6]

Shaw's hatred of poverty is indeed hard to distinguish from
his hatred of the poor. From first to last he was totally out
of sympathy with the aspirations of the working class, in the
sense that he was convinced workers were not the best judges
of their own interests. This did not stem from lack of knowledge
of the lives of the poor—as we have already seen. All the
same, he never failed to distinguish between the just aspirations
of the working class and its political capacity (or incapacity)
to achieve those aspirations for itself.[7]

> As to the working classes I believe neither in their virtues
> nor their intelligence, on the contrary my objection to this
> existing order is precisely that it inevitably produces this
> wretched, idolatrous, sentimental, servile, anti-socialist mass
> of spoiled humanity which we call the proletariat and which
> neither understands, believes in us nor likes us. I am no
> friend of the working class. I am its enemy to the extent
> of ardently desiring its extermination.

For Shaw socialism was not about giving power to the people.
It was not about taking up cudgels on behalf of one class
against another. 'We have never advanced the smallest preten-
sion to represent the working classes of this country', he said
of the Fabians. He rejected out of hand the possibility of the
working class's forming a base for revolutionary or evolutionary
change, and he believed passionately that capitalism was directly
to blame for the creation of this 'mass of spoiled humanity'
because of the general ineptitude and selfishness of its political
leaders.

In a sense Shaw's position is diametrically opposed to that
of many 'moral socialists', in that he sees the working class
as an impediment to the growth of socialism as well as an
indictment upon capitalist inefficiency.[8]

> I do not believe there is a single member of the Fabian
> Society who would face the consequences of placing the
> government of England in the hands of the vast majority
> of the English people: that is to say, of the labouring classes,
> unless his real objective were to achieve a reductio ad absur-
> dum of democracy and have done with it for ever.

Shaw considered it ludicrous to imagine that any society could
be better governed by a million fools than by one able man,
a view from which he never departed throughout his long
career. In short, Shaw believed that the existence of the proletariat condemned capitalism.

Equally, Shaw was convinced that the capitalist system was
incapable of producing able, efficient leaders. In his play *Heartbreak House*, for example, which he wrote as the clouds of war
were gathering over Europe in 1914, Shaw attempted to depict
the deficiencies of the ruling class by means of a Chekhovian
house-party. In *Heartbreak House* there gathered together the

rulers of capitalist society. First there were the cultivated and leisured aristocracy.[9]

They took the only part of our society in which there was leisure for high culture, and made it an economic, political, and, as far as practicable, a moral vacuum; and as Nature, abhorring the vacuum, immediately filled it up with sex and all sorts of refined pleasures, it was a very delightful place at its best for moments of relaxation. In other moments it was disastrous.

But the inhabitants of Heartbreak House were not the only holders of power; there was also Horseback Hall to be considered, which consisted of 'a prison for horses with an annexe for the ladies and gentlemen who rode them, hunted them, talked about them, bought them and sold them, and gave nine-tenths of their lives to them, dividing the other tenth between charity, churchgoing (as a substitute for religion), and conservative electioneering (as a substitute for politics)'.

In conclusion there was little to be expected from the traditional rulers of capitalist society for:

In short, power and culture were in separate compartments. The barbarians were not only literally in the saddle, but on the front bench in the House of Commons, with nobody to correct their incredible ignorance of modern thought and science but upstarts from the counting-house, who had spent their lives furnishing their pockets instead of their minds. Both, however, were practised in dealing with money and with men, as far as acquiring the one and exploiting the other went . . .

When its traditional leaders failed capitalist society dramatically—as they did, according to Shaw, between 1914 and 1918—these 'useless people', the incumbents of Heartbreak House and Horseback Hall, 'set up a shriek' for 'practical business men' to run affairs. By this they meant those who had become rich by placing their own interests before those of country, and by 'measuring the success of every activity by the pecuniary profit it brought to them and to those on whom they depended for their supplies of capital'. But they too, failed the nation, and their conspicuous failure gave 'the whole public side of the war an air of monstrous and hopeless farce. They proved not only that they were useless for public work, but that in a well-ordered nation they would never have been allowed to control private enterprise.'

We could scarcely imagine Shaw placing much faith in democracy as a corrective for this deplorable condition of the body politic. And indeed he does not. 'It is said that every people has the Government it deserves. It is more to the point that every Government has the electorate it deserves; for the orators of the front bench can edify or debauch an ignorant electorate at will. Thus our democracy moves in a vicious circle of reciprocal worthiness and unworthiness.'

The plot, such as it is, of *Heartbreak House*, need not concern us, but the characters should, for, as is often the case with Shaw, each may be taken as representing what the author considered to be the most important movements and opinions in contemporary society. Captain Shotover, the owner of the house, has taken to alcohol and cynicism, and can only regret the dominance within capitalist society of those who make money, like Boss Mangan. 'What is to be done?' he asks. 'Are we to be kept for ever in the mud by these hogs to whom the universe is nothing but a machine for greasing their bristles and filling their snouts?' Mazzini, the disillusioned but mellowed ex-revolutionary, has been engaged in business ventures with Mangan, and takes a different line. He fully appreciates Mangan's grasp of the realities of commerce. 'We'—by which he means 'idealists'—'would spend too much on everything. We should improve the quality of the goods and make them too dear. We should be sentimental about the hard cases among the workpeople. But Mangan keeps us in order. He is down on us about every extra halfpenny. We could never do without him.' Mangan's undoubted commercial acumen seems to be accepted as an appropriate qualification for governing, for he is not corrected when he says to the representatives of the old order, Hectore Hushabye and Hastings Utterword, simply: 'Who else is there but me?'

Mazzini seems content to give Mangan his support, reflecting: 'Every year I expected a revolution, or some frightful smash-up: it seemed impossible that we could blunder and muddle on any longer. But nothing happened ... Nothing ever does happen. It's amazing how well we get along, all things considered.' But Shotover himself is by no means so complacent.

He says to Hector, towards the end of the play: 'The captain is in his bunk, drinking bottled ditch-water; and the crew is gambling in the forecastle. She will strike and sink and split. Do you think the law of God will be suspended in favour of England because you were born in it?' The play ends with death and the sound of bombs, and we are reminded of the time at which it was written, and of Shaw's comment in the Preface:

> Heartbreak House, in short, did not know how to live, at which point all that was left of it was the boast that at least it knew how to die: a melancholy accomplishment which the outbreak of war presently gave it practically unlimited opportunities of displaying.

Shaw's analysis of contemporary capitalist society, then, shows it to comprise selfish incompetence among the leadership and selfish ignorance among the led. The two components are held together in a ramshackle arrangement by the belief that nothing better can be hoped for. It is not so much the morality of the system which Shaw criticises as its crass incompetence. The aristocracy seems bent on marching to join Wells's Eloi and the working class towards a bestial kind of existence similar to the Morlocks though without their technological competence. The idealists have accepted that revolution is not going to save the world. Who is there to save them all but Boss Mangan, the captain of industry?

2

H. G. Wells was a scientist by training and although his studies came to an unsuccessful conclusion at the Royal College of Science, his outlook on life, and indeed his very imaginative powers, were always coloured by science. We shall see later that Wells's faith in the redemptive qualities of science contrast him with Shaw, whose faith was in political science rather than pure science, but their sharply critical analyses of the inefficiencies of capitalist society were made from similar positions.

When we consider Wells's attitude to the working class, the images of Moreau's beast people and also of the Morlocks inevitably spring to mind. But perhaps his most damning statement concerning 'the common man' in capitalist society is to be found in *War of the Worlds*. The artillery-man, who has escaped the Martian war machines, refers to an 'oafish crowd . . . a gaping, stinking, bombing, shooting, throat slitting, cringing brawl of gawky undernourished riff-raff', and ventures the opinion that they will be much better off under the Martians who, though they would eventually eat them, would in the meantime provide them with 'nice, roomy cages, fattening foods, careful breeding, no worry'. The majority of men will wonder however they managed before the Martians arrived.

To set against this the characters of Kipps and Polly, though, is to appreciate that Wells's view of the common man was ambivalent. He is compassionate and understanding on the one hand and deeply critical on the other, on the one hand a moralist and on the other a scientist. Perhaps we can make better sense of his position if we remember that Wells was prepared to extend compassion to those underprivileged who spiritedly tried to improve themselves, even if they failed. Mr Polly, for example, whose act of social rebellion leaves him 'plumper, browner, healthier', looks back on his previous life resentfully: 'And it seemed to him now that life had never begun for him, Never! It was as if his soul had been cramped and his eyes bandaged from the hour of his birth.'[10] Nobody knew better than Wells that the majority of its citizens grew up in Edwardian England 'through a darkened joyless childhood into a grey, perplexing, hopeless world that beats them down at last',[11] because he was an avid reader of many reports and surveys of the time into social conditions. But to earn his support the down-trodden had to take strenuous steps to improve their lot—just as Remington in *The New Machiavelli* and Wells himself had done. But mass man, the creature of capitalism, frightens Wells. Only in so far as he becomes conscious of his self and his capacity to act does he gain Wells's respect and sympathy.

Wells, like Shaw, saw the First World War as providing a decisive indictment of capitalism's incapacity to organise itself for any great purpose. Wells went so far as to distinguish between British inefficiency and German efficiency; the latter's experiments in state socialism and general social cohesion gave Germany a sense of purpose which the British lacked. This is shown clearly in the didactic novel *Joan and Peter* (1918) in which a number of examples are given of this German sense of purpose and resultant ability to organise.[12] Peter Stubland becomes a pilot and is twice shot down. Given plenty of time to think, he comes to see that although British technical expertise is a match for that of the Germans, and although the bravery of British fighting men is beyond reproach, the sheer muddle and inefficiency and snobbishness of the ruling class put the entire fighting force at a grave disadvantage.

Peter's thoughts are shared by his godfather, Oswald Sydenham, who reached his conclusions by observing civilian society, where he notes that the workers are 'bored by the boss's face, bored by his automobile, bored by his knighthood, bored by his country house, and his snob of a wife—'. His godson agrees. 'They not only sweat labour but won't stir a finger to save [labour] from jerry-built housing, bad provisioning, tally-men, general ugliness . . . every kind of rotten thing.'

What Wells is attempting to do is to castigate not this or that military or political leader or group but the system at large. We are reminded that the worst of individual leaders can be nothing more than 'the indicating pustule of a systematic malaise'. Wells's most telling phrase in this context, which encapsulates his entire argument, occurs in another novel concerned with the First World War, *Mr Britling Sees It Through* (1916) when Britling says: 'What's the good of all this clamouring for a change of Government? We haven't a change of Government. It's like telling a tramp to get a change of linen.' It is the capitalist system itself, then, which is at fault.

Wells found it intolerable that this waste and inefficiency should be coupled with such self-confident complacency among the leaders. He saw the world as threatened by grave dangers of a global nature to which it was oblivious. He articulated these fears frequently enough, and we shall be discussing some of them later, but he also gave them imaginative form in *The War of the Worlds*. How totally ineffective are the attempts of the establishment to deal with the Martian threat! We witness the death of one stout well-dressed man, who, only a few days before, 'must have been walking the world, a man of considerable consequence'. But like all the others he is eaten by the Martians who began a 'sustained cheerful hooting'. No doubt he had been, like one of the characters in another novel, 'one of those men whom modern England delights to honour, a man of unpretentious acquisitiveness, devoted to business and distracted by no aesthetic or intellectual interest'.[13] The curate, another pillar of the establishment, is held up for our contempt; he cannot understand or bring himself to believe what has happened. 'Did you think God had exempted Weybridge?' asks the narrator.[14] The Martians, by way of contrast, are shown to be totally efficient in all their operations.

It is appropriate to conclude Wells's analysis of the waste and inefficiency of capitalist society by referring to the analogy to which he often returned when trying to contrast capitalist and socialist societies. Socialists wanted a society which was planned, 'as one designs and lays out a garden, so that sweet and seemly things may grow, wide and beautiful vistas open and weeds and foulness disappear'.[15] In the garden of the capitalists Wells saw only 'gamblers, fools, brutes, toilers, martyrs. Their disorder of effort, the spectacle of futility fills me with a passionate desire to end waste, to create order, to develop understanding . . . Socialism is to me no more and no less than the awakening of a collective consciousness in humanity.'[16]

The story of Wells's life continually serves to illustrate the extent to which he took upon himself the mantle of prophet and seer. The development of the world towards this common consciousness which he called socialism was reflected in Wells's own spiritual and emotional state. Indeed each was seen by him as part of the same process:[17]

I dismiss the idea that life is chaotic because it leaves my life ineffectual, and I cannot contemplate an ineffectual life patiently . . . I assert therefore that I am important in a scheme, that we are all important in that scheme . . .

3

Wells and Shaw wrote not only in general or allegorical terms about the inefficiencies of the capitalist social and political system; they also wrote about the system directly, 'at work', so to say. In the books we shall now consider, the waste and inefficient management of capitalist society form the central theme. For simplicity's sake we shall deal with the works in the chronological order of their publication, the first being

Wells's *Tono Bungay*.

Tono Bungay tells the story of the Ponderevo family; of Uncle Edward, his wife Susan, and the hero, nephew George. George is brought up in a country house, Bladesover, where his mother was in service. Bladesover symbolises style and culture; it stands for something. But it stands for a system which in the end is unacceptable because it rests upon a structure of rigid hier-archy in which all have a place and have to know it. Young George discovered this when he fought the owner's son in a rough and tumble, and was justly punished and cast aside. But whilst the old aristocratic system may have been insupport-able, the capitalist system which replaced it is worse. Bladesover contrasts favourably with the world around it. When it is finally sold and bought by a family of Jewish nouveaux-riches, George reflects that its new owners 'could not have made it, they cannot replace it; they just happen to break out over it—sapro-phytically.'[18]

The pressure to succeed financially has broken the spirit of the residents of the small country town to which George is sent by his mother, to live with his aunt and uncle. But Uncle Edward does not succeed and is obliged to leave the town he loathes and try his luck in London. When George follows, his coming into London is described by Wells in terms similar to those in which Orwell later described Wigan, but George's concluding comment is that of a scientific socialist, more than a moral socialist. 'It is a *foolish* community that can house whole classes, useful and helpful, honest and loyal classes, in such squalidly unsuitable dwellings.'[19]

Uncle Edward succeeds in London, and the means by which he does so constitute a cynical indictment of capitalism, for Edward invents a cure-all cough mixture, Tono Bungay, which, chiefly through astute advertising, became enormously popular and made Edward's fortune. The point is, the mixture is bogus and everybody associated with the venture knows this. Even Edward himself admits Tono Bungay's shortcomings: 'I grant you Tono Bungay *may* be—not *quite* so good a find for the world as Peruvian Bark, but the point is, George, it makes trade! And the world lives on trade. Commerce. A romantic exchange of commodities and property. Romance. 'Magination. See?' George's view is a different one, and he steadfastly refuses to make his fortune through the quack medicine.

'£150,000—think of it!—for the goodwill in a string of lies and a trade in bottles of mitigated water. Do you realise the madness of the world that sanctions such a thing?' The Ponderevos realise that so far as the better-off are concerned, 'acquisition becomes the substance of their lives', and George concludes that British capitalism is 'all one spectacle of forces running to waste, of people who use and do not replace, the story of a country hectic with a wasting, aimless fever of trade and money making and pleasure seeking'.

Tono Bungay crashes, and Edward pursued by the law, dies on the continent in rather squalid surroundings. His bubble, big and bright enough to fill the book with its colour, bursts. George comes out of the crash with some credit and devotes his life to science. His political experiences, which include a visit to a Fabian meeting with a socialist friend, together with a nodding acquaintance with many in parliament, can offer him very little confidence for the future. At the end of the book he sails down the Thames in a new destroyer which he has largely designed. As they pass the Houses of Parliament he reflects:

> There in that great pile of Victorian architecture the landlords and the lawyers, the bishops, the railway men and the magnates of commerce go to and fro—in their incurable tradition of commercialised Bladesovery, of meretricious gentry and nobility sold for riches. I have been near enough to know. The Irish and the Labour-men run among the feet, making a fuss, effecting little; they've got no better plans that I can see. Respect for it indeed! There's a certain paraphernalia of dignity but whom does it deceive?

It is, says George, just 'a feudal scheme overtaken by fatty degeneration and stupendous accidents of hypertrophy'. But above all else, George's major criticism, and Wells's of course, is that 'amidst it all no plan appears, no intention, no comprehensive desire. That is the very key of it all.'

In *The New Machiavelli*, which appeared two years later, Wells was to develop the political criticism with which he concluded *Tono Bungay*. The book has an entirely political setting, concerning the fortunes of a young man called Remington who becomes a leading light in the Liberal party, on its radical wing. We follow Remington's progress from the Liberals to the Conservatives, and his reasons for changing parties are made plain to us by means of a lengthy analysis of the three political parties, and this forms our chief interest here. Eventually, Remington deserts politics altogether in the name of love; such is his general disillusion that he has only a few regrets.[20] What Wells does, through Remington, is to show us the total incapacity of the political machinery to undertake the tasks of efficient government in the age of democracy, and to suggest where hope for future progress might be found.

Let us begin, then, with the traditional champions of individual liberty, the Liberals.[21]

> What but a common antagonism would ever keep these multitudes together? I understood why modern electioneering is more than half of it denunciation. Let us condemn, if possible, let us obstruct and deprive, but not let us do. There is no real appeal to the commonplace mind in 'Let us do'. That calls for the creative imagination, and few have been accustomed to respond to that call. The other merely needs jealousy and hate, of which there are great and easily accessible reservoirs in every human heart . . .

On two occasions Wells stresses this underlying disunity among the Liberals. 'Liberalism', he says, 'never has been nor ever can be anything but a diversified crowd.' It is essentially the party of criticism, what he calls the Anti-party. As far as Wells is concerned this criticism is damning, for leadership and planning are, as we have seen, the essential tasks of government; this becomes even more vital in an age of democracy. 'We liberals', said Remington—when he was one 'know as a matter of fact—nowadays everybody knows—that the monster that brought us into power has, among other deficiencies, no head. We've got to give it one—if possible with brains and a will.' But even as a Liberal Remington realises that the party of which he is a member is unlikely to provide this kind of leadership because of the lack of determination on the part of its leaders, for whom politics is a 'make-believe' world. 'What they want to do . . . is to sit and feel very grave and necessary and respected on the Government benches. They think of putting their feet out like statesmen, and tilting shining hats with becoming brims over their successful noses . . . That's their reality.' Remington becomes keenly interested in Fabianism and in the Labour party, and frequents the Baileys' house. Here Wells indulges himself in an unprincipled personal attack upon the Webbs, for it is clearly they whom the Baileys represent. Altiora Bailey is shown to be a snob with little respect for the working-class MPs. One of Remington's tougher-minded Liberal colleagues, Britten, remarks of Altiora: 'Your Altiora's just the political equivalent of the ladies who sell trace cloth for embroidery: she's a dealer in Refined Social Reform for the Parlour.' The Fabian Society is written off as 'foolery . . . prigs at play'. It is worth pointing out here that Wells's experiences with the Fabian Society were anything but happy. He joined the Society full of enthusiasm, with great plans for building it into a mass movement, the very thing which the 'old gang' (as he called them), including Shaw and the Webbs, had striven to avoid. There were a series of confrontations, several of them public, in which Shaw's superior tactical and debating skills proved too much for Wells. Unable to make the Fabians into a large scale organ of education and propaganda, Wells became disenchanted. All the same, one aspect of Fabianism which appealed to Remington, and clearly appealed to Wells himself, was the idea of a small scientifically-trained élite taking part in decision-making, even if in an advisory capacity. The idea of society's most gifted 'progressive' thinkers meeting regularly on an informal basis was congenial to Wells; it took firm root in his political imagination. Nevertheless, Remington feels that the Baileys are not up to their responsibilities because they have little contact with reality. They 'go through queer little processes of definition and generalization and deduction with the completest belief in the validity of the intellectual instruments they are using . . . Cocksurists—in matter of fact; sentimentalists in behaviour.'

As for the parliamentary Labour party, Remington meets its members during an attempt at 'bridge-building' among progressives and comments on the socialists acidly: 'I could not have imagined that it was possible for half so many people to turn their backs on everybody else in such small rooms as ours.' Remington (like Wells) continues to believe in his own form of socialism, but has no faith in any of its mouthpieces. He concludes: 'To understand Socialism, again, is to gain a new breadth of outlook; to join a Socialist organisation is to join a narrow cult.' In so saying Remington articulates a feeling which was to pervade the whole of the second half of Orwell's *Wigan Pier* some twenty-five years later.

Remington's passion for progress brings him at last to the Conservative party. Traditionally, he feels, the Tories have been subjected to two cross-pressures, the one characterised by a 'certain rude benevolence of public intention', indicated for example by the party's 'constructive and collectivist' attitude towards social reform, in which it had a good record. The other consisted of a pressure to prevent reform when it involved the confiscation of property or increases in taxation on property. 'Then the Conservative Party presents a nearly adamantine bar. It does not stand for, it *is* the existing arrangement in these affairs.' All the same, it is to Tories, though not to the Conservative party as such, that Remington looks. He wants to become a part of an intellectual renaissance on the Conservative side. Remington's wife Margaret, a staunch Liberal, becomes heartbroken when her husband changes parties, realising no doubt that other possibilities of desertion may follow as well, and Remington's attempt to explain his action to her give us a clear indication of Wells's rejection of the parliamentary system and of his hopes for the future. 'Do you really think', he asks, 'that the Tories and peers and rich people are to blame for social injustice as we have it today? Do you really see politics as a struggle of light on the Liberal side against darkness on the Tory?' A little later he goes on:

> These Tory leaders are better people individually than the average; why cast them for the villains of the piece? The real villain in the piece—in the whole human drama—is the muddle-headedness, and it matters very little if it's virtuous-minded or wicked. I want to get at muddle-headedness. If I could do that I could let all that you call wickedness in the world run about and do what it jolly well pleased. It would matter about as much as a slightly neglected dog—in an otherwise well-managed home.

Remington sums up his political development as moving towards an acceptance of the principle of aristocracy, 'not of privilege but of understanding and purpose', drawn from the ranks of the economically powerful and the intellectually able. Thus his general conception of politics becomes: 'The constructive imagination working upon the vast complex of powerful people, clever people, enterprising people, influential people, amidst whom power is diffused today, to produce that self-consciousness, highly selective open-minded, devoted aristo-cratic culture which seems to me to be the necessary next phase in the development of human affairs.'

It might appear strange that Remington still holds to the 'great constructive scheme' of socialism, incredible that he believes his new aristocracy will be drawn towards socialist policies, but we must remember that he is a mouthpiece for Wells's own belief that socialism constitutes 'the scientific idea, the idea of veracity—of human confidence in humanity—of all that mattered in human life outside the life of individuals'. Remington's socialism, that is to say, forces itself upon the imagination of the nation's real leaders. The party system could not of itself achieve anything beyond incremental change; the struggle against muddle and inefficiency was not to be won by this or that party, still less by aspirations of the 'muddle-headed many', but by the interaction between intellectuals and wielders of 'real' (i.e. economic) power which would lead to an awakening of the new aristocracy to their social responsibi-lities. As we shall see later, Wells called this movement an 'open conspiracy' and it acquired a central importance; we might note, before passing on, the similarity between the open conspiracy and concepts like Coleridge's 'clerisy' and Disraeli's socially-conscious aristocracy; each was élitist and to none would socialist policies have necessarily been anathema.

4

The first of Shaw's plays we shall be looking at is *The Apple Cart* (1929), which concerns the attempt of a future cabinet to strip the British king of all political influence and make him nothing but a constitutional rubber stamp. Shaw uses this plot to explore the limitations of democratic government in a capitalist society; to indicate its probable development into a political front for large pressure groups, and to contrast this irresponsible and inefficient 'facade-democracy' with the efficiency and integrity of benevolent autocracy.

Shaw's first major point is the growth under democracy of pressure groups. Plutocracy, says Shaw, destroyed the power of the monarchy through physical force; now it has 'bought and swallowed' democracy. Plutocracy in *The Apple Cart* is represented by Breakages Ltd, a giant transport company with extremely wide interests. It has spokesmen in the cabinet and is able to exercise considerable influence over other cabinet members. This state of affairs has arisen, Shaw tells us, because democracy, in order to prevent rulers acting tyrannically, prevented them acting at all, 'thus leaving everything to irresponsible private enterprise'.[22] The power of Breakages Ltd is sufficient to thwart the ambitions of the most talented member of cabinet, the Powermistress General, Lysistrata. Indeed the only politician able to withstand Breakages is the Postmistress General, Amanda. Yet her method is not likely to commend itself to democrats. The chairman of Breakages contested Amanda's seat at the previous election, with all the support of his company's financial and organisational resources. He made a most impressive speech to a large local meeting, but Amanda, addressing the same meeting the following week, chose simply to mimic all the more high falutin' passages, causing uproar, and then asking the meeting to join her in a song. Breakage's chairman fled the battle.

The other representative of large pressure groups are the trade unions, more precisely the trade union leader Bill Boanerges. Boanerges is as sceptical of democracy as King Magnus, and tells that his approach to 'the people' is to remind them: 'You have supreme power'. They reply: 'Yes, tell us what to do!' Boanerges is completely confident of his position, saying: 'No king on earth is as safe in his job as a Trade Union official. There is only one thing that can get him sacked; and that is drink. Not even that, as long as he doesn't actually fall down.'

In the face of this enormous growth of private power, cabinet meetings have become a mockery; ministers are described as 'the nearest thing to a puppet in our political system' and their work looked down upon by men of ability as 'dirty work'. 'What great actor', King Magnus asks, 'would exchange his stage? what great barrister his court? what great preacher his pulpit? for the squalor of the political arena in which we have to struggle with foolish factions in parliament and with ignorant voters in constituencies?' Politics, he continues, once the centre of attraction for men of ability,

> has become the refuge of a few financiers of public speaking
> and party intrigue who find all the other avenues to distinction
> closed to them, either by their lack of practical ability, their
> comparative poverty and lack of education, or, let me hasten
> to add [for fear of offending his audience of cabinet ministers]
> their hatred of oppression and injustice.

Shaw's position here is substantially different from both
Wells's and his own position in, for example, *Heartbreak House*
and *Man and Superman*, for then it was the ruling class, principally, which was the target for attack. Here, in a work written
after two Labour governments, the target is capitalist democracy. In fact Shaw attacks the whole basis of representative
democracy when he argues:

> An election at present, considered as a means of selecting
> the best qualified rulers, is so absurd that if the last dozen
> parliaments had consisted of the candidates who were at
> the foot of the poll instead of those who were at the head
> of it there is no reason to suppose that we should have
> been a step more or less advanced than we are today.

We may want to quibble with this, since fringe parties usually
finish at the bottom of polls, but we surely have little reason
to doubt the substance of the general point. In short, bearing
in mind the inefficiencies of the electoral system, parliament,
and the government machinery, together with the ability of
large monopolies to control the political system for their own
advantage, we might feel inclined to accept Shaw's advice:
that we should look upon democracy as 'a big balloon, filled
with gas or hot air, and sent up so that you shall be kept
looking up at the sky whilst other people are picking your
pockets'.

Shaw's alternatives will be examined in depth later, but
it is worth pointing out here that Magnus is able to present
a sound argument for benevolent autocracy. As king, he is
not obliged to play the 'democratic game' and can therefore
champion what he calls the great abstractions—the eternal
against the expedient, and so on. Monarchs, says Shaw, whilst
they may not, like Elizabeth I, be the natural superiors of
their ministers in terms of political genius, are all the same

'superior to them in experience, in cunning, in exact knowledge of the limits of their responsibility . . . in short, in the *authority and practical power* that these superiorities produce'.[23] It is in precisely these terms, practical power—the ability to get things done—that capitalist democracy stands condemned.

The second play we shall consider here is *On The Rocks* (1933). This play, as the title suggests, tells of a society in a state of crisis, not unlike that which confronted Britain in the early 1930s and, arguably, the mid-1970s. Sir Arthur Chavender is the Liberal leader of an all-party coalition which has palpably failed to solve the twin problems of mass poverty and unemployment. At the beginning of the play Sir Arthur is discussing with the Chief Commissioner of Police, Broadfoot Basham, the problems of controlling the crowds of workers whose continuous demonstrations are posing a threat to law and order. Basham wants to arrange for the mobs to be addressed by politicians, reasoning that they can do nothing mischievous when listening and that politicians are disinclined to do anything but speak.

At this point in the play, a deputation from the workers of the Isle of Cats appears. Among the deputation are to be found a scruffily dressed red Viscount and an old trade union leader Hipney, whose words we have heard already, and who stays behind to offer the Prime Minister some advice. Hipney speaks out not for democracy or power-sharing but for better material conditions for the workers. Chavender listens with polite interest. His next visitor of importance is a female doctor of somewhat mystical manner and speech, who convinces Chavender to go into retreat in the Welsh mountains for two weeks. Fortified by the help of his new psycho-medical guide and by two weeks of reading Marx in solitude (on Hipney's advice) Sir Arthur bounces back to his problems, setting out a fully socialist plan to get the nation back to work. By making concessions to the armed forces and the police he is able to secure their support, together with that of an impoverished aristocracy and of the representatives of the business community, who believe the plan will promote industry. In fact only the Conservative party, in its role of champion of individual liberty, opposes Sir Arthur. But at this crucial point the deputation from the Isle of Cats makes its return and, on behalf of the workers, sides with the Conservative leader, Sir Dexter Rightside. The mayor of the Isle of Cats believes Chavender's schemes are simply an attempt further to bully the working class. 'But if you think that the British working-man will listen to compulsory labour and putting down strikes you don't know the world you're living in; and that's all about it.'

This confrontation is a perfect illustration of one of Shaw's major criticisms of capitalist democracy; the working class form the major anti-progressive element and are the natural allies of those who seek, for ideological reasons or for personal gain (sometimes for both) to limit the power of the state. But Chavender tries to defend the people against their representatives. The people are 'sick of being told that, thanks to democracy, they are the real government of the country. They know very well that they don't govern and can't govern and know nothing about Government except that it always supports profiteering and doesn't really respect anything else, no matter what party flag it waves.' Hipney sides with the Prime Minister, advising him not to concern himself with seeking to use his power in a parliamentary manner: 'The only man that ever had a proper understanding of Parliament was old Guy Fawkes.' Chavender should act as a dictator and place his confidence not in a parliamentary vote but on the strength of his own values: 'All this country or any country has to stand between it and blue hell is the consciences of them that are capable of governing it.'

At the end of the play Chavender's problems remain unresolved, but his last major speech is significant because it not only outlines Chavender's own position but is probably one of the clearest statements of Shaw's personal position. Chavender recognises that his career as a Prime Minister has amounted to a 'whitewashing job', at which he feels he was very adept— whitewashing over the slums. Yet he knew that poor as the East End was, the West End was 'chock full of money and nice people all calling one another by their Christian names'. He knew this but did nothing because he genuinely believed that nothing could be done, or at best very little and very slowly. He tells his wife that:

I know better now; I know that it can be helped. And rather than go back to the old whitewashing job, I'd seize you tight round the waist and make a hole in the river with you . . . Why don't I lead a revolt against it all? Because I'm not the man for the job . . . And I shall hate the man who will carry it through for his cruelty and the desolation he will bring on us and our like.

In Shaw's view it is the inefficiency of the capitalist system which produces misery for the masses and permits it to continue. There is no doubt in his mind that poverty not only should but could be abolished, but that this will not be done as the result of majority votes in a corrupt and venal parliament.

For Shaw as for Wells there is no hope for socialism within the fabric of capitalist democracy, neither from the representatives of the old social order nor from the democratically elected representatives of the people, and certainly not from the political parties. Both men look towards able individuals who will act for the common good, but almost certainly without common support, and who will lead us into a new era of efficient legislation. Shaw's description of politically inept leadership in capitalist democracy will serve as an apt conclusion.[24]

On the whole, what with our old traditions and new circumstances; our plutocratic legislators trained in nothing but the art of organising the labour of the masses for the benefit of the classes; our acceptance of hero worship, monomania, and partisanship as policy and statecraft; and our ideal cabinet consisting of a lord, a smart debater, a blockhead, and a successful tradesman (representing gentility, brains, the national character and our great industries) with the necessary padding of experienced office seekers to do the hard work, it is not wonderful that the opposition is never at a loss to substantiate the charge of vulgarity, imbecility, cruelty, mismanagement and muddle upon which it demands the dismissal of the government, and on which it will in due course be dismissed. . . .

If we are to believe Wells's Mr Britling, so long as the present social-political system continues, it will be replaced by a cabinet remarkably similarly in all respects.

WHICH WAY FORWARD?

The various criticisms of capitalist society which we considered in Section One gain more force when seen as what they were, parts of coherent systems of thought which not only recognised the shortcomings of society as it existed but also considered how they were to be overcome, and what life might be like when they were. However, we have observed already that fundamental differences existed between the way in which some socialists interpreted the ills of bourgeois society and hence how they sought to cure them. One of the most fundamental differences, which we will discuss in this section, can be put simply: could socialism be established without a revolution? There was hardly a socialist who did *not* believe in *some kind* of revolution and who did not speak about (for example) revolutionary changes in the education system. What divided them was whether or not a violent overthrow of the bourgeois state was necessary in order to establish a socialist society. One of the early champions of the revolutionary tradition, Babeuf, argued that throughout history classes and groups had guaranteed their pre-eminence by controlling the agencies of 'governmental coercion'. No such group, he argued, would yield peacefully to a rival and would thus need to be overthrown violently by superior force. This argument in favour of revolution is, as one writer put it, 'always an apology for violence from within the precepts of rationalism and never a vindication of it';[1] revolution, that is to say, is seen to be a sad necessity.

Others, however, of whom Moses Hess is an example, would argue that only in its struggle with others could a group realise its own consciousness. Here revolutionary violence is advocated not apologetically but positively, as being fundamentally a creative agency through which individuals or groups can fulfil themselves. Marx believed that only the traumatic experience of revolutionary violence itself could free the proletariat from the illusion that its interests and those of the bourgeoisie were reconcilable. 'The violence of the revolution clarifies the issues, obliges millions to declare their positions, it enormously accelerates the growth of consciousness.'[2] This line of argument holds particular attractions for colonial and ex-colonial societies and has been advanced forcefully by revolutionary writers like Franz Fanon of whose celebrated *Wretched of the Earth* Eldridge Cleaver wrote: 'What this book does is to legitimize the revolutionary impulse to violence. It teaches colonial subjects that it is perfectly normal for them to want to rise up and cut off the heads of the slave-masters, that it is a way to achieve their manhood, and that they must oppose the oppressors in order to experience themselves as men.'[3]

The appeal to violent men of the arguments of both apologists for and advocates of violence is obvious enough, but it must be realised that they have a more general attraction especially for those we have described as moralists. The revolutionary situation admits of no prevarication. It is necessary to take sides, necessary to side with the exploited against their exploiters. As George Orwell wrote: 'I have no particular love for the idealized "worker" as he appears in the bourgeois Communist's mind, but when I see an actual flesh-and-blood worker in conflict with his natural enemy, the policeman, I do not have to ask myself which side I am on.'[4]

To the scientific socialist the prospect of controlling a revolutionary movement which would establish rule by a socialist élite holds considerable attractions. But he will be aware, like Swift, that the world was a 'den of dangerous animals' over whom, in a situation of violence, he could exercise little control except through even greater violence. 'A mob of desperate sufferers', wrote Shaw, 'abandoned to the leadership of exasperated sentimentalists and fanatic theorists may, at a vast cost of bloodshed and misery, succeed in removing no single evil except perhaps the existence of the human race.'[5] Even under the leadership of scientists rather than sentimentalists the practical difficulties would be enormous. 'Demolishing a Bastille with seven prisoners in it is one thing; demolishing one with fourteen million prisoners is quite another.'[6] At first sight it might appear strange that few socialist writers were willing to emphasise the inherently distasteful nature of revolutionary violence but preferred to concentrate on practical matters. It is worth emphasising that most would have considered society itself to be acting with unacceptable violence towards the great majority of people in keeping them in poverty and degradation.

For the majority of scientific socialists, then, a controlled and gradual transition towards socialism was the only possible way forward; the complex mechanisms of control of the socialist state could scarcely come into being spontaneously as the result of a violent overthrow of the existing order. Far better for socialists to propagate their beliefs and in the meantime to win as many concessions as possible from the bourgeois state in the effort to build socialism slowly.

For moralists like Orwell and Morris a socialist revolution could unlock the true consciousness of the working class and transfer real power, as no other means could, to the hands of the people. In this section we shall be examining attitudes to revolution and to evolutionary change. It would be facile, and for that matter quite wrong, to imagine that moralist writers were pro-revolutionary and scientists anti-revolutionary; we can only say that the possibility of revolution held certain attractions for the moralists and evolutionary change for the scientists. But none of the writers we shall be looking at (with the possible exception of Wells) was dogmatic on this issue; each explored the tensions inherent within their own arguments and in the end, perhaps, none was fully confident of his own position.

5 'Revolution, Revolution is the one correct solution'

Not many novels or plays with a revolutionary theme have been influential in Britain. Revolutionary experiences have been hard to come by and where writers have used their powers of imagination to recreate from history they have tended, like Dickens in *A Tale of Two Cities*, to use a revolution as a background for adventure and romance. But revolution *as a theme* is quite uncommon. In this chapter we shall be dealing in the main with William Morris and George Orwell, and to a lesser extent with Jack London and Arthur Koestler. One distinction needs to be drawn before we continue: that between the revolution itself and the period following, which, for convenience, we shall call the post-revolution, when the revolutionary government, having achieved power, seeks to establish itself firmly and permanently and to begin to implement the policies based upon the objectives of the revolution. The first two sections of this chapter will deal with revolution, then, and the third with post-revolution.

I

The best-known of William Morris's works is *News From Nowhere*, a visionary novel about future socialist society. He wrote the book for general inspirational purposes, but more particularly to counter the views set out by Edward Bellamy in his popular work *Looking Backward* (1888). Bellamy envisaged a highly cen-

tralised and regimented socialist society developing slowly and
naturally in response to changing circumstances. Bellamy's
socialism was anathema to Morris and he could not believe
that the governing class would relinquish power willingly, however much circumstances changed. Morris's views on the inevitability of revolution are not unambivalent but there was clearly
a period in his life when he very firmly believed in the need
for a violent overthrow of the capitalist social order: this period
followed the events of Bloody Sunday (1887). Morris took an
active part in that ill-fated demonstration and his experiences,
set out in 'London in a State of Siege', in *Commonweal*,
(19/11/1887) led him to believe that the ruling class was prepared to defend its privileges by violence and that its supremacy
could thus only be terminated by violence. The fact is, though,
that Morris did not undertake to drill, train or organise for
the revolution and his commitment to it, though it remained
for the rest of his life, became shallower—or perhaps less enthusiastic.

All the same, the socialist society depicted in *News From
Nowhere* was the result of a bloody revolution, and the course
of that revolution is explored in detail. The book concerns
a nineteenth-century socialist—Morris himself, to all intents
and purposes—who awakes one morning to find himself transported several hundred years into the future. He lives as a
guest from abroad in this new, socialist paradise for a short
while and his experiences and observations will be considered
in detail in a later chapter. For present purposes, though,
his discussions with Hammond, an intellectual figure of great
eminence, are of most interest, for Hammond tells his guest
(whom we shall refer to as Morris) about the revolution itself
and the developments which led up to it. Morris's other writings
on the subject[1] leave us in little doubt that he sets out here
his belief concerning likely future events in Britain. Hammond
tells Morris of the successes, prior to the revolution, of 'meliorist'
socialists in securing what he calls an era of state socialism,
when considerable concessions were wrung from the governing
class by organised pressure. But state socialism turned out to
be inefficient itself and, equally important, its existence prevented the efficient functioning of capitalism. In short, state
socialism was a sort of half-way house which could only prove
to be temporary. The successes gained by the socialists, though,

had provided the organised working class with important experience in the tactics of combination. Eventually all workers had
formed into a federation which held and periodically used the
power to close down whole industries for tactical purposes.

Meanwhile their representatives in parliament had gained
important concessions as a result of this industrial power, such
as shorter working hours, with a higher wage rate to compensate,
and a national minimum wage. Eventually the government
was obliged to take control of certain basic industries because
private enterprise, hamstrung by the new legislation, was incapable of running them at a profit. In the meantime the socialists
had been achieving success in spreading their 'communistic
theories'. When trade became slack and industry began to
stagnate the workers' leaders (not their parliamentary representatives) passed a resolution calling for the socialisation of all
natural resources and the means of production. A great meeting
was called and duly held at Trafalgar Square. As a result
of incompetence and police brutality a number of workers and
policemen were killed. This first serious incident had the effect
of beginning to polarise the supporters of the establishment
and of the workers; London was in turmoil and riots took
place, or were threatened, everywhere. Public confidence in
the government began to crumble and business came to a
standstill. The government of the day, a progressive one, felt
obliged to declare a state of emergency and to bring sections
of the army to London. For their part the workers set up
a Committee of Public Safety and in some areas took control
of bakeries and began to ration and distribute bread.

At this point the industrialists decided to put pressure on
the government to act against the workers. Fearing that the
industrialists might take the law into their own hands the government did indeed take the first opportunity to show its strength.
A large meeting of workers in Trafalgar Square was fired on
by frightened soldiers and over one thousand workers killed.
Surviving members of the Committee of Public Safety were
imprisoned and brought to trial. But the jury found the workers'
leaders not guilty and moreover made a presentment decrying
the 'rash, unfortunate and unnecessary' action of the soldiers.
Free again, the Committee members pressed new demands upon
the government and, in the meantime, prepared a complete
network of local worker organisations. The government had

by now reached a point of crisis, not knowing whether to act resolutely against the workers or to give way to their further demands. Amid the indecision the Tory opposition took over the government and a number of progressive MPs defected to the workers. The new government immediately imprisoned the members of the Committee of Public Safety but they had already completed their preparations and the newly-fashioned workers' organisation, comprising 'a great number of links of small centres', called for a general strike. Whom was the government to act against? How was it to communicate to and secure the loyalty of the public, since there were no newspapers? Only the communist broadsheets appeared, setting out the doctrines and practices of the workers' movement with what Morris, in an inspired turn of phrase, called 'May-day freshness'. The government's position was further undermined by the knowledge that the army would be unlikely to act against the workers as it had in Trafalgar Square. In any event the drama was now being played out locally not nationally, around the many relief centres formed by the workers, to which even the wealthy were forced to turn in order to get the necessities of life. So the government decided to free the workers' leaders in the hope that they might take an initiative to which the government could respond. But they did not, and the government found itself in a situation rather like that of the British general staff after the first year of the Boer War, when their enemy would not confront them in the open field but preferred to fight in small commando units.

The government, then, could do nothing but come to terms with the Committee of Public Safety—at least for the time being. It was at this point that a right-wing movement, The Friends of Order, was established. The movement attacked the local worker organisations and the resulting bloodshed obliged the government to act at last: it threw its weight behind the Friends of Order. The resulting civil war produced enormous physical destruction and great loss of life. Those who could not accept the prospect of a new social order fought to the last; but in vain, for the civil population opposed the government forces and the defeat of the old order was inevitable.

Dreadful though it was the civil war had proved necessary in two respects and happily advantageous in a third. First, to quote Hammond, it was very doubtful 'whether, without this seemingly dreadful civil war, the due talent for administration would have been developed among the working men.'[2] Second, the war permitted the development of a 'true consciousness' among the workers which would be of the greatest assistance in building socialism; and third the massive programme of de-urbanisation necessary for the development of the small-community socialism of Nowhere was made possible coincidentally, by the large-scale destruction of factories.

It has to be said that this account of the 'revolution' is not in the least important to the structure of the novel, such as it is; it is simply one of Hammond's many stories. Its interest lies in its providing the scenario for a possible socialist revolution in Britain, and it is in these terms we need to discuss it. The first point to be made is that Morris seems prepared to accept that the political nose of the governing class will betray it. Through its agents, the police and the army, it will over-react—will make a crass mistake and provide the workers with martyrs. Yet Morris's own 'real-life' experiences in Trafalgar Square on Bloody Sunday seem to have led him to a very different conclusion; that the forces of law and order were extremely well organised and extremely shrewdly led. Tactical skill coupled to strategic incompetence is an unlikely though not impossible combination, and certainly not one that revolutionaries could bank on. Moreover, when he builds on Marxist theory rather than personal experience in depicting the nature of government in the 'state-socialist' half-way house, he does not foresee the problems created for socialism by the inclusion of numbers of its representatives in the elected government; for they, too, would surely strive to defend the legitimacy of a system which had provided them with a measure of power.[3] The legitimacy of the constitutional system is simply not made into an issue by the government of the day and yet an appeal to the people, and of course to the armed forces, on such grounds would clearly have won wide support. We are asked to believe, then, that the government would make a crass mistake in the first Trafalgar Square riot, follow this by not using its chief psychological weapon, an appeal to legitimacy, and be so out of touch as to be nonplussed by the jury's decision to free the Committee of Public Safety (!); and to crown all this by allowing the soldiers such freedom of action that over one thousand workers are killed. By the standards of common experience this represents an unlikely sequence of events. It is also strange that the government makes no appeal for outside assistance. This would make sense only if the major industrial nations had already undergone similar revolutions and would thus be unwilling to recognise the government in Britain as legitimate. But foreign intervention, after all, is a major feature of most revolutionary movements and one could expect such intervention in the British revolution on one and possibly both sides.

There remains a further difficulty which Hammond, in his story, leaves unresolved. Given the success of the revolution, are we to conclude that the Committee of Public Safety simply allowed itself to wither away? Are we to believe that the new scheme of things—in which 'the spirit of the new days, our days, was to be delight in the life of the world; intense and overweening love of the very skin and surface of the earth on which man dwells, such as the lover has in the fair flesh of the woman he loves'—sprang up spontaneously? In other words, Morris deals with the post-revolution by ignoring it almost entirely.

Morris's version of the socialist revolution, based chiefly on what he imagined might, perhaps ought to have happened after Bloody Sunday, seems realistic only insofar as many people lose their lives. In other respects it seems romantic and far-fetched. Certainly stranger sequences of events have occurred, but it is surely unlikely that Morris would have won many over to the cause of socialist revolution on the strength of Hammond's account and this, surely, was his intention. The socialist revolution, for Morris, would be a short, sharp shock, a cold shower in the morning of the socialist day.

For Jack London the socialist revolution was to be a much more drawn out and painful affair and in his celebrated novel *The Iron Heel* (1907), influential among British intellectuals of the thirties, London depicts the events leading up to the establishment of an oligarchy in the United States and the early attempts of socialist workers' movements to overthrow that government. As in *News From Nowhere* the victory has already gone to the socialists, and we are, in fact, retracing the steps of history. The novel is supposed to be a long-lost manuscript written by the wife of an early socialist leader by the name of Ernest Everhard and not discovered until 'long after the final triumph of socialist democracy'. In most other respects

London's story is quite different from Morris's. To begin with, London's novel, like Malraux's *Man's Estate* (1933), is about revolution and revolutionaries and, as a consequence, violence, not simply as part of a theory, but as a series of bloody acts, dominates the work.

Everhard (the name parodies the man) is described as a 'natural aristocrat ... He was a superman, a blond beast such as Nietzsche had described, and in addition he was aflame with democracy.'[4] The basic flaw in capitalist society, as Everhard sees it, is that a conflict between the interests of labour and capital is inevitable since both are straining to maximise rewards in a situation in which rewards are strictly finite. 'That is what we socialists are trying to bring about—the abolition of the conflict of interests', says Everhard somewhat optimistically. All the same, Everhard presents the socialist case to members of the governing class of the American West Coast not as a basic bargaining position but as an implacably hostile philosophy. He rightly predicts that as socialism gains ground amongst the workers, the oligarchy will take firm action to maintain its position. 'We will grind you revolutionists down under our heel', says Wickson the industrialist, 'and we shall walk on your faces. The world is ours, we are its Lords, and ours it shall remain.'

In order to achieve this objective the oligarchy forms an organisation known appropriately as The Iron Heel whose task is to infiltrate and break working class 'revolutionary' cadres. It sets up paramilitary groups known as Black Hundreds to smash socialist presses and disrupt meetings. The socialist political leaders, including Everhard, are discredited by the planting of a bomb in the House of Representatives and an attempt is made to bring them to trial. More long-term strategies include the recognition of 'favoured unions' whose members become a kind of labour aristocracy and who thus may be counted upon to support the oligarchy. Moreover the oligarchy sheds its earlier inefficiency and indolence and comes to see itself as the guardian of civilised values. 'I cannot lay too much stress upon this high ethical righteousness of the whole oligarch class', says Everhard. 'This has been the great strength of the Iron Heel and too many of the comrades have been slow or loath to realise it.' What London is suggesting is that the governing class would in fact place a great deal of emphasis upon legitimacy, not simply as being the lawful government but as possessing the ark of the covenant of all civilised values. But though they may be the champions of the rule of law, the oligarchs are not prepared to extend its advantages to the socialists. In fact they oblige them to act illegitimately; they drive them towards revolutionary action on a large scale.

The situation is a totally confused one, for although the revolutionaries are successful so long as they restrict themselves to a kind of urban guerrilla war, their groups are riddled with *agents provocateurs* and they are eventually persuaded to organise a premature and abortive uprising in Chicago which the oligarchs crush with great bloodshed. In *The Iron Heel*, then, London's governing class is far more bold and skilful in dealing with the socialist revolutionaries than Morris's had been. London shows an awareness of the international dimension, in that both government and revolutionaries are in contact with overseas counterparts and co-operate with them. He shows us how the oligarchy is able to divide the working class against itself. All in all, he convinces us that the battle for socialism will be long and ferocious. Yet that the battle is worth fighting is never in doubt for London; the socialist and the capitalist simply inhabit different plains of existence.

Joseph Conrad wrote two novels not actually about revolution, but about revolutionaries. These are *The Secret Agent* (1907) and *Under Western Eyes* (1911). It would be fair to say, though, that Conrad was above all interested in the psychological make-up of his socialist and anarchist characters rather than in the *raisons d'être* or the fates of the revolutionary movements. His characters are somewhat larger than life and more than a little repulsive, as is well shown by the descriptions of the revolutionaries in *The Secret Agent*: Michaelis, who was 'round like a tub, with an enormous stomach and distended cheeks of a pale, semi-transparent complexion, as though for fifteen years the servants of an outraged society had made a point of stuffing him with fattening foods in a damp and lightless cellar'; Yundt the terrorist, 'old and bald, with a narrow, snow-white wisp of a goatee hanging limply from his chin. An extraordinary expression of malevolence survived in his extinguished eyes'; finally Comrade Ossipon, 'a bush of crinkly yellow hair topped his red, freckled face, with a flattened nose and prominent mouth cast in the rough mould of the Negro type. His almond-shaped eyes leered languidly over the high cheek-bones.'[5] Conrad suggests to us that the character of those who may lead revolutionary movements will be formed more by psychological tensions than social idealism. It is a valid observation; revolution, by definition a time of violence, is likely to attract the sons and daughters of violence.

This is a theme which finds echo in two of Aldous Huxley's novels, *Point Counter Point* (1928), which we have already looked at, and *Eyeless in Gaza* (1936). In the former, Illidge the communist is spurred on by Spandrell, a Satanist figure, to commit a revolutionary act—to assassinate Everard Webley, the fascist leader. Huxley clearly shows the roots of Illidges's bitter discontent to be as much psychological as social. Huxley speaks of Illidge's impotent hatred being the result of a subversive face and general social ineptitude. Illidge 'resented the virtues of the rich much more than their vices.' Mark Staithes, in *Eyeless in Gaza*, is a revolutionary for the sake of revolution. It is the violence, the quest for power and the opportunity to imprint his personality on the course of events which make Staithes a revolutionary.

Huxley later goes on to analyse the make-up of revolutionary parties, through Anthony Beavis's comments on the communist movement, which he calles 'organized hatred'. They comprise:[6]

> Idealists with an exceptional gift for self-deception. Either they don't know that it's organized hatred, or else they genuinely believe that the end justifies the means, genuinely imagine that the means don't condition the end . . . They form the majority. And then there are two minorities. A minority of people who know that the thing's organized hatred and rejoice in the fact. And a minority that's ambitious, that merely uses the movement as a convenient machine for realizing its ambition.

Obviously it would not be circumspect to place too much faith in any such movement's ability to create a new kind of society!

2

Of all the writers we have labelled moralists none wrote more perceptively or at greater length about the nature of revolution than George Orwell. Orwell, after all, had first-hand experience of a revolutionary struggle, having fought and been all but killed in the civil war in Spain. In his book *Homage to Catalonia* (1938) Orwell sets out his revolutionary experiences and his reflections on them with considerable clarity and honesty and we find the 'real' Orwell in the 'real' revolution reacting in much the same way as London's fictional hero Everhard. Orwell was captivated by the atmosphere in Barcelona on his first visit, and later, at the Aragon front.

Although he tended to over-romanticise, Orwell was able to detach himself and analyse his feelings. He notes at one point, for example: 'The revolutionary posters were everywhere, flaming from the walls in clean reds and blues that made the few remaining advertisements look like daubs of mud',[7] but comments a little later: 'There was much of this that I did not understand, in some ways I did not even like it, but I recognized it immediately as a state of affairs worth fighting for.' It was worth fighting for because 'human beings were trying to behave as human beings and not as cogs in the capitalist machine.' Yet at the same time Orwell recognised that this particular revolution was doomed to defeat and that the Barcelona he so admired could not last; in fact Orwell fully realised that the whole intensely egalitarian and comradely atmosphere was a passing phenomenon. The Italian militiaman whom Orwell met provides a cameo of Orwell's Spanish experiences. He met the man only briefly but portrays him as a symbol of the warmth, compassion and decency of the proletariat. Yet he commented: 'But I knew that to retain my first impression of him I must not see him again.'

Homage to Catalonia is one of the clearest and fullest accounts we have of the working out of the tensions between the principles which revolution seeks to establish (or in this case maintain) and the methods necessary to win the struggle. For Orwell the main revolutionary principles were equality and 'common decency' and the methods necessary for victory were discipline, efficiency and solidarity. Take the case of the POUM (Trotskyist) militia which Orwell joined. It represented 'a sort of temporary working model of the classless society. Of course there was no perfect equality, but there was a nearer approach to it than I have ever seen or than I would have thought conceivable in time of war.' 'Revolutionary' discipline, he goes on, depends upon political consciousness, an understanding of *why* orders must be obeyed; Orwell believed that it took no longer to instill such discipline than it did to instill what he called 'automaton' discipline. If we accept these assertions we find the conflict between principles and methods (ends and means) to be reconciled. However, later in the narrative, Orwell met a detachment of Andalusians, whom he considered to be extraordinarily simple men: 'Few if any of them could read, and they seemed not to know the one thing that everybody knows in Spain—which political party they belonged to.' We may wonder how long it would take to instill 'revolutionary' discipline in troops such as these! Moreover, although the Spanish Civil War was a primitive affair by modern standards, it was won nevertheless by the efficiency, technical expertise and superior equipment of the Falangists and their Axis allies. To make a general point, when battles depended upon the courage and tenacity of individual soldiers then the principles for which they were fighting *may* have been supremely important but nowadays battles are likely to be won and lost by technical efficiency; the fact that each man understands and supports the reasons behind the orders he receives can become quite irrelevant.

A second and more significant example of the tension between revolutionary principles and winning the war is provided by a comparison of revolutionary (i.e. POUM and anarchist) and communist organisation and policy. The revolutionary policy was to picture the war as a revolutionary struggle against all forms of fascism and on behalf of worker control, and revolution-ary organisation stressed liberty and equality. The communists, on the other hand, laid emphasis on strong central control and argued that: 'Whoever tries to turn the civil war into a social revolution is playing into the hands of the Fascists and is in effect, if not in intention, a traitor.' Orwell seems unable totally to resolve these tensions, for he says that the communists appeared to be the only people capable of winning the war and that: 'The revolutionary purism of the POUM, though I saw its logic, seemed to me rather futile. After all, the one thing that mattered was to win the war.' Yet Orwell thought the attempts of the communists to discredit and even liquidate their revolutionary allies totally obnoxious.

In short, the communists might have been the better organised to win the war, but was the war worth winning on their terms? 'On paper the Communist case was a good one; the only trouble was that their actual behaviour made it difficult to believe that they were advancing it in good faith.' All revolutions may be failures, he decided, but not all the same failure; the *idea* might survive. The end will survive, if it is not sacrificed to the means.

The final tension to be considered is that between the nobility of the principles of revolutionary struggle and the sordid reality. It is commonplace to answer the jingoist with the statements of his victims, such as Remarque's *All Quiet on the Western Front* (1929). It is less common perhaps to confront the revolutionary's equally romantic and equally dangerous idea of the glories of revolutionary struggle with harsh reality. It is the supreme tension of *Homage to Catalonia* that it justifies (indeed occasionally glorifies) revolutionary struggle and yet also paints the reality of violence in the most sombre colours. We remember the awful picture of Orwell's hospital train, for example, as it drew into Tarragona, full of wounded, pitifully cared for. It happened to pass a troop train on its way to the front.

> It was a very long train, packed to bursting point with men, with field guns lashed onto the open trucks and more men clustering round the guns. I remember with particular vividness the spectacle of that train passing in the yellow evening light; window after window full of dark smiling faces, the long tilted barrels of the guns, the scarlet scarves fluttering—all this gliding slowly past us against a turquoise-coloured sea.

As Orwell remarked, this meeting was an allegorical picture of war, or alternatively reality and illusion at the point of intersection—and yet those on the hospital train who were well enough stood and cheered. Somebody waved a crutch out of a window and 'bandaged forearms made the Red Salute'.

Orwell's Spanish experiences gave his attitude to socialism, and more specifically to revolutionary socialism, much more vigour than consistency: the main tensions remained unresolved.[8] He was obviously reluctant to discard his belief in the necessity of revolution and yet he seemed to have little faith in the successful outcome of such a revolution. As we have already seen he believed that ideas could survive failure, and that the successful revolution might one day be accomplished by the proletariat. 'The struggle of the working class', he wrote, 'is like the growth of a plant. The plant is blind and stupid but it knows enough to keep pushing upwards towards the light, and it will do this in the face of endless discouragements.'[9] In a sense Orwell, too, was working towards the successful revolution like the plant towards the light. It has to be said, though, that his political masterpiece, *Animal Farm*,[10] seems to go further than he ever intended in exploring the dimensions of the failed revolution.

As we shall be examining *Animal Farm* in detail it is important to begin by stating why Orwell wrote the book, since his motives have often been misunderstood. He wished to dissociate events in the USSR from the picture of socialism in the popular imagination. He wished to depict the Russian revolution as a failed revolution dominated by an egocentric megalomaniac, and he did so by means of a fable—a simple animal story. The events in the story follow so closely those of the Russian revolution that there can be not the slightest doubt of the author's intention. Marx, Stalin and Trotsky[11]—not to mention Mayakovsky the poet—are clearly represented, as are Germany and the Western Powers. Events such as the Russian revolution itself, the rebellion at the Kronstadt naval base in 1921, the Treaty of Rapollo in 1922 (ending the capitalist boycott of the USSR), the German invasion of Russia in 1941 and the Tehran Conference of 1944 are equally clearly depicted, and so are three definable periods in Soviet history; that of collectivisation (1929–33), that of the Great Purges (1936–8) and that of the rapprochement with Germany (1939–41).[12] In short, there can be not the slightest doubt that the story of Animal Farm is the story of the Russian revolution.

But the matter can hardly be left there. We have to ask whether the fable does more than Orwell strictly intended. *Animal Farm*, it may be argued, stands as an indictment of revolution as such, not of this or that particular revolution. One critic has compared *Animal Farm* to *Gulliver's Travels* in this respect.[13] Swift's satire was aimed at specific contemporary targets and it adds much to a reading of the book if we are familiar with the politics of the late eighteenth century. But the book's powerful interest remains, even without that knowledge, because it has a far wider relevance; it has something to say about the politics of any age. It is hard to imagine that *Animal Farm* will not be read in, say, fifty years from now, when the details of the Russian revolution may have been generally forgotten; for it, too, whatever the author's intent, has something to say about the nature of revolution in any age.

Animal Farm, then, is an account of a revolution which takes place on Manor Farm. The revolution follows a speech made to the farm animals by an old boar named Major. The speech is modelled upon the concluding section of the *Communist Manifesto*. Major states that all animals are equal and that all men are enemies, and he makes it abundantly clear that only by eschewing the customary practices of humanity can the animals maintain a condition of equality. They must never wear clothes, live in a house, drink, smoke, use money or engage in trade. The animal society to which Major's dicta are to apply is a diverse one but whilst it would be nugatory to attempt to draw precise parallels for each animal in human society, we can take two things for granted; clearly animal society as a whole may be taken to represent human society and, equally clearly, certain of the animals *are* meant to be representational. For example, we can confidently assign the label 'intellectuals' to the pigs, recognise in Clover and Boxer that better-off section of the working class whose virtues Orwell extolled in *Road to Wigan Pier*, see the sheep as the unthinking 'proles', the raven as organised religion, and understand that Benjamin occupies the role of the writer—Benda's 'cleric' (almost certainly partly Orwell himself). This is the animal society, stung by Major's rhetoric into a dim awareness of its desperate condition, driven by his analysis towards the first glimmerings of a 'true' consciousness.

Major set the chief task of the days ahead as being to educate the animals for revolution, and it was at this early stage that the pigs began to assume leadership.[14] 'The work of teaching and organizing the others fell upon the pigs, who were generally recognized as being the cleverest of the animals.'[15] The most prominent parts were taken by Snowball, Napoleon and Squealer.

Old Major died before the revolution dawned, but dawn it did—and sooner than anyone had expected. One mid-summer's eve Jones the farmer had got drunk and had forgotten to feed the animals next morning. They became so hungry that they decided to break into the store-shed. Jones and his men attacked them but were scared off and so 'almost before they knew what was happening, the Rebellion had been successfully carried out.' The first stage in the revolutionary agenda had been accomplished with surprising ease, but the task remained to establish revolutionary society.

The majority of the animals were blissfully happy at the departure of their masters but quite oblivious of what was to become of them. 'They rolled in the dew, they cropped mouthfuls of the sweet summer grass, they kicked up clods of the black earth and snuffed its rich scent.' Meanwhile Snowball and Napoleon took effective control. It was revealed that during the past three months the pigs had taught themselves to read and write—not, of course, forbidden by Major—and they wrote on the big barn wall the Seven Commandments, incorporating the spirit of animalism. Thereafter they organised the other animals. We should note two developments in these early days of the revolution. First, what happened to the milk and later on to the apples. 'Never mind the milk, comrades', said Napoleon when asked. It was being taken to the pigs for their exclusive use. So were the apples. Squealer explained to the other animals that this was quite necessary because these particular foods were so important to brain workers, adding, 'this has been proved by Science, comrades.' The second development is that the pigs 'did not actually work, but directed and supervised the others. With their superior knowledge it was natural that they should assume the leadership.' From the beginning, then, a division of labour of the utmost importance came into being.

Orwell is telling us as bluntly as he can that all animals are *not* equal; it is *natural* for the more intelligent to take control. Can we believe that it is not equally natural for them to assume privileges? At any rate they do so naturally enough. Moreover, the commandeering of the apples and the milk was the one issue upon which the two leaders, Napoleon and Snowball, agreed! The source of the pigs' power was intelligence, and Snowball soon had under way many schemes which were likely to increase the pigs' power since their success depends upon technology. In the evenings the pigs studied blacksmithing, carpentering, and so on. They also tended to dominate the meetings of the animals; it was they who put forward all the resolutions which were voted upon. If we compare these developments to those in Morris's Nowhere we are aware of a totally different attitude towards intellectual ability and future industrialisation.

Technological advance was the safeguard of the revolution on Animal Farm and if Snowball realised this before Napoleon, both came to realise it in the end. The new life-style of the revolution would be based upon a high degree of technical sophistication, only possible if Snowball could procure dynamos and cables and other commodities which Animal Farm could not itself produce. How were they to be obtained? How else but through trade? And how could the animals trade? Only by producing more than they themselves required—considerably more—in the way of eggs and crops and so on. But Major had specifically warned the animals against engaging in trade.[16] Snowball's plans, we might say, were those of a scientific not a moralistic socialist, and in his society, just as in Napoleon's, there was no place for equality.

The lynchpin of Snowball's technological society was a windmill, and it was against the building of this windmill that Napoleon took his stand. He offered no alternative plan for increasing agricultural productivity,[17] nor did he raise moral or intellectual objections to building the windmill; he did not attack the plans as a threat to the principles of animalism: he simply urinated on them. The windmill was Snowball's idea and not his own! This was not the only issue between the two leaders. Snowball wished to send pigeons to other farms to encourage the animals to revolt, but Napoleon clearly recognised that Animal Farm might need the help of its neighbours in the future and was more concerned about the well-being of Animal Farm than about spreading the gospel of animalism.[18] The essential point, though, is that Orwell suggests that divisions within the revolutionary leadership are inevitable, and that these differences, whilst they may be presented as doctrinal, are largely personal.

When the animals held a meeting to decide on whether to go ahead with the building of the windmill, with an affirmative decision almost a foregone conclusion, Napoleon produced his most persuasive argument: nine huge dogs with brass-studded collars, trained in complete obedience to him personally. Snow-

ball barely escaped their attentions with his life. After the
latter's departure from the farm Napoleon announced the cessa-
tion of Sunday meetings—a rather farcical attempt at worker
control—and the setting up instead of a special committee
of the pigs to run the farm. Stage two of the revolution had
been reached; the struggle for power was over and the 'debate'
about the direction of social development had been decided.

Napoleon decided that the windmill should be built after
all and the animals on the farm began a year of intense effort.
Orwell writes: 'all that year the animals worked like slaves.'
The choice of simile is tragically significant. What is more,
Napoleon decided upon a new policy of trading with other
farms. Animal Farm began to sell eggs, thus breaking a basic
principle of animalism. Around this time the pigs also broke
the commandments; they moved into the farmhouse and slept
on beds. The natural leadership which they had assumed from
the earliest days of the revolution began to assume a character
similar to that of Jones, in that it clothed itself in the *same
kinds* of privileges. We begin to realise that Animal Farm's
success will not be measured by its ability to establish a new,
egalitarian way of life but by its technical and managerial
efficiency. Yet this very efficiency was in question, for the windmill was blown down in a gale because its walls were too
thin, and the potato harvest was lost because the clamps failed
to keep the frost out over winter. The only clear measure
of increased efficiency was to be found in the area of the
techniques of social control. Whereas Jones had been intermit-
tently cruel and careless Napoleon and the pigs were systematically savage.

He employs Squealer to change the commandments surrepti-
tiously so that the legitimacy of his regime seems always secure.
For example, when the pigs take to alcohol, the commandment
originally forbidding animals to drink is modified by the addition
of the two words 'to excess'! At the first sign of revolt, when
the hens refused to lay the increased numbers of eggs needed
as a basis for trade with other farms, Napoleon acted with
great brutality. This ushered in the period of show-trials in
which animals confessed to crimes which they had almost certainly not committed and which were always said to have
been organised by the banished Snowball. Four pigs who had
previously expressed reservations about Napoleon's policies con-

fessed to having conspired with Snowball.

There seems to be an almost fatal inevitability about the sequence of events on Animal Farm. Only occasionally do we catch a glimpse of possible alternative developments. One such possibility, for example, was provided when Boxer the horse expressed publicly some slight doubts about Napoleon's policies and was attacked by the dogs. He defeated them easily and could have killed them. Boxer was a kindly animal, but though far from stupid was politically naïve. It was within his power at that point to thwart Napoleon. But Boxer was, in fact, one of the latter's strongest supporters and unaware that animalism has been betrayed. Orwell believed in the power of the working class (excluding its 'sheep') but clearly also believed that the workers would be duped by revolutionary leaders skilled enough to appeal to their instinctive loyalties. At any rate, Boxer did not seize his chance.

It is an exercise of personal judgement to say that the revolution on Animal Farm was a failure, still more so to say that its failure was inevitable. All the same, *by its own criteria* it was a failure. The animals worked as hard and probably harder than under Jones and had as hard a life. True, in the early stages they believed that they were working for themselves and this made a great difference, but the feeling did not last. The moral principles according to which the doctrines of animalism had been formulated were slowly perverted, as each proved either impracticable or a hindrance to the aspirations of the pigs. It could be argued that if the revolution on Animal Farm failed, it did so because the animals were catapulted into revolution before they had become sufficiently politically conscious; because, in Marxist terms, history was not ready, the 'bourgeois revolution' not yet complete. Marx also said that the violence of revolution would accelerate the growth of consciousness. Yet the most numerous of the animals on the farm were sheep; who could rouse their political consciousness? Again, we should remember in whose 'hands' the task of political education was placed: the pigs. Perhaps Animal Farm is not a sound analogy of human society, and yet the leader of the Marxist Social Democratic Federation, H. M. Hyndman, once wrote: 'A slave class cannot free itself. The leadership, the initiative, the teaching, the organisation, must come from those comrades who are in a different position and who are trained to use their faculties in early life.'[19] In other words, there are obvious similarities.

It could also be argued that if the revolution on Animal Farm failed it did so because the leadership forsook the principles of the revolution and lost contact with the mass movement. This is to assume, of course, that the pigs did at one stage subscribe to the principles of animalism, which is itself open to question. But ignoring that problem, it is to suggest that as leaders of the revolution the pigs might have worked closer with the mass movement. Yet in the early days of the revolution the only aspiration which the mass movement could put into effect was to crop mouthfuls of the sweet summer grass and snuff the rich scent of the black earth. The animals needed to be organised by their natural leaders—this much seems unarguable. In other words the objectification of the principles of animalism was the task of a leadership who would be unlikely to countenance the canvassing of alternatives. Control of Animal Farm had passed from a social caste—the farmer and his family, to a political caste—the pigs. The gains in this transfer for the other animals were minimal. In fact since the tyranny of pigs was more efficient the animals could be said to be worse off than before. Benjamin the donkey was the only animal with a realistic attitude to life on Animal Farm; he had no illusions about a time when all animals would be free and equal. After all, the choice for the animals on the farm was rule by a drunkard or rule by a pig; Orwell could hardly have presented his view of the choice more forcefully.

3

After the revolution comes the post-revolution, which sounds a truism but in fact represents a recognition that there exists a period after the successful establishment of a revolutionary regime when it must set the guidelines for future social and political development. Most revolutionary writers recognised that these would be hard days. Morris, for example, referred to the masses being guided by 'the reflex of starvation' in the post-revolution, thus enabling the post-revolutionary government to secure obedience as it set up the localised, community-based structure of government which characterised Nowhere.

On Animal Farm the guiding principle was fear. Napoleon had the means to mould the future of Animal Farm much as he chose. He chose, at first, to trade with the neighbouring farms, in much the same way as Stalin entered diplomatic relations with Nazi Germany and with the West. Napoleon, who handled the local farmers with what he believed to be consummate cunning, was outmanoeuvred by Frederick (Hitler) who not only cheated him but invaded Animal Farm the following day. With the loss of the new windmill the animals repulsed Frederick and his men, and were momentarily united as a result. But the fact remained that Napoleon had been trading with humans on a large scale and worse followed when the pigs discovered alcohol and Napoleon sowed a small paddock of barley as a result. Napoleon's greatest treachery, though, was explained to the animals by Benjamin, when his great friend Boxer, who had worked himself virtually to death, was not permitted to spend his last years out to grass, but was sent off to the knackers to be made into hide, bone-meal and glue. The animals shouted to warn Boxer and heard a tremendous drumming from inside the van by way of answer. But Boxer could not kick his way out; the time for a working-class revolt was gone. 'There had been a time when a few kicks from Boxer's hoof would have smashed the van to matchwood.'

Meanwhile the new windmill had been completed and others begun, though no dynamos were installed and the promised electric lights and hot water did not materialise. The pigs seem to have adopted what Morris considered to be an exclusive device of the capitalists; mechanisation leading to increased productivity not shorter working hours. In fact food for the animals became scarcer, though Squealer, performing the tasks of the Miniplenty of *Nineteen-Eighty-Four*, kept producing statistics showing how all forms of production on the farm had risen. 'All the same, there were days when they felt they would sooner have had less figures and more food.' By and large, though, things were much as they had always been. It was not long after the windmill had been completed that the animals saw a thing which turned their world upside-down. They saw Squealer walking on his hind legs, a whip in his trotter. Benjamin informed Clover (whose memory of the original commandments and of the principles of animalism had dimmed, like her eyes) that there was now only one commandment on the wall of the big barn:

> All animals are equal
> But some animals are more
> Equal than others.

The final scene in the book shows the animals drawn to the farmhouse by laughter and singing, only to discover Napoleon and some of the pigs playing cards with local farmers. They were not to know it, but the farmers had been informed that all the remaining trappings of animalism were to be removed from the farm, henceforth to be known as The Manor Farm. There followed a violent quarrel over the card game during which: 'The creatures outside looked from pig to man, and from man to pig, and from pig to man again; but already it was impossible to say which was which.'[20] Animal Farm's has been a full revolution: from slavery to slavery. The sequence of events which Orwell has depicted seems almost inevitable to the reader; the failure of the post-revolutionary phase is as predictable as that of the revolution itself.

Arthur Koestler brought to the reader a set of experiences which no British author could match, for Koestler had participated in the post-revolution in the USSR, and this probably gave him a deeper insight into the nature of that phenomenon. His *Darkness at Noon* (1940) concerns the interrogation of Comrade Rubashov, a high-ranking official within the party hierarchy and a revolutionary comrade of the leader, No. 1. Rubashov is to play his part as the victim in a show trial and the novel plots the development of Rubashov's response to the charges which are levelled against him. Strictly speaking he is clearly innocent but in a more profound sense he is certainly guilty; guilty of the charge that he no longer believes in the party's omnipotence. He believes that the revolution has been betrayed. His is essentially the revolt of the individual spirit against the corporate spirit. For the first time in his life he feels able to assess the party's achievements in terms of the declared intentions of the revolution, and lengthy discussions take place between Rubashov and his interrogators in terms of the traditional means-versus-ends dichotomy, discussions which are pertinent to the nature of the post-revolution.

Rubashov does not excite our sympathy. His post-revolutionary task was to uncover and destroy those who, for whatever reason, were unable to follow the current party line enunciated from Moscow. This brought him into contact with a young German communist Richard, who believed that the German Communist Party had been deserted by its Russian mother body and left to be defeated with great loss of life. Richard's own pregnant wife had been seized by the Gestapo, and Rubashov's task was to tell him that he was not deserted by the party, his judgement was faulty:[21]

> 'The Party can never be mistaken,' said Rubashov. 'You and I can make a mistake. Not the Party. The Party, comrade, is more than you and I and a thousand others like you and I. The Party is the embodiment of the revolutionary idea in history. History knows no scruples and no hesitation. Inert and unerring, she flows towards her goal. At every bend in her course she leaves the mud which she carries and the corpses of the drowned. History knows her way. She makes no mistakes. He who has not absolute faith in History does not belong in the Party's ranks.

The irony of Rubashov's position is that he, too, came to lose faith in the party and to see himself, at least in part, in Richard's position. He came to believe that the party no longer represented the interests of the masses, as he told his first interrogator, Ivanov:

> 'As you quite rightly remarked, we were accustomed always to use the plural "we" and to avoid as far as possible the first person singular. I have rather lost the habit of that form of speech; you stick to it. But who is this "we" in whose name you speak today? It needs redefining. That is the point.'
> 'Entirely my own opinion,' said Ivanov. 'I am glad that we have reached the heart of the matter so soon. In other words: you are convinced that "we"—that is to say, the Party the State and the masses behind it—no longer represent the interests of the Revolution.'
> 'I should leave the masses out of it,' said Rubashov.

A little later Rubashov goes on:

> 'A mathematician once said that algebra was the science

for lazy people—one does not work out x, but operates with it as if one knew it. In our case, x stands for the anonymous masses, the people. Politics mean operating with this x without worrying about its actual nature. Making history is to recognize x for what it stands for in the equation.

As far as Rubashov was concerned, then, the party had ceased to represent the masses but was still prepared to declare, *ex cathedra*, what the interests of the masses were. Having done so, it could brook no alternatives, and must punish 'wrong ideas' as other states punish crime. 'We resembled the great Inquisitors', he continues, 'in that we persecuted the seeds of evil not only in men's deeds, but in their thoughts. We admitted no private sphere, not even inside a man's skull.' But it was precisely inside his skull that Rubashov was himself guilty. He re-interprets his past, re-evaluating the means/ends balance of his action. He once sacrificed his mistress to the party, for example; not out of cowardice but because he believed his future to be more important to the party than hers. In his cell the 'vision of Arlova's legs in their high-heeled shoes trailing along the corridor upset the mathematical equilibrium. The unimportant factor had grown to the immeasurable, the absolute.' It was this substitution of means for ends in the equation which provided Rubashov with a new perspective from which to view the enormous and unprecedented powers of the post-revolution party.[22] Ivanov describes the party as not being composed, like all preceding revolutionary parties, of 'moralizing dilettantes', but as being 'consequent'. Rubashov agrees:

> So consequent, that in the interests of a just distribution of land we deliberately let die of starvation about five million farmers and their families in one year. So consequent were we in the liberation of human beings from the shackles of industrial exploitation that we sent about ten million people to do forced labour in the Arctic regions and the jungles of the East, under conditions similar to those of antique galley slaves. . .
> Acting consequentially in the interests of the coming generations, we have laid such terrible privations upon the present one that its average length of life is shortened by a quarter . . . The people's standard of life is lower than it was before

the Revolution; the labour conditions are harder, the discipline is more inhuman, the piece-work drudgery worse than in colonial countries with native coolies. . . .

That Rubashov agrees eventually to 'settle his account with history' and take part in a show trial, even though Ivanov has been removed and, no doubt, liquidated, is not relevant here. What signifies for us is that, having defined the sole object of the revolution as being to abolish 'senseless suffering', Rubashov concludes that to achieve this in the long term appears to involve an enormous increase of such suffering in the short term. In practice, moreover, the short term seems capable of infinite extension. The party apparatus, built originally to achieve the ends of the revolution, becomes concerned, in the post-revolution, with ensuring obedience to the party line. In short, the 'means' of the revolution become the 'ends' of the post-revolution. Thus the revolution carries with it the seeds of its own destruction.

4

The writers we have considered in this chapter were drawn towards revolution as the most prompt and effective way of redressing the many ills they saw in their society. But in the case of Orwell and Koestler experiences with revolution or revolutionary movements tempered their enthusiasm and led them to question some of the revolutionary's fundamental assumptions. Even Morris became less committed to revolution when he saw the positive advantages that 'gas and water' socialism was obtaining for the working class through constitutional channels, though he never completely forsook his earlier belief that a truly socialist society could only come about as a result of revolution. But then, Morris did not have the benefit of experiencing at either first or second hand the failure of revolutions and post-revolutions.

The basic problem for each of these writers was that of relating the *means* of assuming and retaining power to the *ends* of socialism. Morris seemed least aware of the tensions involved in the relationship; or at any rate he had least to say about them. Orwell probably remained convinced that revolutionary means and ends could be reconciled, though little he wrote would lead others to take a similar position. Koestler seems to have come to believe that such reconciliation was highly improbable assuming that the mass of the people was unlikely to have attained any degree of political consciousness prior to the revolution. Aldous Huxley was even more pessimistic. When Illidge, in *Point Counter Point*, finally persuaded by Spandrell to help assassinate the fascist leader, Webley, contemplates the body, he can find no social justification whatever for his act of violence:[23]

> By the time the body was finally trussed, Illidge knew that Tom's weak lungs and two-hundred guinea coats, that superfluous fat and his mother's life-long slaving, that rich and poor, oppressed and revolution, justice, punishment, indignation—all, as far as he was concerned, were utterly irrelevant to the fact of these stiffening limbs, this mouth that gaped, these half-shut, glazed and secretly staring eyes. Irrelevant, and beside the point.

If revolution involves the socialist in actions which are as odious as those adopted by the state he seeks to overthrow, he has no justification whatever, as far as Huxley is concerned: his actions must stand or fall *on their own terms*. Orwell and Koestler, on the other hand, believe that such actions *might* be justifiable in terms of revolutionary principles. But in practical experience, as the *ends* for which the revolution was undertaken inevitably move into the distance, it is only by the *means adopted* that the revolution and the post-revolution may be judged.[24] On these criteria, the novels we have considered in this chapter do not appear to inspire confidence in the cause of socialist revolution.

6 The Gradualness of Inevitability

Were we to compare those who supported revolutionary social and political change with those who supported evolutionary change in Britain, we should find the latter a more numerous and probably more celebrated group. But we ought not to forget that, unlike revolution, which can be quite specific in meaning, evolution means many things to many people. Indeed, it would be more appropriate were we to present the initial comparison as between revolution and 'not-revolution', for we can be sure of only one piece of common ground as far as the evolutionists are concerned: they believe in the inappropriateness of revolution as a vehicle for social and political change. But their more positive beliefs run a very extensive gamut from paternalistic government of an authoritarian but welfare-conscious stamp to weak federal systems permitting the maximum amount of freedom to citizens to evolve as individuals. In short there may be as many, and indeed as distinct, differences between various kinds of evolutionists as between evolutionists and revolutionists.

In order to make sense of these many and conflicting evolutionary theories it will be necessary to categorise them, and the most appropriate way to do so, initially at any rate, is to consider separately the writing of three exponents of contrasting evolutionary theories. The first of the three is a scientific socialist, Bernard Shaw, and we shall consider separately two strands of Shavian evolutionary theory. We shall then pass on to the theories of another scientist, H. G. Wells, and finally, having dealt with what might be called the mainstream of socialist evolutionary thought, we shall be turning briefly to the writing of Aldous Huxley, who might properly be considered as a moralist. His work provides an example of individualistic evolutionary theories.

I

One of the difficulties in analysing Shaw's work is that he operated at a number of levels more or less simultaneously. First he declared himself to be a man of practical wisdom, talking in everyday language about the world we know and offering (sometimes) practical advice, as in *Everybody's Political What's What* (1944) and *The Plain Woman's Guide to Socialism and Capitalism* (1929). Second he declared himself an advocate of wholesale social reorganisation, undertaken by far-sighted leaders whose virtues his plays so often extol. Finally Shaw wrote as a philosopher-poet with a long-term view of human development leading to a new kind of 'man' as different from bourgeois man as bourgeois man is from Neanderthal man. This three-fold evolutionism makes Shaw appear more inconsistent than he is. Reading him, as one critic said, is like 'looking through a pair of field glasses where the focus is always equally sharp and clear but where the range may be changed without warning.'[1] Moreover such a diverse approach presents problems for the author himself. As the same critic pointed out: 'The Socialist takes sword in hand to battle for a sounder society based upon a redistribution of income; and the long-term philosopher-poet comes to sap the socialist's faith with misgivings as to the capacity for righteousness and soundness of the material of common humanity as contrasted with philosopher-poets.'[2] In the present chapter we shall be more concerned with Shaw as the practical man and Shaw the advocate of wholesale social reorganisation than with Shaw the philosopher. We shall begin, in fact, by training the field glasses exclusively on Shaw the advocate of constitutional change—on Shaw the Fabian.

In the 1908 reprint of *Fabian Essays* Shaw wrote: 'We set ourselves two definite tasks: first to provide a parliamentary programme for a prime minister converted to Socialism as Peel was converted to Free Trade: and second, to make it

as easy and matter-of-course for the ordinary respectable Englishman to be a Socialist as to be a Liberal or a Conservative.'
Shaw wanted the Fabian Society to remain a small élitist group
which might hope to persuade leaders of any political party
of the wisdom of Fabian policies. It was on these grounds
that Shaw successfully opposed Wells's attempt in 1907 to make
the Fabian Society a mass-movement bent upon propaganda
among the mass of the voters. However Shaw seldom attacked
revolutionary socialists, in fact the reverse would be nearer
the truth; but he continually sought to emphasise the advantages
to be gained through piecemeal reform. In *Essays In Fabian
Socialism*, for example, he wrote:[3]

> Let me, in conclusion, disavow all admiration for this inevi-
> table, but sordid, slow, reluctant, cowardly path to justice.
> I venture to claim your respect for those enthusiasts who
> still refuse to believe that millions of their fellow creatures
> must be left to sweat and suffer in hopeless toil and degrada-
> tion, whilst parliaments and vestries grudgingly muddle and
> grope towards paltry instalments of betterment.

'Sordid' and 'cowardly', yes—but the slower way to progress
is 'inevitable', according to Shaw. Moreover, he will venture
to claim our 'respect' for revolutionary socialists—but not our
support.

The Fabian Society and like-minded socialists in the Labour
movement had a noticeable impact upon progressive Liberals
in the two decades leading up to the First World War, especially
in the labour and trade union legislation of the 1906–14 Liberal
government. But when Labour governments took office their
influence was even more direct. In 1929, for example, the
government of MacDonald (himself an ex-member of the Fabian
executive) contained twenty Fabians, no fewer than eight being
Cabinet members. Whether the measures passed by these minis-
tries justified the Fabian policy of persuasion is quite another
matter.

In more general terms, however, a strong case can be made
out for the advantages of gradual, evolutionary change. One
such is provided by Shaw in a short story which first appeared
in the *Clarion* in 1905. The story is entitled 'Death of an Old
Revolutionary Hero' and concerns the demise of one Jo Budgett
of Balwick at the age of ninety. In the story Shaw explains

that the newspapers had reported that Budgett's wife had tried to prevent Shaw's attending the funeral on the grounds that he had once tried to kill Jo. The story goes on to describe the events which provided the foundation for Mrs Budgett's claim.

Jo Budgett had become seriously ill at the age of seventy-five and the then young Bernard Shaw had gone to visit this old lion of revolutionary socialism. Jo spoke at length to his young admirer about his apprenticeship in the revolutionary cause, served, he said, in the struggle against the 1832 Reform Bill. *Against?* asks young Shaw, taken aback. 'Aye, against it', he said. 'Old as I am, my blood still boils when I think of the way in which a capitalist tailor named Place—one of the half-hearted Radical vermin—worked the infamous conspiracy to enfranchise the middle classes and deny the vote to the working man. I spoke against it on every platform in England ...' Jo's indictment of piecemeal reformism continued in the same vein.

> Then came Chartism with its five points (sic) to fool the people and keep them from going to the real root of the matter by abolishing kings, priests and private property. Then there was Bright and Cobden trailing the red herring of Free Trade across the trail of the emancipation of the working classes. I exposed them and their silly lies about cheap bread; and if I'd been listened to, no Englishman need ever have wanted bread again. Next came those black blots on our statute books, the Factory Acts, which recognised and regulated and legalised the accursed exploitation of the wives and children of the poor in the factory hells. Then came a worse swindle than the Reform Bill of 1832—the '67 Bill, that gave just a handful of votes to a few workmen to bolster up the lie that Parliament represents the people instead of the vampires that live by plundering them.

After a sally against the Education Act of 1870 Jo went on to speak against the International, Karl Marx, the Paris Commune and the Socialist movement in Britain, with its 'half-hearted Chartist palliatives', claiming that he had soon seen through Hyndman and that Morris was 'just as bad'. The youthful Shaw's image of the revolutionary giant was by now shattered to the extent that when Jo began to talk about the

Dock Strike of 1889 he could not guess which side the veteran had taken. He soon discovered. 'Could I lie here and see the people led away by a renegade like John Burns?' he exploded. In short, Budgett suggested that all of the socialist leaders were charlatans; only those who had refused to compromise were the true leaders; only they could act with integrity on behalf of the working class.

Jo Budgett did not demur when Shaw concluded that Jo's guiding principle had always been 'all or nothing'. Shaw went on to suggest that since 'all' was out of the question, Jo's revolutionary socialism stood for nothing: it was, in effect, nihilism! What Shaw does in the course of this interview is to indicate how much piecemeal change has affected the political and social contours of the lives of the majority of people, and, conversely, how the policies of revolutionary change would have made that steady improvement impossible. In a humorous way he exposes what he sees as the intransigence of the revolutionary mentality and also explores, if only briefly, a theme which occupied him later, in plays such as *On The Rocks:* the natural alliance between paternalistic conservatism and working-class extreme radicalism. Just as Budgett shared a platform with the Duke of Wellington so, in *On The Rocks*, the Tory leader Sir Dexter Rightside was supported in his opposition to government reforms by the leaders of the workers of the Isle of Cats.

By the end of his interview, Shaw had become quite convinced that Budgett was a sworn enemy to steady progress and so attempted to bring about Jo's death. Jo had said that the slightest noise would be enough to kill him and so Shaw decided to bring down a grandfather clock, making his escape out of the open window. (Hence Mrs Budgett's original charge!) In fact fifteen years of agitation were left to the revolutionary lion and when he finally died it was chiefly as a result of his opposition to a Bill to enfranchise women because it contained a property qualification. He had remained true to his ideal of 'all or nothing' with the fervour of Ibsen's Brand. The moral of the story is that whereas Budgett's absolutist principles bound him 'tighter than . . . a hooligan with a set of handcuffs' to an ineluctable nihilism, others, less ambitious, who pursued the 'sordid, slow, reluctant, cowardly path to justice' actually achieved very substantial progress.

For Shaw, then, the immediate way forward was to permeate the existing political structure with socialist ideas. 'In the first place', he wrote, socialism 'must be a continuing policy for developing our existing institutions into socialistic ones, and not a catastrophic policy for simultaneously destroying existing institutions and replacing them with a ready-made Utopia.'[4] But his involvement in politics led Shaw to the conclusion that, after all, swapping capitalism for socialism by changing the machinery of government was not likely to be very successful, especially bearing in mind the advent of mass democracy. As we have seen Shaw had no faith in the working class, declaring that: 'They make greater sacrifices to support legions of publicans and sporting bookmakers than free political institutions would cost them; and there is no escaping the inference that they care more for drinking and gambling than for freedom.'[5] But not all men were incapable of improvement, according to Shaw, and if democracy was incapable of administering a socialist society, great men were not. What Shaw had to say on the subject of great men is often confusing, but it is possible to be clear about two important aspects. First, Shaw clearly believed in the existence of naturally dominant people, and his plays contain many: Andrew Undershaft in *Major Barbara*, Magnus in *The Apple Cart*, the millionairess in the play of that name, Caesar in *Caesar and Cleopatra*, and so on. These men and women were society's natural leaders 'in whom the "great abstractions" and a genius for practical affairs combine to make a natural monarch'.[6] Like Carlyle's heroes their power lay 'in their transcendence of the ethical codes and spiritual limitations of ordinary human beings.'[7]

Although Shaw recognised the need to exercise some 'democratic' control over these natural leaders—indeed he devised an elaborate hierarchical system of elected 'panels' to perform such a function—he placed his faith in the superior wisdom of the natural rulers to act in the interests of all. There can be no doubt that Shaw cast himself and his fellow Fabians in the role of natural leaders whose task was to organise the whole of society along socialist lines for its own good. He argued: 'Socialism without experts is as impossible as shipbuilding without experts or dentistry without experts.'[8] The criterion according to which these 'experts' would make their decisions was simply wisdom, which, by definition, they possessed to a greater extent than their fellow citizens; thus when they acted they did so in the interests of all. Therefore widespread dissatisfaction with their rule would be unlikely, revolt unthinkable. After all, 'When a railway porter directs me to No. 10 platform I do not strike him to the earth with a shout of "Down with Tyranny" and rush violently to No. 1 platform.'[9] Shaw did not stop to consider that whilst the great majority of men would certainly accept the railway porter's superiority in deciding which is the best train for them, they most certainly will not accept the expert's primacy in deciding what constitutes the wisest course of action in any given event. The criteria upon which the porter reaches his decision are likely to be accepted by all but the most obtuse passengers whereas in politics such general agreement is a very rare occurrence.[10]

Shaw's uncritical support for the men of action of his day is well known. He once declared himself to be a national socialist before Hitler was born[11] and always argued in favour of the man who, like Andrew Undershaft, gets things done. This ability to act was, he considered, the only measure of true democracy, defined as 'a social order aiming at the greatest available welfare for the whole population'.[12] The model for Shaw's expert ruler was his friend and fellow Fabian Sidney (later Lord) Olivier who became Governor of Jamaica, but he often wrote in support of the policies of Stalin (in particular), Mussolini and even Hitler (though he recognised that the latter did not possess Olivier's 'kindly objectivity'). It is at least likely that Shaw's own inability to act decisively lent undue weight to his admiration for those who could. Indeed, it was possibly the decisiveness rather than the 'wisdom' of action which appealed to Shaw.

A second aspect of Shaw's attitude to great men about which we may be clear is that whilst they constitute only a small proportion of unequal capitalist society—between five and ten per cent—they need not always be so few. Indeed one of the chief arguments with which Shaw underpinned his faith in gradual change was that if society's leaders could be persuaded to enact policies leading towards equality of income as well as other socialistic measures of amelioration, the social and political system would be transformed. In his most active years as a socialist Shaw argued continuously for equality of income, stating that it was the only thing about human beings which could be equalised. To those who argued that, given equality of income, nobody would wish to take up either the most demanding or the most unpleasant occupations, Shaw countered that the most demanding jobs were invariably the most inherently rewarding, and that the most unpleasant jobs were generally the least well paid anyway. We need not explore this argument in any great depth,[13] though we should acknowledge its importance; but equality of income, for Shaw, was a necessary condition for the naturally superior to assume their rightful places in the political hierarchy and to multiply. We shall have to return to this argument shortly but it is worth pointing out briefly that Shaw himself retreated from the position of complete equality later on, arguing for twice the standard wage for his 'top ten per cent', so that they could enjoy the leisure and the means to cultivate the arts.[14] Indeed he told Joad in 1943 in an open letter that 'to give everybody an equal share in the national income today would reduce us all to such an overcrowded poverty that science, art, and philosophy would be impossible. Civilization would perish, and with it most of the people . . .'[15]

Thus, by dint of permeating existing political parties and institutions with socialist ideas Shaw hoped to make possible the advent of a planned, socialist society in which naturally gifted leaders would dominate and men of action provide the maximisation of welfare for all. By means of equalising income (almost!) they would then make possible the emergence and eventual growth of groups of previously socially deprived men and women of natural talent until society as a whole would be able to aspire to a totally new kind of life-style.

2

By removing social barriers, by allowing natural leaders to assume responsibility for society, Shaw believed that he could make possible a fundamental change in human nature. Having dismissed the mass of mankind out of hand as a potential evolutionary force—recognising, like Kant, that nothing straight was ever made 'out of the crooked timber of humanity'—he recognised also the long-term limitations even of his men of action. Did not this recognition lead him back to revolutionary change as the only alternative? 'No: what Caesar, Cromwell and Napoleon could not do with all the physical force and moral prestige of the state in their mighty hands, cannot be done by enthusiastic criminals and lunatics. Even the Jews, who from Moses to Marx and Lassalle, have inspired all the revolutions, have had to confess that, after all, the dog will return to his vomit and the sow that was washed to her wallowing in the mire.'[16] History teaches us to give up the idea that '. . . Man as he exists is capable of net progress.' But as G. K. Chesterton pointed out, Shaw's passion for socialism was so strong that he did not wash his hands of progress: he washed his hands of man. 'Our only hope, then, is in evolution. We must replace the man with the superman.' By the turn of the century Shaw had come to accept the central importance of genetics, after reading Blake and Bunyan, Samuel Butler and Schopenhauer, especially the latter's *The World as Will* (1819). It has been said that his evolutionary theories 'gave him simultaneously a fresh sense of individual significance and a cosmic sanction for his socialism'.[17] As far as Shaw was concerned socialism became 'the embodiment and forefront of the upward struggle of the Life Force'.[18]

What was the life force? 'Unless we believe', said Shaw, 'that the life in us is a divine spark that can be nursed into a steady flame and finally into an illuminating fire, then there is really no sense in belonging to a Fabian Society or indeed in taking the trouble to feed ourselves.'[19] This force within us naturally aspires to what Don Juan in *Man and Superman* calls a 'higher organisation, wider, deeper, intenser self-consciousness, and clearer understanding'. By making himself the servant of the Life Force, by willing what it wills, mankind has developed and will develop much further. Shaw rejected Darwin's theory of natural selection, with its emphasis on pure chance, and held to Lamarck's view that a species evolved through the exercise of will, with the characteristics thus acquired by one generation being transmitted to the next. Shaw associated himself with the French philosopher Bergson who in *L'Évolution Créatrice* (1907) spoke of the *élan vital*, a creative life force which dominated evolution. But what Shaw proposed, however, was nothing less than the taking in hand of evolution (and no doubt slinging it in the way it should go!). It is one thing to recognise the reality and supreme importance of evolutionary change, as Teilhard does, for example, in *The*

Phenomenon of Man (1955): it is quite another to offer practical proposals for speeding evolution up by means of deliberately devised programmes. Shaw suggests, in the Preface to *Back to Methuselah* (1921), that since a weightlifter can, by training harder, 'put up' a muscle, an earnest and convinced philosopher ought, with similar dedication, to be able to 'put up' a brain. That Shaw was in earnest should not be doubted. For him 'the only fundamental and possible Socialism is the socialization of the selective breeding of man; in other terms, of human evolution. We must eliminate the Yahoo, or his vote will wreck the commonwealth.'[20]

Shaw examined themes of creative evolution in a number of plays, but it is in *Man and Superman*, one of his major works, that they are most fully dealt with. Shaw begins with an Epistle Dedicatory in which he outlines the reasons behind his belief in progress through evolution. 'I do not know whether you have any illusions left on the subject of education, progress, and so forth. I have none. Any pamphleteer can show the way to better things; but when there is no will there is no way.' The only answer, says Shaw, is to 'breed political capacity,' and the way to do that is to maximise the natural leadership and talent existing in society. He uses the analogy of a domestic electrical system to explain the role of the natural leader. Think, he says, of the

> great quantity of highly susceptible copper wire which gorges itself with electricity and gives you no light whatever. But here and there occurs a scrap of intensely insusceptible, intensely resistant material: and that stubborn scrap grapples with the current and will not let it through until it has made itself useful to you and those two vital qualities of . . . light and heat.

This illumination provided for the benefit of all by the 'self-consciousness of certain abnormal people' is a source of great satisfaction for those involved.

Shaw's naturally talented élite includes not only political leaders but also men of letters. Both in this play and in *Candida* Shaw deals with the place of artists in general in his social scheme. The artist is a man apart, not to be inhibited or restricted by enduring emotional attachments or humdrum domestic arrangements. He must remain aloof so as to be able to 'show us ourselves as we really are. Our minds are nothing but this knowledge of ourselves; and he who adds a jot to such knowledge creates new mind as surely as any woman creates new men.' Yet both Eugene in *Candida* and Tavy in *Man and Superman* are, to some extent, figures of fun. That is to say, they are essentially romantics who, in the rough-and-tumble of the world, are no match for the realists such as Candida herself and Tanner, not to mention the predatory Ann Whitefield.

Tanner can be assumed to personify Shaw's idea of the natural leader, a man with two responsibilities, one of which he is aware of from the beginning of the play and one of which he is slowly made aware of as the play progresses. The first is the responsibility of assuming a political role. It is made clear to us that Tanner will naturally enter parliament, besides which he has a reputation for radical politics, having just written a book entitled *The Revolutionist's Handbook*. The second responsibility Tanner owes to the Life Force. He has to marry Ann and, we may assume, join her in the making of superchildren. He is, in short, a physical embodiment of Shavian evolutionary theory.

Tanner, of course, is a modern Don Juan whose self-awareness causes him to reject the 'primrose path of dalliance' so as to fulfil his life's true purpose—or in Tanner's terminology, the purposes of the Life Force. The importance of the Don Juan myth to understanding the play is underlined by the dream sequence in Hell in which Don Juan, amid sundry interruptions, conducts a dialogue with the Devil on the relative merits of Heaven and Hell. The latter place is depicted as pleasant enough: man can do pretty well what he pleases but he must accept the limitation that there is nothing for him to strive after. Don Juan is bored in Hell. 'As long as I can conceive something better than myself', he complains, 'I cannot be easy unless I am striving to bring it into existence.' The Devil argues the necessity of accepting the impossibility of genuine progress towards a higher form of humanity. 'Beware of the pursuit of the superman', he warns: 'it leads to an indiscriminate contempt for the human.' Critics who argue[21] that this quotation indicates Shaw's awareness of the possible inhumanity of his evolutionary theories would do well to remember that it is the Devil who speaks these lines; in fact they suggest a philosophy totally alien to Don Juan's and, of course, Shaw's.

The central theme, then, of Shavian socialism, is evolution, an ever-continuing, upward thrust towards, at the social level, a higher form of social structure, scientifically organised, and at the individual level, eventually, a higher form of life altogether. The goals to be achieved are long-term, and yet Shaw sets out fairly clearly the immediate steps to be taken, of which equality of income (and despite retreating from this idea later on he did not entirely abandon it) is the most important.

3

Unlike Shaw, H. G. Wells was by training and by inclination a scientist. Both were élitists, both believed that if it were to be 'improved' society would have to depend upon the far-sightedness and organising abilities of its political leaders and its men of ideas. But for Wells the problems which beset men were, in the strictest sense, technical and technological, and mankind's response would be to evolve a higher technology, superior social organisation and so forth, to overcome these problems. Only scientists—not political scientists or social scientists like the Fabians, but physical scientists—possessed the necessary training and disinterested philosophy to succeed. This is borne out by the Wellsian utopias we shall be considering later: they are based upon some great scientific breakthrough, not a social one. Yet, like Shaw, Wells rejected revolution as an agent of real change.

George Orwell once parodied Wells's philosophy as representing a simple struggle between the scientific and the romantic mind. He wrote: 'On the one side science, order, progress, internationalism, aeroplanes, steel, concrete, hygiene: on the other side war, nationalism, religion, monarchy, peasants, Greek professors, poets, horses. History as he sees it is a series of victories won by the scientific man over the romantic man.'[22]

This is an over-simplified view. Wells himself spoke of two casts of mind, but he categorised them as the 'legal' and the 'creative' minds, with the former being concerned with form, custom and tradition, and the latter wishing to 'let the dead past bury its dead'[23] and casting its eyes always on the future. Orwell is correct insofar as when Wells tries to present us

in his best fiction with the contrast between the kind of man
he admires and the kind he despairs of, the contrast often
takes the form of a scientific man against a romantic man.
A clear example of this is in *Tono Bungay*; when George Ponderevo sails down the Thames in his new destroyer, past the
bastion of 'legalism' (as Wells uses the word), the Houses
of Parliament, he symbolises the creative mind's concern for
the future. But he is a scientist. Edward Ponderevo, however,
though he may be said to represent a world concerned with
custom, tradition and the past, is essentially a romantic figure.
He takes the world as he finds it and is, in any terms surely,
a more creative force than his nephew. True Edward is finally
brought down by the forces of 'legalism' but he gives them
a run for their money. Moreover, whilst Wells sustains a sympathetic treatment for some of his scientific heroes like George,
we have only to remember Griffin (the invisible man), and
Dr Moreau, to realise that despite his often stated view that
a scientific training, with its emphasis on the discovery of verifi-
able 'truths' was the best training for political leadership, Wells
clearly became aware that science itself was *not* a value-system.
In short, Wells did indeed see the future of man as depending
upon a successful scientific response to problems of an essentially
technological character, but he also understood that science
in itself could not provide any answer: it provided no more
than a means to an answer.

It is necessary to grasp what Wells had in mind as an objective
when he tried to appropriate science to the cause of social
progress. The analogy which Wells used in a number of his
novels had nothing to do with Orwell's 'aeroplanes, steel and
concrete'; it had to do with gardens. Wells speaks of a garden
planned overall with a view to symmetry, of juxtaposition of
colours and shapes, of a whole which is something more than
the sum total of its constituent parts. Wells's future, as we
shall see later, had more to do with this simple harmony than
with steel and concrete. 'In the future,' he wrote, 'it is at
least conceivable, that men with a trained reason and a sounder
science, both of matter and psychology, may . . . at last attain
and preserve a social organisation so cunningly balanced against
exterior necessities on the one hand, and the artificial factor
in the individual on the other, that the life of every human
being, and indeed, through man, of every sentient creature in

earth, may be generally happy.'[24] To what extent Wells really believed that man could be happy in such a well-ordered environment may be open to question. After all, Alfred Polly, that most human of Wells's creations, is described as feeling 'as the etiolated grass and daisies must do when you move the garden roller away to a new place'; it is almost as if the individual flourishes when in opposition to some general plan for his integrated well-being!

The fundamental difference between Wells's evolutionary theories and Shaw's was precisely this emphasis which the former placed upon mankind's integrated well-being. Man's survival, according to Wells, depended entirely upon his developing a species-consciousness, and he did discern in history a clear pattern, that mankind was slowly groping towards a species-consciousness, and that this was a relatively recent phenomenon. After all, mankind may be hundreds of thousands of years old but philosophy is only three thousand years old. In *Boon* (1915) Wells referred to species-consciousness as 'the Mind of the Race' and commented that: 'It [the human race] begins to live as a conscious being, and as it does so, the individual too begins to live in a new way, a greater, more understanding and more satisfying way. His thoughts apprehend interests beyond himself and beyond his particular life . . .'[25] For Wells, then, the man of the future would be a completely integrated species-being, not a Shavian superman.

The task of the socialist, since the well-ordered world state which would be the home of the new species-being was synonymous with socialism, was, to quote Masterman in *Kipps*, to build the imagination to use socialism—'to create and direct the public will'.[26] Man's progress, small though it may have been, has always depended on the ability 'to evolve the extrinsic, cumulative, transmissible mental environment of civilization'.[27] Civilisation being a 'fabric of ideas and habits', it tends to grow '. . . through the agency of eccentric and innovating people, playwrights, novelists, preachers, poets, journalists, and political reasoners and speakers, the modern equivalents of the prophets who struggled against the priests—against the social order that is of the barbaric age.'[28] In other words Wells assigns a special role to the artist in general in helping to create a species-consciousness. This makes Wells's artist far more important in the process of evolution than Shaw's. Wells was aware of the scope of his claim. He himself was prepared to sacrifice his standing as a novelist in order to promote his political ideas; selling his birthright, it was said, for a pot of message.

If the artist (especially the novelist) as socialist has an important function to perform in stimulating the growth of species-consciousness, all socialists have a similar general task, that of propaganda. When Wells joined the Fabian Society he declared simply: 'Make socialists and you will achieve socialism; there is no other way.' But that was not the declared aim of the Fabians. During Wells's four years as an active Fabian, membership rose fourfold, only to dwindle again on his departure. But he was never able to win the Fabian leaders over to his large-scale propaganda drive aimed specifically at the young.

Although Wells set great store by preparing the majority for socialism he did not for a moment believe that socialism would be brought into being simply by popular acclaim. It was important that there should be a general understanding of what the aims of socialism were, certainly, and to that end Wells was prepared to invest a great deal of time on works such as *The Outline of History* (1920), *The Work, Wealth and Happiness of Mankind* (1932), and *A Short History of the World* (1922). But as to building a socialist state, that was a task for élites. He saw members of these élites forming themselves into an 'open conspiracy' aimed at securing world government based upon rational social and economic planning. The élites he envisaged included professional groups, trade unions, transport and communications authorities, manufacturers and so on.[29] Governments would be sympathetic to these co-operative international developments because three growing pressures would be obliging them to think along similar lines. First, ever-increasing international co-operation would oblige national leaders to recognise the limitations of any national or even purely regional solution to their problems. Second, over-population would cause global problems requiring global co-operation in the effort to solve them. Third, the enormously destructive capacity of modern warfare would oblige major nations to co-operate in order to limit or even eliminate it.

Wells was quite sanguine when discussing the possibilities of a socialist world state. He believed that one would come into being eventually but probably only after mankind had failed to respond to the world-wide problems he outlined, thus bringing about some great catastrophe. From the ashes, as of necessity, would arise the phoenix of world socialism. Wells pursued these theories relentlessly; together with his scheme for mass propaganda, they are part and parcel of his general concept of the growth of species-consciousness (the Mind of the Race). Catastrophe as a catalyst became part of the theory only after the 1914-18 war, an event so damaging to the growth of species-consciousness that it had to be accommodated somehow into the general theory. In *Boon* Wells coined the phrase that it had been the war to end war, and in this sense catastrophe, too, was given a positive role in Wells's evolutionary theories. Indeed, it is interesting to note the part catastrophic events play in Wells's earlier novels; it is only through catastrophes that Kipps, Polly and George Ponderevo, for example, are able truly to discover themselves. For the story of the advent of world socialism, however, we are best advised to turn to *The Shape Of Things To Come* (1933). Here the diplomat, Dr Philip Raven, sets out the details of dreams he was having about the future before his death in 1930. Wells, a friend of this fictitious diplomat, undertakes the task of editing the notes Raven has made of his dreams and the book is supposed to be the outcome of his efforts. It tells of the inevitable collapse of competitive capitalism 'absolutely incapable of controlling the unemployment it had evoked and the belligerence it had stimulated' and of the emergence of the world state.[30]

> It has been a chronicle of disaster, wherein particular miseries, the torment and frustration of thousands of millions, are more than overshadowed by its appalling general aimlessness. We have seen the urge towards unity and order, appearing and being frustrated, reappearing and again being defeated. At last it reappeared—and won. The problem had been solved . . .
>
> It was no great moral impulse turned mankind from its drift towards chaos. It was an intellectual recovery. Essentially what happened was this: social and political science overtook the march of catastrophe.

It appears that Wells's attitude to the social sciences had mellowed or that, more likely, he believed that the response of social scientists to catastrophe would be more truly 'scientific' than some of their earlier analyses.[31] In any event Wells sets out his faith in the eventual triumph of species-consciousness clearly.

These, then, were Wells's theories of evolution. It remains only to add that we cannot fully understand the sudden burgeoning of species-consciousness unless we grasp the central role which Wells had set aside for himself in the process. He was to be the great sage and prophet who would rescue mankind from catastrophe. This is why Wells, as he got older, became less optimistic; his pessimism grew in direct proportion to his own apparent failure to arouse mankind. Perhaps, though, the world will not be faced with the simple choice of catastrophe or rapid transition to world socialism. Perhaps world government will come—much as Wells suggested—but more gradually. perhaps mankind will muddle through, as often before. But if it does, then maybe the evolutionary theories popularised by Wells in the first half of this century will have played no small part. George Orwell, a perceptive critic who had a personal distaste for Wells, wrote: 'The minds of us all, and therefore the physical world, would be perceptibly different if Wells had never existed.'[32] Wells was wrong to accuse humanity of not allowing him to deliver it. The epitaph he is said to have considered for himself, 'God damn you all. I told you so', would have been most inappropriate, belittling his significant achievement in the growth of what he called the Mind of the Race.

4

There remains one last theory of evolutionary change to be considered and it is, unlike the preceding ones, essentially moralistic. Like moralistic revolutionary theory, it looks for a change in the character of man as we know him. Unlike the scientists, proponents of this theory hold that change can only be internally and not externally induced. Change comes about as a response to a new understanding of the relationship between man and his environment, an understanding of religious or quasi-religious dimensions. The exemplar of moralistic evolutionary theory we shall consider is Aldous Huxley, and the novel in which he sets out his theory most concisely and pertinently is *Eyeless in Gaza*. The leading character, Anthony Beavis, in stating

his own personal problem, states mankind's: 'The problem
is: how to love?'—how to feel a persistent affectionate interest
in people? If the individual can learn to solve this problem,
his relationship with his environment—and hence his environment—will be transformed. Miller, the anthropologist, reinforces
the closeness of the connection between individual man and
society at large: 'States and nations don't exist as such. They
are only people. Sets of people, living in certain areas, having
certain allegiances. Nations won't change their national policies
unless and until people change their private policies. All governments, even Hitler's, even Stalin's, even Mussolini's, are representative. Today's national behaviour—a large-scale projection
of today's individual behaviour ... Or rather, to be more
accurate, a large-scale projection of the individual's secret wishes
and intentions.'[33] For Miller, as of course for Huxley, the important fact in the relationship between man and society is that
the former plays the dominant role: 'society' is simply a representational image of man in the particular. For society to change,
men must change. Miller is not without hope of such changes
because of what he takes to be four empirical facts. First that
we are all capable of love. Second that we impose limitations
upon our love. Third that we can transcend these limitations
if we choose. Fourth that love when expressed is returned. If
men acted on these facts, society would be transformed. Miller
goes on to describe Hell as 'the incapacity to be other than
the creature one finds oneself ordinarily behaving as', a definition which would appeal to Shaw's Don Juan.

Later in the book, Miller analyses English politics, suggesting
that most reforms have been made without the principles underlying them ever being accepted. 'There are no large-scale plans
in English politics, and hardly any thinking in terms of first
principles.' This absence, he continues, has resulted in a tolerant
and good-natured political system.

Deal with practical problems as they arise and without reference to first principles; politics are a matter of higgling.
Now higglers lose tempers but don't normally regard one
another as fiends in human form. But this is precisely what
men of principle and systematic planners can't help doing.
A principle is, by definition, *right*; a plan *for the good of
the people*. Axioms from which it logically follows that those

who disagree with you and won't help you realise your plan
are enemies of goodness and humanity.

This analysis is completed by the indictment that a government
with a comprehensive plan for the betterment of society is
a government that uses torture! But Miller goes on to argue
that, whether it wills it or no, a government today is obliged
to plan, at least to some degree, because of the constantly
accelerating speed of technological advances and because of
the universal ability to prevent conception. In such circumstances, the lack of broad planning would, says Miller, simply
lead to breakdown. But in devising plans, governments must
think in concrete and not ideological terms, 'For if you
begin by considering concrete people, you see at once that
freedom from coercion is a necessary condition of their full
development into full-grown human beings.' But most modern
governments plan very differently. They fail to realise that
an economic prosperity based on the possession of 'unnecessary
objects' does not lead to individual well-being; that a leisure
filled with only passive amusement is not a blessing; that
the urban life-style which people are encouraged to strive
for can only be gained at a high psychological price; that
an education system which 'allows you to use yourself wrongly'
has no real value. Yet modern man accepts readily all these
undesirable aspects of planning as natural and unavoidable.
Why?[34]

> Because he is so little aware of his own interests as a human
> being that he feels irresistibly tempted to sacrifice himself
> to these idols. There is no remedy except to become aware
> of one's interests as a human being, and, having become
> aware, to learn to act on that awareness. *Which means learning
> to use the self and learning to direct the mind.*

Miller's argument, then, accepts the inevitability of planning
but clearly wishes planning to be merely skeletal, allowing
as much scope as possible to the individual. The individual,
however, must make a response, must learn to become a complete individual, acting out of love for his fellow men. Only
then will society be transformed. 'Wouldn't it be nice', says
Miller, '. . . if there were another way out of our difficulties!'
But of course there is not, no 'salvation from outside, like
a dose of calomel.'

One who wrote more explicitly about the importance of love, and who tended to emphasise *eros* at the expense of *agape*, was Huxley's mentor during his early years as a writer, D. H. Lawrence. Lawrence's politics were clearly not socialist in any accepted sense. Yet just as Lawrence shared (indeed helped to form) many of Huxley's views on the ills of capitalist society,[35] so he also shared Huxley's view on the nature of political and social change. For Lawrence, too, men had to change the nature of their relationships with each other. He wrote: 'If our civilisation had taught us how to let sex appeal flow properly and subtly, how to keep the fire of sex clear and alive, flickering or glowing or blazing in all its varying degrees of strength and communication, we might, all of us, have lived all our lives in love, which means we should be kindled and full of zest in all kinds of ways and for all kinds of things.'[36] Democracy, as far as Lawrence was concerned, had to concern itself not so much with redistributing property as with allowing each man to be spontaneously himself. Man would then rediscover his wholeness. Only then would he be moved by a new impulse to *free himself* from the[37]

extraneous load of possession, and walk naked and light. Every attempt at pre-ordaining a new material world only adds another last straw to the load that has already broken so many backs. If we are to keep our backs unbroken, we must deposit all property on the ground and learn to walk without it. We must stand aside. And when men stand aside, they stand in a new world; a new world of man has come to pass. This is the Democracy; the new order.

Those, like Huxley, who argue that society can only change as individuals change, cannot provide us with a plan of action to be analysed in depth. By definition, they have none.[38] But what they have to say, though we deal with it briefly here, is nonetheless important. They advance a very different view of evolutionary change to those of the scientists. Huxley's theory, for example, puts him in direct opposition to Shaw, who argues that only the natural leaders in society are capable of achieving progress, and to Wells, who emphasises communality at the expense of individuality. But for all three, as indeed for all who believe in evolutionary change, the process is inevitably gradual. 'A change is a slow flux, which must happen bit by bit', wrote Lawrence. 'And it must *happen*. You can't drive it like a steam engine.'[39]

VISIONS OF SOCIALISM

'A map of the world that does not include Utopia is not worth even glancing at,' said Oscar Wilde, 'for it leaves out the one country at which humanity is always landing.' Although the scrupulous political theorist might want to argue that the dreams of a classical utopia had ceased to exercise imaginations long before Wilde, it remains true that the majority of men who would like to be regarded as 'progressive' (in the political sense) continue to possess in their minds a picture of a world substantially different from their own. It is in this broader sense that Wilde used the word, and we shall follow his example here. Classical utopia was, after all, a place with no room for original sin. It represented, in Judith Shklar's words, an 'expression of the craftsman's desire for perfection and permanence.'[1] Classical utopia was not so much an indication of faith in the future but of criticism of the present. For writers like Thomas More[2] the object was to contrast the crudeness and dissolution of contemporary Europe with the unity and virtue of classical antiquity, and to heighten the contrast between the indicative and the normative by giving no idea of how utopia was to be arrived at. Classical utopia, more often than not, was a picture painted for intellectuals, and was inspired by a belief, which the intellectuals by and large shared, in a universal, rational morality; a belief, incidentally, which did not outlive the French Revolution, or so Shklar claims. Marx and Engels, for example, believed that they understood fully the course of bourgeois history and could *predict* future developments with scientific accuracy. 'In short', says Shklar, 'it was ideology that undid utopia after the French Revolution.'

Yet if nineteenth- and twentieth-century socialist writers were not utopian in the strict, classical sense, they did, all the same, paint pictures of the kind of society they hoped to achieve, and they also intended these pictures to be understood as criticisms of contemporary society. Not merely this, of course, but they hoped their utopias might inspire men to change society in the expectation of bringing their hopes to reality. 'The Golden Age lies before us and not behind', said Edward Bellamy, 'and it is not far away.' Those who were to make these dreams reality, moreover, were not always—nor even usually—just the intellectuals. The socialist 'utopians' aimed at as wide an audience as possible; they had little to say which could not have found its way into a party manifesto.

All the same, like their classical predecessors, the socialist 'utopians' needed faith in man's capacity for justice and rationality. As one critic writes: 'In general the hope of an earthly utopia can exist at all only because the dreamer assumes that he and his neighbours are good enough and rational enough to sit down and plan a better world. Not merely plan it, but build it.'[3] The role of the socialist writer, then, is to stimulate the public into seeking and working for the kind of future he perceives and portrays. It is the task of the artist to provide a vision of the future powerful enough to promote a reaction. He must 'perceive slight tremors in the air and give them objective expression before the average person is aware of them.'[4] As a visionary, then, he will be in advance of public opinion, but a general sympathy, however vague, must exist in the public mind already if he is to be successful.

The future for the writers we have been looking at is clearly a socialist future, but what sort of socialist future? C. P. Snow aptly remarked of Wells that he sought to create the kind of society into which his own life-style would fit snugly, and *that* would require 'a pretty major transformation of society, for his life was a very odd one.'[5] What is true of Wells is, as we shall see, true of others. On the other hand, there are certain features which are common to socialist utopians, in fact to all utopians. Walsh lists ten such features, the most important of which are: man is by nature good (Wells remarks in *A Modern Utopia* that 'the leading principle in the utopian religion is the repudiation of the doctrine of original sin'); as a consequence there need exist no conflict between the interests of the individual and those of a fair and just society; man is also rational and therefore capable of solving such social and technological problems as the future might hold and thus be able to create a fair and just society; the purpose of this society will be to provide for the earthly welfare of all men, with an emphasis usually upon cultural or spiritual rather than material welfare. We can add to Walsh's list another feature of very considerable importance: that nothing which is in demand is scarce, and therefore there is no divisive competition. Not all utopians are egalitarian; in fact most are not. But there are no 'haves' and 'have-nots'—only 'haves' and 'have-mores'.

So we can expect that the visions of the future to be considered in this section will be individualistic to some extent but at the same time bound together by some of these common features we have discussed. They will also tend to emphasise one or other of the 'tendencies' we have been concentrating on in this book; that is to say, they will tend to be moralistic or scientific.[6] The moralist's utopia will emphasise equality, and the freedom of the individual to shape his own life within the framework of a community. For the scientists, utopia will be more regimented; emphasis will be placed not so much upon the individual as upon society, or mankind, ordered and disciplined, striving for some collective good beyond the good of individual men. High technology is more likely to have a place in the scientist's vision of utopia and technologists and social scientists to be accorded high status within the leadership. But in principle there is no reason why a moralist utopia should not be based upon high technology, so long as that technology is clearly subordinated to the needs of the individual.

The task of providing a picture of a future society that is worth striving after is clearly an important one, and one which merits detailed consideration. Moreover, since we have said that these pictures are likely to be individualistic, our time will be better spent considering one example of each kind of utopia, the moralist's and the scientist's, in as much detail as possible, using each as a framework within which to make appropriate comparisons with other utopias. The utopian visions we shall be examining belong to the moralist William Morris and the scientist H. G. Wells.

One point more. For reasons which we have not the time to go into, the period after the 1914–18 war is better known for its dystopias than its utopias. Creative writers have been more intent to show how societies *should not* develop than how they *should*. To say that nobody wrote about utopia after 1918 would be wrong; we should have to ignore much that has been written in the science fiction genre, and much else besides to make such a claim. But the fact remains that the most memorable pictures of the future depicted by imaginative writers in this period have been dystopias. We shall therefore take advantage of two of the best-known dystopias in order to show more fully the dangers and pitfalls of moralistic and scientific utopias.

7 'No Masters and no Masters' Men'

William Morris, we have seen, believed men to be 'artists' by nature, by which he meant that their basic instincts were creative and not, for example, political, in the Aristotelean sense. The most fulfilling thing a man could do was to create, and the job of society was simply to maximise his opportunity to do so. Morris himself, it will be remembered, resorted to politics chiefly because he believed that bourgeois society was structured in such a way as to restrain man's creative instincts and thus prevent him from becoming a complete man. Indeed, Morris was persuaded to become a socialist precisely because the men he saw about him were stunted and incomplete and in no way compared to his vision of the full man. 'In the times when art was abundant and healthy', he wrote, 'all men were more or less artists; that is to say, the instinct for beauty *which is inborn in every complete man* had such force that the whole body of craftsmen habitually and without conscious effort made beautiful things . . . and the audience was nothing short of the whole people.'[1] It is important to attach a precise meaning to the word art, but before we attempt this task we should note the words in italics. Morris was firmly committed to the idea that every individual possessed creative ability and, despite the impact of capitalism, was still capable of making himself a complete man by using that creativity. 'Three hundred years, a day in the lapse of ages, has not changed man's nature thus utterly, be sure of that: one day we shall win back art, that is to say the pleasure of life; win back art again to our daily labour.'[2] Potentially, at least, we are all artists; but what exactly is art?

I

'Art', says Morris, echoing Ruskin, 'is man's expression of his joy in labour.'[3] In other words, Morris identified art not as a category of human activity but as a frame of mind in which activities may be undertaken; so that most activities are susceptible to artistic performance. Because one takes pleasure in doing a particular task, cooking a meal, sowing a crop or whatever, it becomes an art form. Some tasks, he conceded, are inherently distasteful and are therefore not to be performed artistically. These must be shared around as much as possible, so as not to burden any particular individual or group. But wherever it can be managed they are to be performed by machines. Since art is joy in labour, the question now posed by Morris is: how is joy to be restored to man's labours? His answer is to give man once again 'the pleasure of working soundly and without haste at *making* goods that we could be proud of . . . such a pleasure as, I think, the world has none like it.'[4] Now most of these art forms open to the labourer are, actually or potentially, to some extent decorative, and for Morris the decorative arts have two specific functions. The first is to give pleasure to men in the things 'they must perforce *use*' and the other to give men pleasure in the things 'they must perforce *make*'.

So man's pleasure, drawn from art, should be two-fold: pleasure in the making and pleasure in the using. Yet certain important preconditions inhere in this pleasure. First, for man to take pleasure from making an object he must know that its use is beneficial to society and second he must be able to make the object under agreeable conditions. Morris wrote: 'It would be an instructive day's work for any one of us who is strong enough to walk through two or three of the principal streets of London on a weekday, and take accurate note of everything in the shop windows which is embarrassing or superfluous to the daily life of a serious man. Nay, the most of these things no one, serious or unserious, wants at all.'[5] Secondly, Morris was opposed to the mass manufacture of 'shoddy' goods, and the existence in capitalist society of a large underprivileged class seemed to necessitate the production of such goods. Men can take no pleasure from making shoddy goods. So, for men to take pleasure in making goods, they must live in an egalitarian society in which only the apparent needs of a people living a simplified existence are met. 'No one would make plush breeches', Morris argued, 'when there were no flunkies to wear them.'[6]

Morris's second precondition was that men must work under agreeable conditions. He was keenly aware of the significance of the relationship between dingy homes, dingy factories and dingy lives. He believed that those factories which continued to operate—the majority, being currently given over to the production of either shoddy or luxury goods, would be unnecessary in a just society—should become 'centres of intellectual activity' providing a wide range of social and recreational facilities. But the working day must be a short one for 'when class robbery is abolished, every man will reap the fruits of his labour, every man will have due rest.'[7] Finally, Morris argued for variety of work. Under the capitalist system men are 'educated' to play a certain role in the system. But this is not 'due' education which should enable young people to become proficient in a variety of handicrafts, thus allowing them, in the first instance, to take up a task for which they are suited and later to turn their hand to something else should they wish. In Morris's just society these conditions would be fulfilled, so that it would be possible to envisage labour's becoming 'a real tangible blessing in itself to the working man, a pleasure even as sleep and strong drink are to him now'.[8] We begin to understand, then, that much is necessary in the way of new political arrangements if Morris's new man is contentedly to indulge his creative instinct in work.

We have already discussed why Morris believed that man could not achieve fulfilment in a capitalist society. It is appropriate now to examine the utopian socialist society which Morris created in *News From Nowhere* in order to see what life is like for the whole unalienated man.

2

The simplest way to treat *News From Nowhere* is to follow the story as Morris tells it and to make some general observations along the way—much as the author himself does. The traveller, whom we shall call Morris, as in Chapter Six, awakes one morning to find himself transported to a London quite different from the one he knows; he has travelled forwards in time. Only slowly does Morris begin to realise what has happened, and so his first reactions give us some good clues as to the nature of the changes which have taken place. First, Morris notices how clean and bright the Thames looks. When he sees an oarsman on the river he is immediately arrested by the man's physical appearance. He describes Dick, the oarsman, who is one of the book's central characters, as being of berry brown skin with well-knit muscles, a 'specially manly and refined young gentleman'. The socialist world of Nowhere, we are given to understand, is a much cleaner, brighter and healthier place, and soon we discover it to be a place of abundance also. There are, for example, salmon nets in the river. Perhaps this is less surprising in the fourth quarter of the twentieth century than Morris would have imagined, but what *is* surprising is that the nets are not in use. 'We don't want salmon *every* day of the season', Dick explains.

But it is the dress and demeanour of those he meets on his first morning that impress Morris most. 'Almost everybody was gaily dressed, but especially the women, who were so well-looking, or even so handsome that I could scarcely refrain my tongue from calling my companion's attention to the fact.'[9] Throughout the book it is dress and demeanour which symbolise the life-style of Nowhere; indeed Morris's characterisation of the fashion in dress would provide an equally accurate description of the kind of society in which the people live: 'somewhat between that of the ancient classical . . . and the simpler forms of the fourteenth century, though it was clearly not an imitation of either'. The presence of such comeliness is the more pleasing to Morris since he finds, on his journey into the centre of London, no contrasting poverty. In fact when he tackles Dick on the subject, the latter does not understand the meaning of the phrase 'poor people' and can only imagine that his guest is alluding to sick people.

Morris's journey into the centre of London turns out to be a source of constant visual pleasure. 'This whole mass of architecture which we had come upon so suddenly from amidst the pleasant fields was not only exquisitely beautiful in itself, but it bore upon the expression of such generosity and abundance of life that I was exhilarated to a pitch that I had never yet reached.' Yet the architecture is not imposed upon the people, so to speak; it forms part of their everyday lives and is integrated into a generous and in many ways noble life-style. It is a life-style which extols the virtues of spontaneity and inspiration rather than tradition. In the field of education, for example, Nowhere's children educate themselves at their own pace. Morris and Dick pass groups of children playing in the woods, and Dick explains that in the summer months the children live in the forests and learn to master the skills of swimming and tumbling. Formal education, though it can hardly be so called, concerns the acquisition of skills in, for example, carpentering. As for reading, Dick assures Morris that: 'Most children, seeing books lying about, manage to read by the time they are four years old.' Foreign languages they pick up from the children of 'guests from oversea', and along with these, in some secret manner we never discover, Latin and Greek too.

Finally Morris can restrain himself no longer; he draws Dick's attention to the beauty of one young woman. Dick replies: ''Tis a good job there are so many of them that every Jack may have his Jill.' This is a comment which should not pass unnoticed for reasons which will become apparent later. Another remark of Dick's is worth remembering; he expresses a fear that work in Nowhere is beginning to become scarce. In the zero-growth utopia the need for labour is small and continually diminishing, and this fact seems to worry the more thoughtful citizens.

Just before they reach their destination Morris and Dick come upon a gang of workers mending the road. The foreman calls out to the gang: ' "Spell ho, mates! here are neighbours want to get past." Whereupon the others stopped also, and drawing round us, helped the old horse by easing our wheels over the half undone road, and then, like men with a pleasant task on hand, hurried back to their work, only stopping to give us a smiling good-day.' As they pass Dick looks in envy at the lucky workers and again one senses a vague anxiety about the scarcity of 'real' work in Nowhere.

Morris's and Dick's journey ends at the house of the latter's kinsman, old Hammond. The discussions which Morris has with Hammond form the central core of the book and we have already referred in detail to that part of the discussions concerning the revolution which created Nowhere's egalitarian society. But before we go on to deal with other, equally important aspects, it is appropriate to consider what we have gleaned so far about life in Nowhere.

A striking feature, surely, is that we have not yet met any 'individuals'. That is to say, the characters we have met are easily distinguishable by the clothes they wear but not by any characteristics to which we may allude by the word 'personality'. Boffin the dustman stands out, but, once again, chiefly because of the brightness of his dress. As for the others, they are all more or less brown, healthy and happy—on the face of it a race of Alfred Pollys—though in fact possessing none of the latter's depth of personality. They are extremely friendly people, but we are given no examples of any personal relationships based upon anything more abiding, such as love, or indeed hatred. Moreover we gather from the picture of education painted by Dick that no attempt is made to transmit any cultural values, such as loyalty, honesty or patriotism, or any religious or spiritual values. In short, we gain an impression of a people who are charming but entirely lacking in any depth. When Hammond somewhat later tells Morris that: 'We pass our lives in reasonable strife with nature', he hits the nail squarely on the head. Life for the citizen of Nowhere is something of a game, and the score does not signify. Unfortunately Morris is sometimes less than honest with himself concerning the implications of this easy-going atmosphere. For example, it is feasible that the young would learn some important aspects of any foreign language from children whose mother tongue it is; but Morris could not have believed it possible to acquire any knowledge at all of the classical languages in the process. He cannot have it both ways; the citizens of Nowhere must either do without the classical heritage or they must study it formally. Much of the cultural heritage of a civilised society is not capable of being transmitted orally. It is either lost or it is inculcated into the young by skilled teachers.

In any event, Morris now finds himself ensconced with old Hammond, the sage of Bloomsbury, an historian of considerable repute in Nowhere. Hammond's task is to explain to Morris— and thus to the reader—how the ugly, brutal and divided society of Victorian Britain transformed itself into the colourful, pleasant and completely egalitarian society of Nowhere. Moreover he will explain how social and political arrangements are organised. We have already discussed the revolution which destroyed capitalism in the middle of the twentieth century. The first great post-revolutionary change was the movement of population from the towns to the country. This had begun to happen even before the revolution, but after it people 'flung themselves upon the . . . land like a wild beast upon his prey'. Agriculture had been badly neglected prior to this. Now people found what they were fit for and did it. The consequence was that although the population remained much as it had been in Victorian times it became far more evenly spread and the differences between town and country became increasingly few. This process of general equalising was not restricted to the physical appearance of the country, although the emancipated people of Nowhere destroyed everything which had a desolate or miserable appearance, and so totally changed their environment. The style of life became more simplified everywhere and differences of status and function fell off society like dead scales. We have already seen democratised education in action, but the mistrust of book-learning has led to the eclipse of all seats of learning such as universities: no great loss, these, says Hammond, for they were merely 'breeding places of a peculiar kind of parasites, who called themselves cultivated people' but who were in fact treated by the middle classes with 'a kind of contemptuous toleration with which a mediaeval baron treated his jester.'

Academic institutions are not the only ones to have ceased to exist. There is no legal structure in Nowhere whatsoever. With the abolition of private property, and the hierarchical system (and its defences) which the system of private ownership implies, the whole structure of civil law and the court system becomes redundant. Hammond examines the implications of the relationship between property and crime not merely at the social level but also the private. In marriage, for example, the absence of property permits the establishment of relationships based upon love and not law, affection and not ownership. Maternity is highly honoured among the citizens of Nowhere, though the problem of eradicating hereditary illnesses seems to have exercised their minds. 'How to take the sting out

of heredity, has for long been one of the most constant cares
of the thoughtful men amongst us.' Indeed, according to Hammond, a study of photographs taken in the nineteenth century
allows him to confirm Morris's own view: that the citizen
of Nowhere is a more beautiful and healthy individual than
his predecessor.

In a society free of unnatural constraints the only crimes
to remain are crimes of passion. These, as Hammond points
out, cannot be eliminated by any legal system. In Nowhere
they are regarded not so much as the actions of habitual enemies
of society, but as the transgressions of friends. They are not
punished, since punishment achieves nothing in such cases.
Within the atmosphere of 'true communities', such as those
which exist in Nowhere, such transgressions are never repeated
because remorse overtakes the transgressor. Hammond is careful to point out, though, that 'there is no code of public opinion
which takes the place of . . . courts, and which might be as
tyrannical and unreasonable as they.' Quite how Nowhere steers
its happy middle course is not made clear.

As with law so with government: the equal society has no
need of it. The Houses of Parliament, the centre of a government
of a mighty empire in Morris's day, has become the Dung
Market . . . 'fertility may come of that', jokes Hammond,
'whereas mere dearth came of the other kind . . .' Hammond
continues that in reality parliament had represented nothing
but a sort of watch committee 'sitting to see that the interests
of the upper classes took no hurt'. They were 'a sort of a
blind to delude the people into supposing that they had some
share in the management of their own affairs.' Hammond habitually uses his knowledge of Victorian capitalism to illustrate
by comparison how things are arranged in Nowhere. So when
he speaks about politics, for example, after his arresting introduc-
tory assertion: 'We are very well off as to politics because
we have none', he suggests to Morris that the Victorian two-
party system was a myth. How else could politicians have
'eaten together, bought and sold together, gambled together,
cheated other people together?' In Nowhere, by comparison,
differences of opinion are real enough, yet they 'need not,
and with us do not, crystallise people into parties permanently
hostile to one another, with different theories as to the build
of the universe and the progress of time.' In Nowhere decisions

are taken by local community councils— at least, this is the only decision-making process which is described. They are taken communally, after each has voiced his opinion, and since all are equal, individuals are prepared to accept the verdicts of the majority of their peers.

The citizens of Nowhere lead a simplified life. There is no commerce (that is, no buying and selling), only a system of barter and exchange which is self-regulating and guided by general custom. The use of machinery is restricted to the performance of such tasks as would prove irksome to do manually. In short, the citizen of Nowhere is free as well as equal. The apparatus of the state has withered away. Everything that is produced in Nowhere is either for the direct use of the citizens or else for bartering. The fear of foreign domination is unknown, since the world is full of equally peaceful neighbours, and so are the pressures of competitive capitalism for 'Success in besting a neighbour is a road to renown now closed, let us hope for ever.' It is a world in which man-the-creator can lead a full and unalienated life, making only the things which he and his neighbours need and value. In the remainder of the book Morris describes at length what this full life is like, but it is worth pausing before we consider his description to discuss further the social and political arrangements of Nowhere —or more accurately, the lack of them.

It is surely strange to find Hammond, the sage of Bloomsbury, attacking academic institutions with such vigour. His own life's work is the study of books, and clearly his knowledge is a source of prestige; he is widely known. Moreover we can see that Hammond's knowledge is a source of power. There is, in fact, a clear difference in status between Hammond and those around him which is no more than one would expect. In primitive societies knowledge is a major source of power and the monopoly of knowledge was always much prized by priestly castes, and Morris is quite unrealistic in portraying the pursuit of knowledge as something of no general consequence. He is also being inconsistent, because if machinery is used at all, its construction and maintenance require expertise and thus knowledge. True, the use of machinery is limited to the performing of unpleasant tasks, but this restriction in no way rules out developments of increasing sophistication. There is a role, then, and a necessary one, for the expert in Nowhere.

But all this is shadow-boxing. The most contentious of Hammond's assertions is that the equal society has no need of administrators of any kind—nor of lawyers nor civil servants nor policemen nor soldiers. It is this Marxian assertion of faith which needs to be examined most carefully, for it provides the keystone of Morris's future society. We can see why Morris wishes to exclude the administrator. He is an expert. He has a skill which the ordinary man does not possess, and all forms of expertise necessarily divide men. But his claimed expertise is in the field of organisation; he organises the lives of others. This, of course, makes him a double threat to the egalitarian society. The modern industrial state demands all kinds of expertise, administrative among them: but Nowhere is anything but a modern industrial state. Its communities are small, its life-style uncomplicated. Can it not afford to turn its houses of parliament into dung markets? But we must be certain, more certain than we shall discover Morris to have been, about the consequences of doing without administrative expertise.

By far the most important would be the rudeness of life for the citizens. Any form of trade between communities, and more especially between countries, obviously necessitates a high degree of organisation, even on the basis of barter. Morris seems quite unaware of this. After dinner, for example, Hammond and Morris resume their talk with the aid of what is described as a 'good bottle of Bordeaux'. Are we to assume that the Thames Valley has begun to produce its own Bordeaux in abundance? Or has the knowledgeable Hammond secured 'good' Bordeaux as a result of barter whilst his neighbours make do with poor Bordeaux? Or do all neighbours get an equal supply of the good and the poor? Let us assume the latter to be the most likely. It is not conceivable that this whole process of procuring quantities of Bordeaux wine could be undertaken without a detailed system of arrangements concerning the trade agreement itself, the classifying, carrying, delivering and equal distribution of the wine. Such an enterprise, concerning a fairly trivial aspect of life in Nowhere, would clearly require a high level of organisation and administration, for which there is no provision whatever. Morris seems quite unaware, in fact, that life without administrators would not properly be described as simple but as rude at best, and more

realistically as brutal. Morris believed, with good reason, that
those in authority over others frequently abuse their authority.
But to abolish authority altogether is simply not a possibility.
And once we grant authority to experts we require a legal
system to ensure that they do not abuse that authority. We
must establish rights for individual citizens *vis-à-vis* those in
authority and try to sustain those rights in courts. Moreover,
society requires the provision of many essential services, such
as medical services, which demand expertise and dedication
at a variety of levels. Where are these dedicated experts in
Nowhere?

After their first day on the river, a day savoured by Morris
because of the beauty and abundance of the countryside through
which they pass and the pleasure of the company, they stay
overnight with a 'grumbler' and his beautiful grandaughter
Ellen. A grumbler is one who hankers after the old ways of
capitalism. These men and women do not pose any threat
to the existing order and are thought of as harmless eccentrics.
The grumbler speaks highly of competition, believing it to
produce a brisker and more alive society, more notable
than their own in terms of the great works of art it produces,
and so on. Ellen argues that for the ordinary citizen, herself
for example, the world of competitive capitalism would be
far harsher, reducing her rapidly to a grey middle age, whereas
she now is at the height of her beauty. As for the cultural
achievements of competitive capitalism, she declares: 'Books,
books! always books, grandfather! When will you understand
that after all it is the world we live in which interests us;
the world of which we are a part, and which we can never
love too much?'

Ellen is not merely a young lady with forceful opinions;
she possesses a beauty rare even by the standards of Nowhere.
Her beauty produces an air of tension the next day when she
decides to join the party on its way to the hay-harvest. Clara
clearly feels threatened by her presence and, equally clearly,
her presence excites Dick. Morris, himself excited, nevertheless
tries to ease the tension, by himself sharing a boat with Ellen.
Ellen later explains to Morris that '. . . even amongst us, where
there are so many beautiful women, I have often troubled
men's minds disastrously.' This, she explains, is why she has
been living alone with her father and now her grandfather.

There are three other points worth making about Morris's progress up the Thames. The first is the absence of machinery. For one thing the railway has disappeared, and for another the lock gates have not been at all improved. 'You see, guest' Morris is told, 'this is not an age of inventions.' The second is that even Morris is surprised—and despite himself not pleasantly surprised—that all those he meets talk at such great length about country matters. At one stage he finds himself commenting that they talk about the weather like children. Finally, the shortage-of-labour question appears again, and again we feel a sudden frisson in the atmosphere. On this occasion Morris's party come upon a group who are decorating the interior of a fine house. One of the sculptresses remarks to another: 'Now, Phillipa, if you gobble up your work like that, you will soon have none to do; and what will become of you then?' This is said in jest but it carries a note of earnest.

It is not long before Morris is spirited away from Nowhere and we feel his sense of remorse at leaving; all the same we need, once again, to examine closely what he has to say about the life-style of the people to whom he has become so attached.

'I demand a free and unfettered animal life for man first of all',[10] Morris once claimed, and there will be little argument that man enjoys just such a life in Nowhere. The country is full of buxom girls and broad-shouldered youths, beautiful, strong and healthy. The consolations of life for the citizens of Nowhere may be summarised as: freedom, happiness, energy, beauty of body and artistic environment. No mean attributes these, but it is surely a major criticism that the life of the spirit has no place in Nowhere. Looked at from a spiritual point of view, life in Nowhere is not so remarkably different from Huxley's *Brave New World*. As Maurice Hewlett commented: 'A race of fleshy perfection, worshipping phenomena, relying on appearance, arguing from sensation; a nation of strong men and fair women, conscious of their own growth and of their country's, owning an art which springs from and is directed to Nature, Simplicity, Truth, which yet sees no significance, no shadow behind these comely forms, dreams no future, owns no standard, accepts no explanation, needs no justifying.'[11]

Nowhere is open to another criticism which, though it may

be stated briefly, is important; for a socialist society it seems
to be highly individualist. Although its citizens call each other
'neighbour', share all things in common and have no private
property, they seem to be remarkably untouched by any community spirit. That is to say, the community as such contributes
little to their way of life beyond providing the most effective
environment for each to explore the limits of his individuality
and creativity.

Linking these two criticisms together we find in Nowhere
a people who are individuals only at a superficial level, forming
part of communities which do not appear to be anything more
than the sum of the individuals composing them. Possibly this
represents an artistic failure on Morris's part but it is also
possible that he misunderstood the nature of community.[12] Does
there exist, in the entire span of human—or indeed animal—experience, an example of a community of complete equals? Does
not community imply division of function and perhaps of status?
In any event, Morris's communities appear to be mere shells
and their members disappointingly superficial. Ellen, it will
be remembered, points to her beauty as an example of how
much better things are in Nowhere than they were in nineteenth-
century Britain: how quickly it would have deteriorated in
the 'bad days'! Maurice Hewlett comments: 'It is as if a
pheasant were endowed with sensibility and lamented the moult-
ing season.'[13]

Morris believed passionately in the creative vitality of folk
art and culture and hence felt it necessary that all the citizens
of Nowhere should feel an appreciation of beauty in nature.
But it is surely unacceptable to sacrifice the entire cultural
heritage of a people simply because to absorb and transmit
it involves not communion with nature but communion with
art galleries, libraries and concert chambers. Even Morris comments to Ellen, in a cautionary way, that the citizens of Nowhere
are too 'careless of history', though what he fears is not the
loss of part of the cultural heritage so much as the possibility
of some citizens becoming 'bitten with some impulse towards
change'.

We have seen already that the success of Nowhere's social
arrangements rests upon a largely contented citizenry, although,
judging by past experience, there is little reason to expect
such all-round contentment. One of the principal reasons for

general contentment in Nowhere is its natural abundance. We hear from Dick, for example, that there are enough beautiful women in Nowhere for 'every Jack to have his Jill'. Yet Ellen is of such beauty that she feels obliged to live outside the community because she causes bitterness among men. In short, where personal relationships are not governed by the law but by personal proclivity, as in Nowhere, a woman's beauty may be a source of infinite friction. Morris seems to have been aware, then, that abundance was no guarantee of harmony. But in fact there is no guarantee of abundance. We have already observed that many citizens in Nowhere are acutely aware that opportunities for 'real' work are diminishing. Hammond explains that work will always be available but his analysis does not seem to correspond to the facts. In any event Morris seems to be apprehensive that the socialist man of Nowhere may not have buried his old self-interest so deep as not to be able to resurrect it in order to compete for a scarce commodity!

There remains one final criticism to be levelled at Morris's Nowhere. We have been told that the people are not inventive; they have no railway system left and they have not improved such machinery as they have a use for. We have also been informed that the people talk much about country matters such as the weather and not about much else. In a word, Society is stagnating: the citizens have no 'dreams of the future', in Hewlett's words. They are concerned with beauty, of course, especially with creating beautiful buildings, but the temptation is strong to compare the people of Nowhere with Wells's Eloi from *The Time Machine*. Magnificent buildings exist in the land of the Eloi, but they were built long before and the Eloi have since lost the requisite skills. The Eloi, too, are concerned with beauty, but almost exclusively physical beauty. They have fine libraries, but the books have decayed through lack of use. The Eloi could well be the citizens of Nowhere several generations on; a people who live together in 'communities' which lack the sense of drive and purpose that breathes life into a community; a people who have degenerated to the level of beautiful animals who sing and dance in the sunlight. In Morris's *A Dream of John Ball* (1887), Ball the hedge-priest asks of the peasants:

What shall ye lack when ye lack masters? Ye shall not lack for the fields ye have tilled, nor the houses ye have built, nor the cloth ye have woven; all these things shall be yours, and whatso ye will of all that the earth beareth.

Ball is quite right; in the 'fundamental egalitarian'[14] society of Nowhere there are no masters and no masters' men; instead all share equally a life of pleasant but primitive superficiality in a land of eternal sunshine. (What a different picture would have emerged had it been raining during those June days which Morris spent in Nowhere!)

3

Hammond declared that the objective of the revolution in Nowhere had been to allow the citizens to be happy—and hence the best way to prevent a counter-revolution was to keep the people happy. For Morris, as we have seen, it would be impossible for a people to be happy if they were not all equal; there would have to be no masters and no masters' men. But what if people could be happy in an unequal society? Morris attempted to depict a society in which men are free to do the things they like doing. But what if they are persuaded, instead, to like doing the things they have to do? What if a society were able to provide its citizens with 'the secret of happiness and virtue—liking what you've got to do.'?[15] In *Brave New World* (1932), Huxley describes a political and social system in which: 'All conditioning aims at that: making people like their unescapable social destiny.' It will seem strange at first sight to discover *Brave New World* in a chapter dealing with moralistic socialist visions of the future, but in effect Huxley's task is much the same as the moralists—to produce an unalienated man. It is true that a very high degree of sophisticated technology underpins Huxley's society, but it does not dominate the lives of the citizens. Indeed they enjoy their work, even though for most of them it is purely mechanical, and they have a wide range of leisure facilities in which all may participate. The objective of the state, according to the Director of the Central London Hatchery and Conditioning Centre, is to maintain social stability—an impossibility without individual stability. The way to keep an individual stable is to keep him happy. Thus the objective of the Brave New World is precisely that of Nowhere: to keep the people happy. It is because of the light that Huxley throws upon such ideas as happiness, fulfilment, stability and community, ideas which feed the very roots of moralistic socialism, that we shall be considering the Brave New World in this chapter.

Huxley introduces us to the brave New World by taking us, along with a party of new students, on a tour of the Central London Hatchery and Conditioning Centre. The Director is explaining the various processes by means of which children are 'decanted' and then 'conditioned'. First ovaries are taken from certain female volunteers (who gain six months' salary as a bonus) and eventually immersed in a bouillon containing free-swimming spermatozoa, then replaced in the incubators and finally bottled. However, the lower castes are brought out again after only thirty-six hours to undergo Bokanovsky's Process. By checking the normal process of growth, it is possible to encourage budding in the fertilised egg. As a result, instead of obtaining one individual human from each egg it is possible to obtain as many as ninety-six. 'To what end?' one of the students asks the Director.

'Can't you see? Can't you *see?*' He raised a hand; his expression was solemn. 'Bokanovsky's Process is one of the major instruments of social stability!' For the first time in history, went on the Director, planning became a real possibility. He quoted the planetary motto. 'Community, Identity, Stability.' Grand words. 'If we could Bokanovskify indefinitely the whole problem would be solved.'

Solved by standard Gammas, unvarying Deltas, uniform Epsilons. Millions of identical twins. The principle of mass production at last applied to biology.

The intention, then, is to produce a society to order; the required number of each kind of caste, each as nearly identical as possible.

From the Decanting Room the students are taken to the Neo-Pavlovian Conditioning Rooms at the Infant Nurseries, so that they can see the various processes of social conditioning which build on the pre-natal conditioning. First they witness how a group of Delta babies are conditioned to hate literature and the countryside for the rest of their lives. Books and roses are set before them and the babies crawl towards them. When they reach them, however, they are given an electric shock and bombarded with noises. 'Books and loud noises, flowers and electric shocks—already in the infant mind these couples were compromisingly linked; and after two hundred repetitions of the same or a similar lesson would be wedded indissolubly. What man has joined, nature is powerless to put asunder.' As the children grow older, so they are subjected to the technique of hypnopaedia: that is, of being indoctrinated whilst asleep. The Director describes hypnopaedia as: 'The greatest moralizing and socializing force of all time.' Suggestions are made and repeated to the child constantly until 'the child's mind *is* these suggestions, and the sum of these suggestions *is* the child's mind.'

Finally, the students are fortunate enough to be addressed by Mustapha Mond, the Controller for Western Europe and one of the Ten World Controllers. Mond gives the students a history lesson, explaining to them what 'homes' were like in the terrible days when children were brought up by parents. The home and family of the 'pre-moderns' made them 'mad and wicked and miserable. Their world didn't allow them to be sane, virtuous, happy.' Theirs was a life of prohibitions, temptations and remorse, disease, uncertainty and poverty—and consequently strong emotions. 'And feeling strongly (and strongly, what was more, in solitude, in hopelessly individual isolation), how could they be stable?' He concludes with an axiom of fundamental importance for the philosophy of government in the New World: 'No civilization without social stability. No social stability without individual stability.'

Thus, from the beginning, we are provided with a clear idea of the differences between the New World and our own and of the basic assumptions according to which those differences were brought about. So we are equipped for the examination of the life styles of the upper castes of the New World with which Huxley provides us. First we meet two young women, Lenina and Fanny, who are discussing their love lives. We gather that enduring personal attachments are frowned upon, and Lenina is regarded as acting rather immorally because she has maintained a relationship for several months with the same man. She complains that she has not been feeling very keen on promiscuity lately, but has to agree with Fanny who reminds her that, after all, everybody belongs to everybody else! Promiscuity, the gratification of sexual impulse virtually at will, is the basis of inter-personal relationships. Lenina is described by one of the men as '. . . a splendid girl. Wonderfully pneumatic. I'm surprised you haven't had her.' Lenina and Fanny, like all the other women in the New World, are encouraged to buy new clothes regularly, in order to keep production high. (Some of the hypnopaedic chants, in fact, encourage high consumption: The more stitches the less riches; Ending is better than mending; I love new clothes, I love new clothes . . .) Lenina's current pride is her silver-mounted green morocco-surrogate cartridge belt, 'bulging . . . with the regulation supply of contraceptives'.

There is as much abundance in the brave New World as there is in Nowhere. Moreover technology opens many more possibilities to the people of the New World in terms of pleasure pursuits. But the citizens are not only programmed for self-indulgence; they are programmed for community awareness. Even the Alphas believe firmly that all men are equal—psycho-chemically equal of course—and that everyone not only belongs to everyone but also that everyone works for everyone else. 'We can't do without anyone. Even Epsilons are useful.' In a more profound sense, though, the citizens of the New World *are* equal: they are equally happy. As Lenina and her companion fly over the Slough Crematorium they catch a column of hot air, the result of a human 'going up in a squirt of hot gas'. 'It would be curious to know who it was—a man or woman, an Alpha or Epsilon . . . Anyhow . . . there's one thing we can be certain of; whoever he may have been, he was happy when he was alive. Everybody's happy now.' Boredom and depression, however, are not unknown, but the citizens can relieve mild cases with a plug of sex-hormone chewing gum and more severe cases with a ration of the drug soma. Soma helps men to live only for the present: 'Was and will make me ill, I take a gramme and only am ', or 'One cubic centimetre cures ten gloomy sentiments.' Finally, the New World has its religion. Whilst there is no real equivalent of the Church Militant in the New World there is a faith, known as Fordism—sometimes Freudism—which provides the citizens with their Solidarity Services at which six males and six females drink from the Loving Cup, swallow their soma tablets and try to achieve

Oneness. Finally, when the soma begins to take effect, the participants join in an orgy.

> Orgy-porgy, Ford and fun,
> Kiss the girls and make them One
> Boys at one with girls at peace
> Orgy-porgy gives release.

It works. For the majority the Solidarity Service brings a sense of oneness and satisfaction. 'Hers was the calm ecstasy of achieved consummation, the peace, not of mere vacant satiety and nothingness, but of balanced life, of energies at rest and in equilibrium. A rich and living peace.'

There are two men, however, who are not contented, who search for something which life in the New World does not offer them. Bernard Marx is an Alpha Plus psychologist who feels himself isolated as a result of being small and rather stunted—too much alcohol in his blood surrogate perhaps—and of being 'too able'. His friend and confidant is Helmholz Watson who composed hypnopaedic rhymes for the Bureau of Propoganda. Helmholz is described as suffering from a mental excess and he feels himself to be capable of saying something important but he does not know what it is. In any event, both are dissatisfied with life and need only a catalyst to prompt them into some kind of action.

The catalyst is provided by John, a savage from one of the Indian Reservations, in which the people are permitted to live according to their traditional, primitive customs. John is the son of Linda, a woman of the New World who once visited the reservation on holiday and got lost. She was pregnant at the time, accidentally of course, and had the child on the reservation. She was obliged to live on the reservation thereafter and to bring up her son. John had nothing in the way of formal education beyond the customs of the Indians, but he did possess the collected works of Shakespeare and read them intemperately: he became, in short, a particularly noble savage. Bernard Marx visited the same reservation with Lenina, also on holiday. He met John and his mother, and received permission to bring both back to the New World. John's experiences in the New World provide Huxley with a series of opportunities to criticise its social customs without detracting from the narrative. Linda, his mother, pined for her past life of ease and comfort from the time her son was born; more correctly, from several months before he was born, because one of the first facilities she missed was that provided by London's Abortion Centre. 'Is it still down in Chelsea, by the way', she asks, 'and still flood-lighted on Tuesdays and Fridays? ... That lovely pink glass tower!'

Linda's stay back in the New World is short. To the people who see her she is grotesque. Her life becomes a soma holiday, and before long she is taken to the Park Lane Hospital for the Dying. John finds her, propped up with an expression of 'imbecile happiness' watching the semi-finals of the South American Riemann-surface Tennis Championship, quite unaware of what is happening to her. To make matters worse, before Linda dies she is visited by a group of Delta twins on a death-conditioning visit. They come to watch people die and in the meantime enjoy a good play and a chocolate eclair. For them death will hold no sting, nor grave a victory. But for John, trying to snatch a moment of dignity, the whole episode of his mother's death is like a nightmare. 'Their faces, their repeated faces—for there was only one between the lot of them—puggishly stared, all nostrils and pale goggling eyes. Their uniform was khaki. All their mouths hung open. Squealing and chattering they entered. In a moment, it seemed, the ward was maggoty with them.'

The fact is that although John manages to establish some contact with the disillusioned Helmholz Watson and Bernard himself, especially the former, he never feels that he properly understands them or, more important, that they properly understand him. For example, when he reads extracts from *Romeo and Juliet* to Helmholz, the latter 'broke out in an explosion of uncontrollable guffawing'; he found its 'smutty absurdity' to be 'irresistably comical'. Similarly when John expressed his love to Lenina, he is horrified by her response:

> Zip, zip! Her answer was wordless. She stepped out of her bell-bottomed trousers. Her zippi-camiknicks were a pale shell of pink ... Zip! The rounded pinkness fell apart like a neatly divided apple. A wriggle of the arms, a lifting first of the right foot, then of the left: the zippi-camiknicks were lying lifeless and as though deflated on the floor ... 'Darling. *Darling*! If only you'd said so before! She held out her arms.

But instead of also saying 'Darling!' and holding out *his* arms, the Savage retreated in terror, flapping his hands at her as though he were trying to scare away some intruding and dangerous animal.

Lenina's departure from his bedroom is hastened by a prodigious slap on the buttock and cries of 'Whore!' 'Impudent strumpet!'

John's private failure to understand or be understood properly by the people of the New World is followed by a public failure. After Linda's death he attempts to raise a revolt in the name of freedom among the menial staff of the Hospital for the Dying. But these Bokanovskified Deltas do not want freedom; they want their soma ration, and John, who stands between them and its consolations, is almost torn limb from limb. He is rescued, in fact, by the timely intervention of Watson. The only person with whom John can communicate intelligibly is the Controller, Mustafa Mond, who has also read Shakespeare and knows enough history to be able to understand John's predilection for liberty. He explains John's failure to him:

> The world's stable now. People are happy; they get what they want and they never want what they can't get. They're well off; they're safe; they're never ill; they're not afraid of death; they're blissfully ignorant of passion and old age; they're plagued with no mothers or fathers; they've no wives, or children, or loves to feel strongly about; they're so conditioned that they practically can't help behaving as they ought to behave. And if anything should go wrong, there's *soma*. Which you go and chuck out of the window in the name of liberty, Mr. Savage. *Liberty*! He laughed. 'Expecting Deltas to know what liberty is!'

Happiness, Mond concedes, may be squalid in comparison with the glamour of a good fight against misfortune, but it provides a far more stable basis for social arrangements. Mond also shows the necessity of the caste system by referring to the 'Cyprus Experiment' when that island was populated exclusively with Alphas. Within six years a bloody civil war had killed off three quarters of the population and the remainder had petitioned the World Controllers to resume the government of the island. 'The optimum population', he explains, 'is modelled on the iceberg—eight-ninths below the water line, one-ninth above.'

Mond explains why art, science (except that which deals with 'the most immediate problems of the moment') and history are forbidden to the citizens of the New World: each can lead men to be dissatisfied. Above all, God has become redundant. After all, religion traditionally provided men with a refuge when the world turned against them but in the New World 'there arent't any losses for us to compensate; religious sentiment is superfluous.' When John suggests that 'God's the reason for everything noble and fine and heroic' Mond retorts simply: 'My dear young friend . . . civilization has absolutely no need of nobility or heroism. These things are symptoms of political inefficiency.' The conversation ends with an agreement to differ. John claims that he does not want comfort: he wants God, poetry, real danger, freedom, goodness and sin. He claims, in Mond's words, the right to be unhappy. Mond goes on:

> Not to mention the right to grow old and ugly and impotent; the right to have syphilis and cancer; the right to have too little to eat; the right to be lousy; the right to live in constant apprehension of what may happen tomorrow; the right to catch typhoid; the right to be tortured by unspeakable pains of every kind. There was a long silence.
>
> 'I claim them all,' said the Savage at last. Mustapha Mond shrugged his shoulders. 'You're welcome,' he said.

The story ends with Helmholz Watson and Bernard Marx being transported to far-off islands where 'dissidents' are allowed to live in freedom. John is not permitted to join them; he is to assist Mond with some experiments. But he is not willing to co-operate and runs away, setting up home in an old lighthouse. He is so pestered by the media, though, that his already unpleasant life becomes quite intolerable and he ends it.

4

The task of the moralistic socialist is to make man happy. This may be a simplification but it is not, surely, a distortion. It is true that Morris says as much only once in *News From Nowhere*, when Hammond states that the objective of the revolution was to make men happy. Usually Morris prefers words like fulfilment and wholeness. But he uses these words, basically, to make the idea of happiness more explicit. For Morris man is at heart a creator and if he is not able to create objects which are aesthetically pleasing—and we have seen the kind of social preconditions which inhere in designating objects as aesthetically pleasing—he is alienated. But man does not create in order to create; he creates in order to fulfil himself, in order, that is, to be happy. What Huxley does in *Brave New World* is to strip down the idea of an unhappy, or alienated man, and to remove as far as possible all the hindrances, all the pressures, which alienate man. This leads him to conclusions very different to Morris's. The technological base of the New World allows the Controllers to condition men to like the environment in which they live, whereas Morris would have men create the environment they like. But in both cases a congenial environment exists and the people of both worlds live contented in it. Again, Morris states categorically his belief in fundamental equality whereas the New World is rigidly hierarchical. But the main virtue of equality in the eyes of its advocates, surely, is that it precludes the less fortunate from working at jobs they do not enjoy, living in miserable conditions, and so on. The conditioning processes in the New World produce much the same result. In short, although superficially Morris's and Huxley's worlds are totally different, in important ways they are very similar.

The most important, perhaps, is the lack of any spiritual values in both societies. In Nowhere, it is as if Morris believed that man's spirit would receive sufficient nourishment from the act of creation itself; in the New World, Mond simply rejects spiritual values, as an impediment to stable government.[16] What Huxley suggests, through the medium of the Savage, is that alienation is part of man's nature; it is man's alienation that turns him to love, to religious feeling and indeed to creativity. We have already examined the possibility that Wells, in depicting the life-style of the Eloi, was indicating the likely development of a society in which the struggle for life had been won; in which all men were whole. Eventually it becomes too tiresome to create, too tiresome even to defend oneself. Remove alienation and you may remove man's creative instinct! When the Savage claims the right to be unhappy he raises a fundamental criticism of moralistic socialism: that the unalienated man may not be a complete *man* at all.[17]

Two points are worth making, by way of conclusion. First, when our objections to Nowhere have been raised and applied there remains at the back of many readers' minds an image of a society of natural and architectural beauty, peopled by free men whose relationship with each other and with the natural world is basically harmonious.[18] Second, when we consider the butterfly-like life-style of the citizens of the brave New World, so clearly meant as a warning, it is worth pondering how many people in twentieth-century Britain would have good reason to prefer the New World, even with its gross defects, to their own.

8 The Benefits of 'Regimen'

For the scientific socialist it is not enough that man should be happy; he must have a sense of purpose.[1] Every individual is part of a scheme of things which is, in Wells's terminology, kinetic and not static. The essence of the scientific socialist's utopia is that it never ceases to develop; it must 'shape not as a permanent state but as a hopeful stage, leading to a long ascent of stages.'[2] In Wellsian language the most appropriate metaphor for a utopian society is not the citadel but the ship of state. On board that vessel the importance of the individual resides only in his specific functions as crew-member, though, of course, it is advantageous to have a robust, contented crew, for they will be all the better sailors. The voyage on which the ship of state is embarked is no pleasure cruise; it is a journey through dangers and discomforts towards a way of life quite different from that which we know.

Nothing more clearly distinguishes the scientific socialist than his emphasis on species-consciousness: his belief that society is organic and that it ought to think and act as a whole. That is why scientific socialists such as Shaw and Wells continually emphasised the importance of élite leadership, for at the early stages of the development of a socialist society, only the most politically-conscious elements would be capable of deciding for all, the direction in which society ought to be heading. Thus Orwell was only partly right when he argued that Shaw and the Fabians wanted to turn the world into

'a sort of super garden city'. Shaw's Perivale St Andrews was
nothing more than the first stage in a long development which
would eventually lead to nothing less than a world of pure
intellect: 'Lives that have no use, meaning or purpose', said
Shaw, 'will fade away.'[3] But Orwell was completely right to
point out that to believe a scientific élite would necessarily
be capable of deciding on the direction of future social and
political developments is to equate science with common
sense. Scientists like Wells, went on Orwell, may be justified
in assuming 'that a "reasonable", planned form of society,
with scientists rather than witch doctors in control, will prevail
sooner or later but that it is a different matter from assuming
that it is just around the corner.'[4] But even this assumption
assumes something more: that such an élite would not abuse
its powers over the rest of society nor usurp its authority
in the quest for privilege, neither would it retain its power
longer than was necessary. The fact is, of course, that the
models which scientific socialist writers like Wells and Shaw
used for their politically-conscious élite-members were none
other than themselves; they were, that is to say, simply taking
their own political and species-consciousness, their own reason-
ableness, their own common sense, for granted. If we grant
them and their like as much as they granted themselves, they
would still have to convince us that the rest of society would
be equally reasonable and common-sensible in recognising the
benefits of their rule. We may feel a little better qualified
to exercise judgment on these issues after a consideration of
Wells's scientific society in some detail. It is appropriate,
therefore, to turn now to his *A Modern Utopia*.

I

Wells begins by telling us that this book is 'neither the set
drama of the work of fiction you are accustomed to read,
nor the set lecturing of the essay you are accustomed to evade,
but a hybrid of these two.' It is, in fact, a rather unsuccessful
attempt to weld together political commentary and fiction,
though one cannot deny that the fictional element provides
an extra critical dimension.[5] Wells's companion in the adventure, a botanist, continually intrudes into the narrative. When,
for example, Wells stands in a Utopian township, his whole

being taken up with 'speculative wonder', his companion would be 'lugging my attention persistently towards himself, towards his limited, futile self'.[6] In many respects the botanist may be seen to represent the petty but all too real selfishness of common humanity which seems always to intrude between the scientific socialist and the realisation of his schemes. 'This thing perpetually happens to me, this intrusion of something small and irrelevant and alive, upon my great impressions', Wells went on. The story, such as it is, is simple to relate. Wells and his botanist friend are making a walking tour in the Swiss Alps.[7] They have just had a pleasant lunch, and Wells is turning his mind to consider various aspects of the perfect world when: 'And behold! in the twinkling of an eye we are in that other world.' This Utopia is a replica of Earth down to the smallest feature, but in manner, custom and social arrangements, it is quite different. Yet Wells takes pains to have us believe that his Utopia is not simply a dream. He is dealing with 'realities' in a way that Morris, for example, never did. He takes Morris to task for changing the nature of man altogether, making 'the whole race wise, tolerant, noble, perfect . . . every man doing as it pleases him, and none pleased to do evil, in a world as good in its essential nature, as ripe and sunny, as the world before the fall.' Wells, on the other hand, builds his Utopia upon man as we know him: 'We are going to accept this world of conflict, to adopt no attitude of renunciation towards it, to face it in no ascetic spirit, but in the mood of the Western peoples, whose purpose is to survive and overcome.' Indeed, when he wakes up on his first morning in Utopia he is aware of having had some 'vague nightmare of sitting at a common table with an unavoidable dustman in green and gold called Boffin.' No: Wells will have us believe that his is a world of 'real' men as we know them.

When we come to consider these 'real' men in their Utopian world, however, we have to dispose of an immediate problem. Wells's novel is far more discursive than even Morris's. He continually switches from narrative to general discussion about this or that aspect of Utopian society, which is taken so far, only to be dropped and picked up again at a later stage. Meanwhile the author turns his attention to some general impression about the flavour of life in Utopia. We cannot, therefore, simply follow the book, but must divide it into themes and

follow Wells's thought through, more or less under section headings.

One theme about which Wells has much to say at the beginning of the book, and to which he continually returns, is the
atmosphere of Utopian life. We should begin, perhaps, by recognising that Wells's Utopia is on a grand scale in every sense.
It cannot be contained within a valley hidden in the mountains
nor on a remote island. It cannot be local in character, as
Nowhere certainly is, but needs a whole planet upon which
to manifest itself. It is also worth pointing out now that Wells
believed that his Utopian life-style, unlike that of Plato's, More's,
or Morris's, would recommend itself to his contemporaries.
We may judge for ourselves. Early in the story, Wells and
his botanist friend meet a rather idiosyncratic Utopian walker,
whose total inconsequentiality annoys Wells. The man seems
out of place in Utopia and causes Wells to muse:

> The pervading quality of the whole scene was a sane order,
> the deliberate solution of problems, a progressive intention
> steadily achieving itself, and the aspect that particularly occu-
> pied me was the incongruity of this with our blond-haired
> friend.
>
> On the one hand there was a state of affairs that implied
> a power of will, an organising and controlling force, the
> co-operation of a great number of vigorous people to establish
> and sustain its progress, and on the other, this creature of
> pose and vanity. . . .

Thus Utopian efficiency and species-consciousness does not
exclude ordinary individuality even where it is quite unproduc-
tive and, in fact, rather stupid. All the same, the emphasis,
in the main, is upon collective efficiency, and for Utopia to
operate efficiently there must exist a collective spirit which
'wills' that efficiency, for: 'No single person, no transitory
group of people, could order and sustain this vast complexity.
They must have a collective if not a common width of
aim . . .'

The technical efficiency and technological mastery of Utopian
society creates an atmosphere of calm and order, but above
all, of the total mastery of nature. There are 'faultless roads
and beautifully arranged inter-urban communications, swift
trains or motor services', so that travel is both cheap and

highly efficient. Utopian industries are set in clearly defined geographical areas, other areas remaining unpolluted. Yet the Utopian retains his own castle—his private house. Here Wells takes issue not only with the communist utopia of Morris but also with the principle enunciated by Thomas More, who said of private houses in his *Utopia* that 'Who so will may go in, for there is nothing within the houses that is private of anie man's owne.' Wells's ideas resemble more those of, for example, Schopenhauer, who likened men to hedgehogs clustering together for warmth but not wishing to become too closely packed. Wells's Utopian man has a house in which he may arrange his private property as he wishes. 'We are too much affected by the needy atmosphere of our own mismanaged world', he says. 'In Utopia no one will have to hunger because some love to make and own and cherish beautiful things.' Indeed, the Utopian may, if he chooses, 'own' some small business enterprise, though his proprietary rights will be circumscribed. In addition to house and personal property the citizen of Utopia also has a right to a garden of his own in addition to the communal land which surrounds all urban localities. But if our mind turns to comparisons with Nowhere we are soon brought back to realities, for Return-to-Nature, as Wells calls it, is no part of the Utopian scheme. Indeed Wells again attacks Morris specifically, claiming that he and his mentors were indulging in 'bold make-believe' when they claimed that all labour could be made a joy. (They claimed, in fact, that *most* and not *all* labour could be made a joy, though Wells's objection still stands.) 'If toil is a blessing, never was blessing so effectively disguised. . . . It needed the Olympian unworldliness of an irresponsible rich man of the shareholding type, a Ruskin or a Morris playing at life, to imagine as much. Road-making under Mr Ruskin's auspices was a joy at Oxford no doubt, and a distinction, and it still remains a distinction; it proved the least contagious of practices.' Indeed, in Wells's Utopia man as a source of energy has been dispensed with altogether, a labouring class having become 'unnecessary to the world of men'. And whilst no leisured class exists either, there will certainly be found men and women of leisure. Each Utopian is required to undertake a certain minimum workload and anyone undertaking more than this minimum is entitled to more privacies, more space in which to live. 'The modern

Utopia will give a universal security indeed, and exercise the minimum of compulsions to toil, but it will offer some acutely desirable prizes.' When we come to consider social arrangements we shall look a little closer at these provisions.

Another important characteristic of the Utopian life-style is that women are no longer in any sense inferior. Marriage continues, though with ample provision for divorce without disgrace, but it is based upon a far greater degree of feminine independence. A housewife receives a wage and, in addition, a family benefit which increases with each child who attains more than the minimum state requirements in terms of health and physical and mental development. Not only does the state thus provide an incentive for the physical and mental well-being of the young but it also enables a wife to prosper irrespective of the fortunes of her husband. Not surprisingly the citizens of Utopia impress Wells with their physical well-being. 'Everyone one meets seems to be not only in good health but in training; one rarely meets fat people, bald people, or bent or gray. People who would be obese or bent on Earth are here in good repair, and as a consequence the whole effect of a crowd is livelier and more invigorating than on Earth.'

Wells's earlier descriptive passages concern the countryside, but it is only when he comes to describe the Utopian London that he interests us, for his London is as different to the actual London as was Morris's:

> There will be a mighty University there, with thousands of professors and tens of thousands of advanced students, and here great journals of thought and speculation, mature and splendid books of philosophy and science, and a glorious fabric of literature will be woven and shaped, and with a teeming leisureliness, put forth. Here will be stupendous libraries, and a mighty organisation of museums. About these centres will cluster a great swarm of people, and close at hand will be another centre, for I who am an Englishman must needs stipulate that Westminster shall still be a seat of world Empire, one of several seats, if you will—where the ruling council of the world assembles.

Wells then goes on to give us an inkling of the atmosphere of this mighty and beautiful capital city:

Great multitudes of people will pass softly to and fro in this central space [Rich with palms and flowering bushes and statuary], beautiful girls and youths going to the university classes that are held in the stately palaces about us, grave and capable men and women going to their business, children meandering along to their schools, holiday makers, lovers, setting out upon a hundred quests.. . . .

The contrasts between Morris's and Wells's London are enormous, none greater than in the prestige accorded to institutions of learning and of government, absent in Morris but central in Wells. There is a sense of order and cleanliness in Wells's Utopia, of everything in its proper place, which calls to mind Orwell's comment in *Road To Wigan Pier* that many intellectuals are drawn towards socialism through the desire to create an orderly, clean society. Indeed, when Wells wakes up in Utopia for the first time he describes in considerable detail how spotlessly clean his room is, and how easy to keep clean. 'A little notice tells you the price of your room', he adds, 'and you gather the price is doubled if you do not leave the toilet as you found it.'

So much for the Utopian life-style. There is a life of sufficiency for all and for those who are prepared to work harder than the state requires, a life of considerable comfort. As one would expect in a scientific socialist state, the 'collective spirit', as Wells calls it, is the driving characteristic, though Wells tries to show that there is room, within limits, for personal initiative. 'The state is to be progressive', says Wells, and 'no longer to be static, and this alters the general condition of the Utopian problem profoundly; we have to provide not only for food and clothing, for order and health, but for initiative.' All the same, one cannot help but wonder what Alfred Polly would have made of life in Utopia.

2

In Utopia scientific discovery is encouraged at every level of society. Research, for example, is on an entirely different footing. 'In Utopia, however, they will conduct research by the army corps while we conduct it—we don't conduct it! we let it happen.' In Utopia, he continues, 'a great multitude of selected men, chosen volunteers, will be collaborating on each new step in man's struggle with the elements'—in many ways this is reminiscent of Bacon's House of Saloman—so that Utopian research will progress 'like an eagle's swoop in comparison with the blind man's fumbling of our terrestrial way'. This research will certainly not be restricted to physical science. Indeed, the whole basis of scientific socialism is the application of scientific techniques to social organisation. Perhaps the most significant difference between terrestrial social and political arrangements and those of Utopia result from the latter's ability to select for office 'the best possible government, a government as merciful and deliberate as it is powerful and decisive.' Wells elaborates this point by example. In the narrative he and his companion are asked to prove their identities by means of thumb-prints. It transpires that Utopia possesses a central catalogue containing the thumbprints of every citizen in the world. The identity of any individual could be established very quickly by having his print taken and checked with the central catalogue. No doubt, given recent developments in computerised information services this system is much closer to reality than would have seemed possible to Wells's contemporaries. Moreover, not only does science provide Utopians with a government as beneficent as it is strong but it also makes possible the creation of an extensive bureaucracy celebrated for its efficiency and humanity. Because they had 'systematised their sociology', Utopians had been able to give attention to the 'psychology of minor officials'!

Thus science has made possible the blossoming of the paraphernalia of government in Utopia to much the same proportion as it had withered in Nowhere. The World State is the only landowner of any size, though local authorities hold land feudally, as landlords. Much of industry is run by the state, and all energy resources are vested in public ownership. In parenthesis, and this is an excellent example of Wellsian prescience, the Utopians use energy (not gold or dollars) as the standard of value, money being tied to the amount of surplus available energy.

If we pause for a moment and take stock of the Utopian system of government we see that the whole apparently scientific edifice is built upon one quite unscientific foundation—indeed Wells readily admits as much—that of the expectation of good government. We shall deal shortly with the means by which

Utopians rise to positions of authority, but it is surely worth asking at this point whether Wells is being true to his original intention of depicting a future society filled with men as we know them. There is an assumption that those Utopians who have the ability to rise to positions of authority will have overcome every tendency to abuse their privileges. They will be beyond reproach, like Plato's guardians. Whilst it may be perfectly legitimate for Wells to devise programmes to produce such a class of leaders, it is as well for us to bear in mind that no such élite has yet existed. It may be that government is the most suitable arena for the exercise of virtue, but to suppose that virtue is synonymous with political or administrative talents is to ignore the lessons of history. In many ways it implies an even grander supposition to suggest that when a state has 'systematised' its sociology—whatever that may mean—it can then turn its attention to producing minor officials with a psychological make-up suited to their bureaucratic tasks. In many respects, though, it is as important for a scientific socialist state to produce a bureaucracy with a human face as it is to produce a virtuous élite, and here we can afford to be even more critical of Wells, for he offers no indication at all of how such a humane and efficient bureaucracy is to be produced. So much for the scientific basis of government in Utopia. Let us now turn our attention to some of the details of Utopian social arrangements.

It is typical of Wells that a belief in not simply the inevitability but the value of competition should be stated in an uncompromising way:

But there must be a competition in life of some sort to determine who are to be pushed to the edge, and who are to prevail and multiply. Whatever we do, man will remain a competitive creature, and though moral and intellectual training may vary and enlarge his concept of success and fortify him with refinements and consolations, no Utopia will ever save him completely from the emotional drama of struggle, from exultations and humiliations, from pride and prostration and shame. He lives in success and failure just as inevitably as he lives in space and time.

The task of Utopian social arrangements is to make endurable the margin of failure, not to abolish competition. Thus every citizen who agrees to fulfil the minimum quota of labour imposed by the state will be guaranteed good housing, a sufficiency of food and clothing, good health and sanitation. Every citizen will be educated and trained by the state, and insured against ill-health and accidents. The application of scientific management principles will make it possible always to balance the 'presence of disengaged labour' with the pressures of unemployment. Thus poverty would be abolished for all but the idle. 'If the work the citizen does best and likes best is not to be found, there is still the work he likes second best.' We notice that capitalism's apparent inability to maintain constant full employment is not reflected in Utopia; once again, Wells offers science as the solution to the problem, and not simply as the means by which a solution might be implemented. To the objection that the increasing application of science to the processes of production will reduce prospects for employment, Wells counters that an increase in available labour (as long as it was not simply a reflection of an absolute increase in the population) would provide 'exactly the condition that should stimulate new enterprises ... in a state saturated with science and prolific in inventions.'

Population control, mentioned in passing above, is central to the continued success of Utopia's social arrangements; like other features, it is a scientifically applied scheme of control:

> The method of nature ... is to degrade, thwart, torture and kill the weakest and least adapted members of every species in each generation, and so keep the specific average rising; the idea of a scientific civilisation is to prevent these weaklings being born.

Where this control is not successful the state will give itself the power to take the lives of deformed and diseased births—though these are the only lives the state may take. In the normal course, however, scientific birth control is exercised by allowing only certain kinds of people to reproduce: 'The state is justified in saying, before you add children for the community to educate and in part support, you must be above a certain minimum of personal efficiency.' Personal efficiency is defined as being self-supporting, mature, physically fit and free of transmissible disease. Wells does not discuss these criteria more precisely nor does he suggest who would be responsible for enforcing the regulations. It is, after all, one thing to make such apparently common-sensible regulations; it is quite another to decide how far the state should go in securing obedience to them. Is it not likely that some proscribed couples might seek to have children clandestinely? This is not an argument worth pursuing further; it is enough to suggest that such a law could prove to be inhuman when implemented. Moreover there is no guarantee that even if it were possible to implement, such a programme would necessarily prove efficacious. For example, the treatment of transmissible diseases has made possible medical advances along very broad fronts in the past; it will continue to do so, no doubt, with considerable ramifications for the treatment of, for example, environmentally induced disease. Moreover, are we to consider it scientific to exterminate the weak in order to produce a race which appears to be 'not only in good health but in training'? Is one of the great benefits of regimen the fact that compassion has been set aside in order that there should not be a single bald head in Utopia? 'The difference between us, Wells, is fundamental', said Joseph Conrad. 'You don't care for humanity but think they are to be improved. I love humanity and know they are not.'[8]

3

The keystone of Wells's scientific Utopia is in its hierarchical social structure. Wells describes this structure in considerable detail and again the narrative adds an interesting dimension to his explanation. Just as the physical features of the Earth are reflected in Utopia, so are the peoples of the Earth. When Wells and his botanist companion are called to account for themselves, their thumbprints are checked at the central data bank and are discovered to match those of two important Utopian citizens. One of the book's more interesting sections is the subsequent encounter between Wells and his Utopian self, and the latter's explanation of the Utopian social structure, together with Wells's comments on it. Utopian-Wells explains that whilst Utopians do not believe that all men are equal, neither do they believe in the accidental categorisation of people into social classes. Instead, Utopians are classified according to temperament. There are four classes, then: the poietic, the kinetic, the dull and the base. The first two classes are thought to constitute the 'living tissue of the state'. Significantly none of these classes is hereditary; people may drift in and out of their own accord—much as the dead may commute between Heaven and Hell in Shaw's *Man and Superman*—though naturally they will tend to stay in the class which seems to suit them best. The characteristics of these classes are as follows. The poietic possess creative imagination: they are the artists and the truly creative scientific minds, the great philosophers and the moralists. We are given to understand that there is more than enough room in this class for 'wayward geniuses' such as Wells himself, whose imagination tended sometimes to outpace their practical abilities. The kinetic class comprises very capable but conventional people. 'The most vigorous individuals in this class', we are told, 'are the most teachable people in the world, and they are generally more moral and more trustworthy than the poietic types.' Utopian-Wells explains that there are two main kinetic types, the mainly intellectual— who comprise, for example, judges and administrators (at best) and rather average scholars and men of science (at worst)—and the mainly emotional—comprising (at best) great actors, popular politicians and preachers. The dull class is made up of men and women of 'altogether inadequate imaginations' described by Utopian-Wells as incompetent, formal and imitative and as counting 'neither for work nor direction in the State'. Lastly come the base, comprising men and women with no moral sense and who, moreover, are frequently inclined towards cruelty. They are characterised by a 'narrower and more persistent egoistic reference than the common run of humanity'. In short, they could be described as the criminal class of Utopia. It is interesting to note that in Utopia criminals are banished to isolated islands and left to their own devices, for they are seen as a threat to society. In *Brave New World*. by contrast, the threat to society is posed by the equivalents of the *poietics*, such as Bernard Marx and Helmholz Watson—and it is they who are banished to the islands!

This classification is accepted by Utopians to be a crude one, and certainly neither Utopian-Wells nor Wells himself indicate precisely how the system operates. We are provided with little more than a vague picture of the interaction of the groups in the setting up of the Utopian state. We are informed that the poietic types in various sectors of public life elucidated the task of combining progress with stability by means of world-wide movements which embraced and absorbed existing governments. They indicated which paths were to be followed, and their pioneering work was sustained, expanded and institutionalised by many kinetic types. Thus, Wells tries to establish a pattern of progress in which the poietic types, through the exercise of creative imagination, point the way ahead, their suggestions being implemented by the more energetic kinetic types.[9] In short, Utopia recognises the value of its poietic types—its H. G. Wellses—much more than do the short-sighted nations of our world. 'My double told me of a great variety of devices by which poietic men and women were given honour and enlarged freedom, so soon as they produced an earnest of their quality, and he explained to me how great an ambition they might entertain.'

The political structure of Utopia, however, is not based upon these social divisions. Power lies in the hands of a voluntary nobility known as the *samurai*, of which, needless to say, Utopian-Wells is a member. The *samurai* are described by Wells as fulfilling functions similar to those of Plato's guardian class. They are not an hereditary class—in fact any intelligent, healthy and efficient adult over twenty-five may elect to follow the Common Rule. First, though, they will have to have followed a course of instruction at college and to have passed an examination. Having then elected to follow the Common Rule they are required to keep themselves in peak physical and mental condition in order to serve the state. 'We prescribe a regimen of food, forbid tobacco, wine or any alcoholic drink, all narcotic drugs.' They are required to sleep alone four nights in every five and to take a cold bath and to exercise every morning. In addition they are obliged to read from the *Book of Samurai* for ten minutes each day. They are not permitted to act, sing or play public sports, neither may they buy or sell or 'avail themselves of the coarser pleasures wealth can still buy'. Finally, every *samurai* is obliged, for one week in each year, to go to some wilder part of the world on his own and to fend for himself entirely. 'We civilised men', says Utopian-Wells, 'go back to the stark Mother that so many of us would have forgotten were it not for this Rule.'

Although the *samurai* are forbidden all the trappings of public

worship, religion plays a large part in their lives. As we have
observed, utopias require a fundamental faith in man's goodness;
Wells's Utopia is no exception. 'The leading principle of the
Utopian religion is the repudiation of the doctrine of original
sin; the Utopians hold that man, on the whole, is good.' For
the *samurai* religion is an intensely personal thing; their god
is transcendental and mystical. When all these things have
been explained to Wells, he concludes: 'I saw more clearly
now something I had seen dimly already, in the bearing and
faces of this Utopian chivalry, a faint persistent tinge of detachment from the immediate heats and hurries, the little graces
and delights, the tensions and stimulations of the daily world.
It pleases me strangely to think ... how near men might
come then to the high distances of God.'

The task of the *samurai* is to 'direct and co-ordinate all
sound citizens of good intent'. Practically all responsible positions in Utopia are held by *samurai*: 'All our head teachers
and disciplinary heads of colleges, our judges, barristers,
employers of labour beyond a certain limit, practising medical
men, legislators, must be *samurai*, and all the executive commit-
tees, and so forth, that play so large a part in our affairs
are drawn by lot exclusively from them.' Although the Order
occupies power—indeed you have to be a *samurai* to vote—at
least one tenth of the supreme legislative assembly must be
elected from outside the Order because it is believed that 'a
sort of wisdom ... comes from sin and laxness.'

Wells has been criticised for being more concerned with
inessential detail than with the more important aspects of his
ideas. His picture of the duties and way of life of the *samurai*
offers a good example of this inconsistency, for although we
know that the *samurai* take a cold bath every morning we
have not the least idea of the nature of the legislative and
administrative machinery in which they work, nor—more im-
portantly—how the Order allocate tasks of varying status among
themselves. We know only of their success in the tasks of government, for war and poverty have been eliminated, disease cut
to a minimum, and the 'order, beauty and resources of life'
enormously increased.

There are many criticisms one might raise against Wells's
Utopia, but it remains true that he does contrive to give the
flavour of an efficiently organised state in which life appears

to be more orderly and vigorous than ours today. The major social and economic problems of modern capitalist society appear to have been solved, though perhaps at the expense of compassion. But we find a question shaping in our minds as the discussion progresses, a question which is never properly answered by Wells: what is the *purpose* of it all? The question is probably most effectively put in the writer's own terminology. We are told that those who comprise the 'living tissue' of the state, the poietics and the kinetics, appear to be 'not only in good health but in training'. In training for what? Could it be that, like virtue, the scientific organisation of society is its own reward, regimen itself the most enduring benefit of regimen?

4

Two basic assumptions underpin Wells's scientific socialist Utopia; indeed, as stated at the beginning of the chapter, they underpin the entire scientific socialist edifice: they are that the scientific élite will always act for the good of all citizens—or at least for the proletariat—and that they will eventually dismantle the sophisticated, centrally organised machinery of power which they have built up. None doubted these assumptions more strongly than did George Orwell and no writer criticised them more ruthlessly than he did in his novel *Nineteen Eighty-Four*. Earlier, in *Animal Farm*, Orwell seemed to be rejecting firmly the possibility of a genuine revolutionary role for an élite. In *Nineteen Eighty-Four* he turns his attention to the élitist socialist society, forged in the revolution and hammered into shape in the post-revolution. Orwell's Oceania represents a form of scientific socialism: it is a society which sees itself as an organic whole with no place for individual aspirations; a society which calls into question the whole idea of individuality. But *Nineteen Eighty-Four* depicts a perverted form of scientific socialism,[10] for in reality Oceanian society is organised and regimented for the sole purpose of maximising the privileges of the élite. Technology provides the basis for the dominance which the élite maintains over Oceanian society but the superstructure which gives specific shape to that dominance comprises psychological techniques of great sophistication. 'The ideal set up by the party', says Orwell, 'was something huge, terrible and glittering—a world of steel and concrete, of monstrous machines and terrifying weapons—a nation of warriors and fanatics, marching forward in perfect unity, all thinking the same thoughts and shouting the same slogans, perpetually working, fighting, triumphing, persecuting—three hundred million people all with the same face.'[11] The idea of the party, then, was to crush individuality for ever, and Orwell sought to show, in writing *Nineteen Eighty-Four*, that this would be the likely effect, and probably intention, of any élitist regime in the technological age. The regime in Oceania happens to be scientific-socialist, but Orwell clearly believed that technology harnessed to a totalitarian government of any political persuasion would produce the same political and social results. In Oceania, at any rate, technology provided the party with the means to keep all citizens under constant surveillance, thus effectively bringing private life to an end. 'The possibility of enforcing not only complete obedience to the will of the State, but complete uniformity of opinion on all subjects, now existed for the first time.'

With present purposes in mind, the most suitable way to discuss *Nineteen Eighty-Four* is to examine this central theme, the crushing of individuality by the élite, under a number of headings. First we need to say something about the nature of the élite itself, its membership, structure and ambitions. Then we need to examine the nature of individuality as Orwell sees it, and to discuss the techniques used by the party to destroy it. Let us begin with the élite.

In Oceania, with its population of 300 millions, the party comprises only fifteen per cent. Of this fifteen per cent, six millions (two per cent of the whole) belong to the Inner Party and thirty-nine millions (thirteen per cent of the whole) belong to the Outer Party. The remaining eighty-five per cent of the population belong to the proletariat. The Inner Party is described as the brains of the state and the Outer Party as the hands. A small amount of interchange between these two sections is permitted, but only so much as will ensure that weaklings are excluded from the Inner Party and that ambitious members of the Outer Party are made harmless by allowing them to rise. The 'proles' are left very much to their own devices—indeed one of the Party mottoes claims that animals and proles are free!—but should any gifted leaders emerge among the proles they are eliminated by the Thought Police. Our understanding of the power structure is helped by the fact that Winston Smith, the 'hero' of *Nineteen Eighty-Four*, obtains a copy of the subversive *Theory and Practice of Oligarchical Collectivism*, by Goldstein—modelled on Trotsky's *The Revolution Betrayed* (published in English in 1937)—which purports to explain the nature of Oceanian society. According to Goldstein the élite is what he calls an adoptive hierarchy. Hereditary hierarchies are inevitably shortlived, whereas corporate or adoptive ones, such as that of the Catholic Church, are capable of surviving for hundreds or even thousands of years. Technology in the hands of the élite had become an enormously valuable weapon; only if industrial-technological development required the education of the proletariat in order to master new techniques could it conceivably become an enemy of élite domination.

It is important, for our purposes at least, to remember that the revolution which established the élite in power was a socialist one. Goldstein points out that it had always been assumed that if the capitalist class were expropriated, socialism would follow. But in the event what happened was quite different. 'The so-called "abolition of private property" which took place in the middle years of the century meant, in effect, the concentration of property in far fewer hands than before: but with this difference, that the new owners were a group instead of a mass of individuals.' But once established in power the élite showed no inclination whatever to share that power with the people nor to improve substantially the living and working conditions of the majority of citizens.

The only member of the élitist Inner Party whom we meet in *Nineteen Eighty-Four* is O'Brien, a man of rather refined appearance whose face 'seemed to cast doubt upon his political orthodoxy'. Winston Smith did not know whether he was to consider O'Brien as a friend or enemy—somehow it did not seem to matter—for: 'There was a link of understanding between them, more important than affection or partisanship.' We are told that somehow O'Brien's mind actually contains Winston's, and that during the latter's interrogation O'Brien knows what Winston is thinking—indeed he seems to know better than Winston. We discover also that long before he actually meets O'Brien, Winston has dreamt of their meeting and of O'Brien's saying: 'We shall meet in a place where there is no darkness.' If

Orwell wishes us to make anything of this, it can only be that Winston was a thought-criminal many years before making his first act of defiance (buying a diary) and that the telescreen and Thought Police surveillance was sensitive enough to register this fact. Thought-crime being 'the essential crime that contained all others in itself', Winston became thereafter a marked man.

O'Brien, unlike Utopian-Wells, does not leave us in any doubt at all as regards the purpose of scientific 'socialism' in Oceania. It is to maximise the power of the Inner Party. O'Brien regards as quite spurious any ideology which posits power as a means to an end—the creating of equality for example. Power is not a means at all; it is an end. 'We are the high priests of power', he says of the Inner Party. He defines power as unambiguously as it has ever been defined: 'Power is in inflicting pain and humiliation. Power is in tearing human minds to pieces and putting them together again in a new shape of your own choosing.' The power of the Inner Party, moreover, is growing steadily, so that the picture of the future which emerges is of '. . . a boot stamping on a human face—for ever.' In short the aims of the revolution have been totally perverted by the élite and the scientific socialist dream has become a nightmare.[12]

5

We shall now consider the nature of individuality, as Orwell sees it, and assess the various ways in which the Party seeks to eliminate individuality. First, Orwell claims for the individual the right to be his own judge of external reality—in essence the protestant's claim to his or her own direct access to God. The Party stands against this claim, demanding of the individual that he reject the evidence of his own senses. 'But I tell you, Winston,' says O'Brien, 'that reality is not external. Reality exists in the human mind and nowhere else. Not in the individual mind, which can make mistakes, and in any case soon perishes: only in the mind of the Party, which is collective and immortal. Whatever the Party hold to be truth *is* truth. It is impossible to see reality except by looking through the eyes of the Party.' What the eyes of the Party might see is very much open to conjecture: 'In the end the Party would announce that two and two made five, and you would have to believe it. It was inevitable that they should make that claim sooner or later: the logic of their position demanded it.'

Winston Smith had a far better opportunity than most to witness the Party's attempts to control external reality, for he was employed in the Ministry of Truth. The Party employed a vast panoply of technological apparatus to ensure that the past was *its* creature so that 'all history was a palimpsest, scraped clean and reinscribed as often as was necessary.' Above all else, it is the Party's ability to pronounce *ex cathedra* on the nature of external reality which destroys the individual, for as Winston says: 'If the Party could thrust its hand into the past and say of this or that event, *it never happened*—that, surely, was more terrifying than torture or death?'

Orwell's second prerequisite for a private domain for the individual is family life.[13] In Oceania family life among Party members had broken down entirely. 'The family had become in effect an extension of the Thought Police. It was a device by means of which everyone could be surrounded night and day by informers who knew him intimately.' The model of Oceanian family life is provided by Winston's near neighbours in Victory Mansions, the Parsonses. Parsons himself, than whom a more stalwart and hearty Party member could not be imagined, was eventually betrayed to the Thought Police by his own daughter. But Parsons's predicament was far from unique. 'It was almost normal for people over thirty to be frightened of their children.' The Party had destroyed love and family loyalties and thus deprived the individual of the sustenance that these provide. One of Winston's most enduring memories is of his mother, dying without reproach so that he might live. This act belonged to a former time 'when there was still privacy, love and friendship, and when the members of a family stood by one another without needing to know the reason.'

Thirdly Orwell claims involvement in a cultural tradition for the individual. He must feel himself a part of that tradition and be able to pass it on to his children. As far as Orwell was concerned the most important component of that cultural tradition was language. Another important component was a past and a future independent of the Party. To deal with language first, it is probably true that Orwell attached more importance to the nature of language than any other politically committed writer. In Oceania the task of the Party philologists, like Syme (a man too creative to survive long), was to control behaviour by systematically controlling vocabulary. It might be argued that Orwell falls too ready a prey to the suppositions of the linguistic analysts, but his thesis suggests that the more the Party contracts vocabulary, the more easily it will control behaviour. 'Don't you see', Syme explains to Winston, 'that the whole aim of Newspeak is to narrow the range of thought? In the end we shall make thought crime literally impossible, because there will be no words in which to express it.' Orwell provides us with an Appendix entitled 'The Principles of Newspeak' in which he offers an illustration of Symes's point. The Newspeak word 'sexcrime' covered 'all sexual misdeeds whatever. It covered fornication, adultery, homosexuality, and other perversions, and, in addition, normal intercourse practised for its own sake.' Before long, intercourse for its own sake would become as reprehensible as, say, raping a minor. As for the past, *Nineteen Eighty-Four* is redolent of Winston's attempts to bring the past to life as a barrier against the Party. The book he bought for his diary was a beautiful old one, with smooth creamy paper. He bought it in Charrington's junk shop, to which he was instinctively drawn. Then he bought a paper-weight, a beautiful but useless object. 'If it [the past] survives anywhere, it's in a few solid objects with no words attached to them, like that lump of glass there', Winston remarks. The room which Winston and his lover Julia rent from Charrington, above the junk shop, is described as '. . . a world, a pocket of the past where extinct animals could walk.' In such an atmosphere Winston became whole again; his nagging leg-ulcer cleared up. Predictably enough, when the Thought Police finally broke into the room, one of them picked the paperweight up and smashed it to pieces on the hearth-stone—thus symbolically obliterating the past. We remember, also, Winston's toast in O'Brien's flat—'To the Past'—and his dedicating his diary 'to the future, or to the past, to a time when thought is free, when men are different from one another and do not live alone—to a time when truth exists and what is done cannot be undone.'

Orwell's fourth claim for the individual is that of a full

emotional life. He believed that totalitarian élites would attempt
to stifle passion. As O'Brien puts it bluntly to Winston during
the latter's interrogation: 'We shall abolish the orgasm. Our
neurologists are at work upon it now. There will be no loyalty,
except loyalty towards the Party.' Julia's great strength, as
far as Winston was concerned, was her simple love of carnal
pleasure. When they are quite alone in the hazel grove, on
their first meeting, Julia, as quick to unzip her clothing as
was Huxley's Lenina Crowe, flings it aside with a gesture which,
as Winston describes it, seemed to be annihilating a whole
civilisation. Julia's vaunted promiscuity was much prized by
Winston himself: 'Listen. The more men you've had, the more
I love you . . . I hate purity, I hate goodness! I don't want
any virtue to exist anywhere. I want everyone to be corrupt
to the bones.' Having already made out a case for relationships
based upon love, Orwell advances here the case for promiscuity.
'Not merely the love of one person but the animal instinct,
the simple undifferentiated desire: that was the force that would
tear the Party to pieces.' Winston is probably not in favour
of promiscuity in fact, but rather against the *total lack* of any
undifferentiated passion: he presents, so to say, an argument
in favour of some sort of balance.[14] After all, he later accuses
Julia somewhat scornfully as being 'only a rebel from the waist
downwards.' In fact, Julia falls asleep when Winston reads
passages of Goldstein's book to her.

Fifthly Orwell claims material sufficiency as a precondition
for a fully individual life. The opening few sentences of *Nineteen
Eighty-Four* tell us clearly that scarcity and not plenty character-
ises Oceania. Winston is convinced that man has a right to
something better. He ascribes this feeling to some ancestral
memory which causes him to reject as unnatural the discomfort,
the dirt and the scarcity, 'the lifts that never work, the cold
water, the cigarettes that came to pieces, the food with its
strange evil tastes'; to reject as unnatural the fact that 'nearly
everyone was ugly, and would still have been ugly if dressed
otherwise than in the uniform blue overalls'.[15] Goldstein argues
that it is deliberate Party policy to maintain scarcity for all
Outer Party members, so as to enhance the importance of
even minor privileges. Competition for these vital day-to-day
necessities, overall scarcity and shoddiness, Orwell suggests,
break down the human spirit and render a truly individual

life impossible.

Lastly, and briefly, Orwell clearly demonstrates the importance of privacy to the individual. In Oceania he has none. He is constantly watched by the telescreens and is obliged to walk about with what Winston describes as an expression of quiet optimism; any other visible emotion might condemn him. It is surely not necessary to elaborate on this obvious but enormously important point. Privacy is the *sine qua non* of a fully individual life.

There is a great deal else in *Nineteen Eighty-Four* which is outside the compass of this present study. What is important for us is that Orwell presents a picture of a scientific socialist society in which all the aspirations of the scientific socialists have been perverted by a malevolent élite which has consistently used the powers gained during the revolution and the post-revolution purely for its own ends. *Nineteen Eighty-Four* is the ultimate warning against trusting the monopoly of technological and managerial expertise to an élite.

6

The scientific socialists have little answer to a moralistic critic like Orwell, for their case rests on the supposition of wisdom and benevolence among the élite. Because of an inherent distrust of élites, which is very marked in writers like Orwell and William Morris, the moralists tend to believe that all political movements not rooted in and dominated by the mass of men are doomed to fail, inasmuch as totalitarianism would, for them (though not for scientists like Shaw) be classified as failure. Although in *Nineteen Eighty-Four* Orwell concentrates on the variety of assaults upon the individual we have been speaking about above, he does allude on a number of occasions to a possible alternative to Party domination. If there is hope, says Winston, it lies with the proles. It is appropriate, by way of conclusion to this chapter, to say just a little about this alternative.

In contrast to Party members the proles have totally escaped the benefits of regimen. They retain a sense of that common decency by which Orwell set so much store. At the beginning of the book we have an example of this from Winston's diary, when he is recounting a visit to the cinema. One of the films shows an Oceanian helicopter bombing a lifeboat full of enemy women and children. There was great applause from the Party seats but '. . . a woman down in the prole part of the house suddenly started kicking up a fuss and shouting they didnt oughter of showed it not in front of the kids they didnt it aint right not in front of the kids it aint until the police turned her out i dont suppose anything happened to her nobody cares what the proles say.' Orwell returns to this theme much later in the book and again compares the residual decency of prole life with the regimen imposed upon Party members.

> What mattered were individual relationships, and a completely helpless gesture, an embrace, a tear, a word spoken to a dying man, could have value in itself. The proles, it suddenly occurred to him, had remained in this condition. They were not loyal to a party or a country or an idea, they were loyal to one another. For the first time in his life he did not despise the proles or think of them merely as an inert force which would one day spring to life and regenerate the world. The proles had stayed human. They had not become hardened inside. They had held on to the primitive emotions which he himself had to relearn by conscious effort.

Winston speaks earlier in the book of his hope that proles might one day initiate a revolution against the Party. 'They needed only to rise up and shake themselves like a horse shaking off flies. If they chose they could blow the Party to pieces tomorrow morning. Sooner or later it must occur to them to do it? And yet—.' But he comes to realise that the importance of the proles is not so much a function of their revolutionary potential as of their sheer survival, for it was their survival which might ultimately defeat the Party.

In conclusion, then, the future society envisaged by the scientific socialist requires a high degree of systematic planning and organisation. This planning and organisation would have to be the responsibility of an élite whose wisdom and benevolence must be assumed. Wells makes precisely this assumption of his voluntary nobility, the *samurai*, and Orwell seeks to show what might happen were that assumption invalid. Moreover, through O'Brien, Orwell seeks to show that a scientific élite would inevitably misuse its powers to the extent, indeed, of destroying humanity. Orwell suggests that it is only in surrendering his humanity that the individual can assume the corporate identity, the species-consciousness, which is the objective of scientific socialism. At the end of *Nineteen Eighty-Four* we are left with a picture of Winston, at last unalienated against himself, his fellows and—above all—against the Party. He sits alone in the Chestnut Tree Café:

> O cruel, needless misunderstanding! O stubborn, self-willed exile from the loving breast! Two gin-scented tears trickled down the sides of his nose. But it was alright, everything was alright, the struggle was finished. He had won a victory over himself. He loved Big Brother.

For Winston Smith the benefits of regimen had come a little late.

9 Conclusion: Socialist Thought in Imaginative Literature

To call the last chapter of a book a conclusion seems logical enough, but perhaps in the present case it may give rise to expectations which are unlikely to be realised, for there are no neat conclusions to be drawn from what has gone before. We began with the ambition of throwing more light on to the relationship between socialism and imaginative literature: if we have succeeded, so much the better. Yet it remains true that throwing more light on a subject will, as often as not, highlight its complexities and ambiguities rather than simplify them. We have sought to illuminate, through imaginative literature, part of the richness of the mixture of 'tendencies' which make up socialism by concentrating on two of those tendencies, the moralistic and the scientific, and to indicate the tensions implied by their juxtaposition.

In this final chapter two tasks will be attempted which, together, will complete our analysis of the relationship between socialism and imaginative literature. The first task will be to consider such empirical evidence as there is to indicate that imaginative writers have any influence upon socialists in Britain. The second will be to attempt a necessarily brief summary of the tensions which our analysis of moralistic and scientific socialism has brought to light.

I

Four studies have been conducted into the influence of imaginative writers upon politics,[1] three having been concerned exclusively with the Parliamentary Labour Party. Each indicated that a significant number of Labour MPs, something like one-third, claim to have read and been politically influenced by imaginative writers. The most detailed of the studies was based upon questionnaire returns from, and interviews with, Labour MPs. The writers who enjoyed most influence were Bernard Shaw and H. G. Wells, an 'order of merit' established by the first and corroborated by the larger study, though the later study indicated a decline in their influence. Another very influential writer was George Orwell. It will be worth our while to consider the findings of the most detailed study, which concentrated chiefly on these three writers, more closely.

Two basic questions upon which the study hoped to throw light were: How does the imaginative writer seek to influence attitudes and events, and to whom should he address himself? Three quotations from the questionnaire returns provide useful guides to finding answers to these questions.

(a) 'Imaginative writers can help to create ... a general climate of opinion.'
(b) 'These writers were able to appeal to the politically sophisticated, the activists, much more so than the heavy, turgid writings of "serious" writers.'
(c) 'They added to the background against which highly influential men made political and social decisions.'

Taken together these statements claim that imaginative writers may influence politically aware members of the general public, thus creating a climate of opinion; that they may influence the political activists, such as MPs; and finally that they may exert influence over the decision-makers. Critics who attempt to analyse the source of particular policies assess differently the contributions of public opinion, the party rank-and-file and the leadership. What is claimed for the imaginative writer is that he is in a position to influence all levels! These three statements, then, merit more detailed discussion.

In what sense could writers be said to create a climate of opinion? Bernard Shaw once said: 'I write plays with the deliberate objective of converting the nation to my opinions ... I have no other effectual incentive to write plays.'[2] Now what did Shaw mean by 'the nation', or to put the question more generally, in what sense can authors be said to influence the public? Obviously they can only be writing for the better-off sections of the public, since it is chiefly the latter who attend the theatre or buy serious novels—though this was much less the case in the past. But writers are surely more restricted even than this. After all, Shaw also described theatre-goers as crowds of unobservant unreflecting people to whom real life means nothing.[3] No; the writer has somebody quite specific in mind when he tries to influence public opinion. Richard Hoggart identified the target reader by the phrase 'the intelligent layman', which, though it appears uncompromisingly simple, is helpful in indicating the nature of the author-reader relationship at this level. But who is the intelligent 'layman'? Inevitably he is, so to speak, a projection of the writer himself back into the 'state of innocence'. That is to say, a writer believes that those for whom he is writing (which is not the same as saying those who read him) will, when led out of their innocence by the information he has to offer, follow *his* argument to *his* conclusions. This is precisely the supposition which a writer makes who wishes to communicate political or social values, and there can be little doubt that the three writers in the study in question did communicate their views successfully. A quotation from one MP is typical of many statements made about Shaw and Wells. 'They influenced changes in the attitude of a whole generation.'[4] But some MPs argued that Orwell achieved the widest measure of public reaction when his *Nineteen Eighty-Four* appeared on BBC television in 1954. Indeed the phrase 'Big Brother is watching you' still has pretty wide currency, as does 'some are more equal than others'.

More pertinent to the second level of political activists, it is nonetheless true that imaginative writers also serve to strengthen the convictions of the already committed member of the public. For the intelligent (but no longer innocent) layman this function of reinforcement is an important one.

Finally, it is worth noting the destructive aspects of the imaginative writer's influence at this first level. By his critical, satirical, iconoclastic view of society he may assist dramatically in promoting public questioning of accepted attitudes. This is a function which seems to come naturally to many imaginative writers. In these ways then the imaginative writer may influence the general climate of opinion.

Considerable though the writer's influence may be with the general public, or at least the intelligent laymen, it is probably at the second level—the level of the party activist—that his influence is at its most marked. At this level the writer possesses a captive audience. He does not create opinions here so much as give them definition. What the writer does then is to lend specific shape to strongly held—and in the case of many, especially older, working-class MPs—poorly structured ideas. 'They are seldom if ever innovators', said another MP. 'They give a higher degree of articulation to what is already being said.'

Bernard Shaw and his Fabian friends set great store by the influence they believed themselves to enjoy with the political establishment. It is interesting to note, therefore, that the survey of MPs indicated clearly that those with positions of responsibility within the party appear to have read more and been influenced more than the party rank-and-file; in both cases not just more but substantially more. Consequently it would appear that, for whatever reason, the ears of the influential have indeed been attentive to the arguments of imaginative writers. Clearly it would be impossible to take this line of argument any further; we could not substantiate any example of policy emanating from a Labour cabinet which was influenced by the ideas of an imaginative writer—though when Shaw's close friends and colleagues Sidney Webb and Lord Olivier sat in the first Labour Cabinet the relationship was direct enough! On the other hand it is difficult not to believe that policies promoted and put into effect by a group of individuals, several of whom owed much to imaginative literature for the shape of their politics, would not reflect these influences in some measure. Prime Minister Balfour, for example, took the Leader of the Opposition to see *John Bull's Other Island*, having previously seen it himself on three occasions, presumably to improve his understanding of 'the Irish problem'.

A second area which the study sought to explore was: *How* do imaginative writers exert political influence? Is it principally the strength and cogence of an argument or is it the vividness of a particular image which transmits an idea or a value most serviceably? Is it possible, after all, to separate the two and to assess their influences separately? From replies to the questionnaire a pattern appeared to emerge which it was possible to test to some extent in interviews. The pattern suggested that MPs who claimed to have been influenced appreciably by imaginative literature felt themselves to have been influenced principally by images rather than arguments. This is an important consideration, because although no writer can always choose his audience he can, to some extent, choose his method of proselytising. H. G. Wells, for example, gave up the imaginative literature of his earlier period to write overtly political novels, and encyclopaedic histories and biologies, in order, so he said, to win over the masses to his brand of socialism; an approach which provoked Lytton Strachey to say that he ceased to think about Wells when Wells became a thinker! Judging by the evidence of the survey his scepticism was well merited.

The imaginative writer's ability to capture in miniature a whole landscape of political and social comment—this, it seems, is what gives them influence. In questionnaire replies and in interviews numbers of examples from the works of all three authors were provided. Among them were Orwell's short story *The Shooting of an Elephant*, which one MP referred to as 'a consummate condemnation of imperialism in a nutshell'; and another Orwell short story *The Hanging*, which a second MP called 'the great unanswerable indictment against capital punishment'. The key word here is 'unanswerable', and a third example shows precisely why. Bernard Shaw frequently argued publicly the case for total equality of opportunity. It would result, he said, in a break up of social stratification and thus make possible a humane and just society which was the prerequisite of socialism. Many could and did take fierce issue with Shaw but nobody could argue the point with Eliza Doolittle! The nub of the argument then is that the imaginative instinct of a writer can enable him to make concrete a whole ideology in an unforgettable character or situation. This image, once having influenced a person's thinking, may prove highly resilient.[5] It seems possible to state that imaginative writers influence principally as a result of their ability to create symbols which people can identify with their own experience and value system, and which therefore serve as a synthesis and reinforcement.

A brief summary of the major points arising from the survey may be helpful here. There is no necessary limit to the breadth or depth of an imaginative writer's influence. He may influence equally any thinking member of the general public (and thus affect party policy indirectly) any member of the Labour movement or any decision-maker.

By appointment: Breakers of Idols and Purveyors of Visions—these were the major functions of imaginative writers in the development of British socialism. In performing these functions imaginative writers helped to provide the British socialist movement with a sense of purpose.

2

Finally, we shall consider briefly some of the tensions which our analysis of moralistic and scientific socialism has brought to light. The first is the tension between equality and material sufficiency. In Section One we examined the criticisms which socialist writers made of capitalist society and although both moralists and scientists were aiming at much the same kind of targets, closer investigation reveals an important difference. Both groups argued that capitalist society was unequal and that it obliged the majority of its citizens to live in considerable hardship. Yet there was a clear difference of emphasis between those who saw inequality as the great evil and those who believed poverty to be the great evil: between the moralists and the scientists. For William Morris, for example, equality was far more important than material sufficiency. He claimed that inequality was worse than the most grinding poverty and that equality of condition ennobled a people, however poor they were. For Bernard Shaw, on the other hand, poverty was the worst crime of all, and its eradication the prime task of any socialist society. Now it was quite obvious to scientists like Shaw and Wells that the poor could not help themselves—not as a class, anyway, though they might as individuals—and that as a consequence they had to be helped by their betters, by men like Andrew Undershaft. The task of these natural leaders was to run society to everybody's advantage. But theirs would be a privileged position, and the society which they governed, whilst it might be less unequal than capitalist society, would certainly not be equal. The tension between these two objectives is clearly brought out in *Animal Farm*. The animals change from a Morrissonian pastoral society in which, theoretically at least, equality in most respects is a possibility, to a technological society in which inequality is unavoidable. The technology planned by Snowball and introduced by Napoleon gives a special role to experts; they hold a virtual monopoly of 'wisdom' when it comes to making decisions regarding the future of the farm. Without technology, on the other hand, the animals would have been condemned to poverty. It is interesting that although Morris considered poverty a price worth paying, his egalitarian society in Nowhere is anything but poor. Mysteriously the scarcity of resources in demand, a problem that has bedevilled most human societies, simply does not obtain in Nowhere.

If we relate this tension to the development of British socialism its importance becomes apparent. The Labour movement clearly possessed greater unity and moral strength when its demand for equality implied greater material sufficiency for the majority of its supporters *as well.* But when the redistribution of wealth through direct taxation comes to imply a transfer not simply from the middle to the working class, but also from one section of the working class to another, the tension between equality and material sufficiency becomes more obvious and more important.

A second major tension we have observed is between a belief in radical social and political change through revolution and a belief in gradual, constitutional change. For the socialist, the main question, we may assume, is which of the two methods is most likely to bring about a socialist society. Orwell's Barcelona and his POUM militia provide the best pictures we have of a socialist society emerging from revolution, though Jack London's revolutionary struggle is vivid enough. As we have seen, there are two kinds of justification for revolutionary violence. The first suggests that it is the only way to remove the incumbent élite, which will not relinquish power willingly. The second is that violence is a force for the growth of political consciousness. Both of these arguments are supported by the moralists Morris and Orwell. But the important questions, which Orwell himself raises in later works, are: first, since revolutions have to be organised by élites, is there any reason at all to suppose that the revolutionary élite will be any more willing than other élites to give up its power (after the revolution, that is)?; second, if violence is a force for political consciousness, is it not also a force for other things, such as greater violence, or violence for its own sake?

On the other hand, to play the constitutional game is to accept the rules drawn up by the ruling class to protect their own interests expressly or implicitly. As William Morris argued so passionately, socialist representation in parliament would only sap the vitality of socialist leaders and eventually make the socialists simply another bourgeois party. Even so, for the scientific socialist, gradualism offers the best prospects for a transition to a socialist society. Some, like Shaw, set great store by their ability to persuade political leaders of all parties of the wisdom of socialist policies, while others, like Wells, argued that the task of the socialist was to convert as many as possible to the cause—to 'go out and make more socialists'.

This tension has been written about so extensively that it is really unnecessary for us to relate it to the development of British socialism. It is enough to say that the Labour party comprises a number of members who, whilst rejecting revolution, support the kind of radical policies which only a revolution could bring about. As well, there are many who believe that the wisdom of socialist policies is sufficiently apparent to win the support of those in established positions of economic and managerial power. There are also those who believe that socialism can only become viable when, through propaganda, the majority have come to support its main tenets. Strong as this tension is within the Labour party, it is stronger within British socialism generally, and although the revolutionary faction is weaker than in most socialist movements, it is clearly alive.

The third and probably most important tension which our analysis has brought to light concerns the basic aim of socialism: should it emphasise the individual or the social good? Most socialists would argue that these goods are not mutually exclusive; rather the opposite in fact, as Shaw indicates here:[6]

> This is the true joy of life, the being used for a purpose recognised by yourself as a mighty one; the being thoroughly worn out before you are thrown on the scrap heap; the being a force of Nature instead of a feverish selfish little clod of ailments and grievances complaining that the world will not devote itself to making you happy.

Yet it remains true that the relationship between the individual and society in *News from Nowhere*, for example, is profoundly different to the same relationship in *A Modern Utopia*. For the moralist the socialist society must allow as much freedom of action to the individual citizen as is compatible with social, political and economic equality. He must be allowed to fulfil himself. As Aldous Huxley remarks: 'For if you begin by considering concrete people, you see at once that freedom from coercion is a necessary condition for their full development into full-grown human beings.'[7] For the scientific socialist it is society itself and not the individual which provides the focus of attention, since the scientist is concerned above all with development, with 'progress' towards a different kind of society. The dispute, to put it at its simplest, is between individual virtue, 'personal salvation', or simply hedonism on the one hand and social purpose on the other. For Morris, Orwell and Huxley the life which gave most satisfaction was one in which the individual was master of his own destiny. For Morris this allowed man to maximise his pleasures through being creative; for Orwell it allowed man to pursue his own pleasures and to practice simple virtues in the context of interpersonal relations; for Huxley it allowed the individual to increase his knowledge of God. For the scientist, however, the individual signified only insofar as he contributed to the process of 'socialist' development. Wells put the point as follows: 'I have come to believe in ... the coherence and purpose in the world, and in the greatness of human destiny. Worlds may freeze and suns may perish but I believe there stirs something within us now that can never die again.'[8]

In practical terms this tension has the widest ramifications. Socialism for Orwell and Morris was rooted not so much in an abstract ideology but in the values of ordinary people—or more precisely what they took the values of ordinary people to be. It is said of Morris, for example, that when asked what Marx's theory of value was he replied: 'To speak quite frankly, I do not know what Marx's theory of value is, and I'm damned if I want to know. It is enough political economy for me to know that the idle class is rich and the working class is poor.'[9] Orwell refused to elaborate any theory of socialism beyond that of 'decency' and 'justice' because he believed that to elaborate an ideology of socialism was, by definition, to take socialism away from ordinary people. For the scientists, on the other hand, socialism represented an elaborate doctrine according to whose theories a modern technological society was to be run. To believe that one had to secure the approval of the mass of men—by definition ignorant—was a palpable absurdity. Admittedly when society's natural rulers had organised a truly socialist society, power could be far more widely dispersed, but that time was a long way off. According to the scientist, what the majority of men wanted was not the rude equality of Nowhere (Morris was entirely mistaken!), but the comfort and convenience of a problem-free Brave New World. Only society's leaders are capable of pursuing the policies necessary to create a socialist society and it would be naïve to imagine that the mass of men had anything to contribute to this exercise beyond providing the physical support to make it successful. Again, the tension has dominated debates between British socialists. It has frequently taken the form of whether the Labour party is 'socialist' or 'labourite' (that is, a spokesman of working-class self-interest).

It is evident that each of these three tensions involved precisely the same relationship, that between an élite—society's natural masters, or the revolutionary vanguard—and the mass of men. The tension between equality and material sufficiency, for example, is much affected by the role of technology. If technology is necessary to create material sufficiency, then a technological élite of some sort would be necessary also. On the other hand, Morris shows us that a society whose people are socially, politically and economically equal—a fundamentally equal society, that is—is likely to be a primitive one, and almost certainly having to tolerate much greater material hardship than he indicated in *News From Nowhere*. It is ironic too, that in arguing for equality come what may, Morris was adopting an élitist attitude, whilst Shaw and Wells, in arguing for élitism and for greater material sufficiency were almost certainly adopting a majority attitude!

The tension between revolutionary and gradual change is also influenced significantly by the relationship between the élite and the majority of men. For any revolution to succeed, the support of the majority is essential, if not initially then eventually. Yet at the same time revolutions have to be prepared for and organised, and, as Orwell shows in *Animal Farm*, this work will fall to the pigs. If Orwell is to be believed, and if history is any guide, the pigs, having led a successful revolution, will be as reluctant to share power as were previous élites. The absence of political consciousness among the majority of the animals made such a result inevitable on Animal Farm. Without political consciousness among the majority, a 'socialist' revolution is impossible: without a socialist revolution, 'true' political consciousness is impossible. Gradual change, on the other hand, must be effected by a parliamentary élite, by definition. Yet again, progress towards increasingly socialist policies would only result from strong pressure from the majority of voters.

Finally, the tension between the individual and the social good is little more than a reformulation of the tension between what the élite believes to be in society's interest and what the majority believes. If it be granted that the main task of government, having created 'equality', is to stand out of the individual's sunshine, then the scope for élitist rule is strictly limited. If, on the other hand, we see society in the scientists' terms, as a ship of state, rather like Wells's destroyer in *Tono Bungay*, sailing out to some technological Utopia, then the élite's role becomes a crucial one.

It ought to be said that the existence of these tensions does not imply that they must, can, or even ought to be resolved, nor that in any given situation it will be necessary to opt either for scientific or moralistic courses of action. It was stated in the introduction that none of the writers we have considered was wholly consistent. We can label a particular writer or a particular book moralistic or scientific, but he or it is never wholly so. Similarly any course of action adopted by socialist movements is almost certain to contain elements of both tendencies within it. Thus we can see that to have adopted a wholly moralistic approach with regard to political leadership would have deprived socialism of its greatest thinkers and best organisers and have turned it into a mere populist party. Not only would such an approach have deprived the Labour party of most of its leading politicians but it would also have denied the socialist movement the contributions even of Morris and Orwell themselves! On the other hand to believe with the scientists that society's natural leaders have a monopoly of political wisdom and are thus endowed with the right to throw the majority in the direction they 'ought' to go, is equally unacceptable. Orwell was right to point out that this would lead to totalitarianism.

In highlighting these tensions within socialism, imaginative writers have added enormously to an understanding of them, and not only on the part of the general reader but, as we have seen, on the part of many within the labour movement. Moreover their relevance is surely as great today as ever it was. It seems almost certain that a second industrial revolution, based upon silicon-chip and solid-state computer technology will change the basis of production in every industrialised country within the next two decades. Perhaps the kind of worlds of which the moralists and scientists dreamed will become real possibilities. Almost certainly work as we know it will become as scarce as Morris suggested, and the discoveries of physical scientists as important to the well-being of us all as Wells predicted. The analysis of the ills of capitalist society—not as great now, certainly, as in the earlier part of our period, but present all the same—which imaginative writers provided, together with their proposals for change and their glimpses of the future, have helped to shape the views of politicians and people in the past. Perhaps, once again, the relevance of their statements about the need for change and the possibilities and dangers of change will be acknowledged. What cannot be doubted is that the student of politics, having studied these writers, will be better able to understand the way in which British socialism has developed in the past and the way it might develop in the future. 'These are the people', say Bellow's Mr Sammler, 'who set the terms, who make up the discourse, and then history follows their words. Think of the wars and revolutions we have been scribbled into.'[10]

Notes

1 INTRODUCTION: 'The Most Effective Means of Propaganda'

1 See S. S. Prawer, *Karl Marx and World Literature* (Oxford University Press, 1976).

2 (London: Macmillan, 1975.)

3 (London: Hodder and Stoughton, 1977.)

4 (London: Macmillan, 1977.)

5 (London: Methuen, 1971.)

6 Preface to *Mrs Warren's Profession*, in *Plays Unpleasant* (Penguin Books, 1972).

7 *Speaking to Each Other*, Vol. 11, *About Literature* (London: Chatto & Windus, 1970) p. 19.

8 'The American Scene', in *The Dyers Hand* (London: Faber & Faber, 1948) p. 313.

9 *Speaking to Each Other*, loc. cit.

10 *The Common Pursuit* (London: Chatto & Windus, 1958) p. 113.

11 Ibid., p. 198.

12 See J. P. Sartre, *What is Literature?* (London: Methuen University Paperback, 1967) p. 124.

13 R. D. Charques, *Contemporary Literature and Social Revolution* (London: Martin Secker, n.d.) p. 5. I have already mentioned Lucas's edited collection of essays entitled *Literature and Politics in the Nineteenth Century*.

14 Op. cit., p. 51, my italics.

15 See for example; 'Why I Write', *Collected Essays and Journalism*, Vol. 1 (London: Secker and Warburg, 1968).

16 'Inside the Whale', *Collected Essays and Journalism*, Vol. 1, pp. 493–526.

17 'Charles Dickens', *Collected Essays and Journalism*, Vol. 1, pp. 413–59.

18 Ibid.

19 See Sartre, *op. cit.*, p. 116.

20 Julien Benda, *La Trahison des Clercs* (Paris: repr. Grasset, 1927).

21 Advanced in a BBC lecture, part of a series entitled *Writers and Society*,

in December 1971.

22   He quotes Franz Fanon as exemplifying artificially exaggerated commitment—he calls it 'untrue rhetoric'.

23   Bernard Shaw frequently claimed that he worked under the shadow
of his public 'persona'.

24   J. Mander, *The Writer and Commitment* (London: Secker and Warburg,
1961) p. 99.

25   *Inside the Whale.*

26   Orwell, 'Writers and Leviathan', *Collected Essays and Journalism*, Vol.
IV, pp. 407–13.

27   Irving Howe sees no difficulty in treating any novel as source material
for politics. He says that he means by a political novel 'any novel
I wish to treat as if it were a political novel'. *Politics and the Novel*
(London: Stevens and Sons, 1961) p. 17.

28   See, for example, Berki's book mentioned below; R. Milliband, *Parliamen-
tary Socialism* (London: Merlin Press, 1972); M. Beer, *A History of British
Socialism* (London: Allen and Unwin, 1940); C. F. Brand, *The British
Labour Party: a Short History* (Oxford University Press, 1965); David
Coates, *The Labour Party and The Struggle for Socialism* (Cambridge Univer-
sity Press, 1975); H. Pelling, *The Origin of the Labour Party 1880–1900*
(Oxford: Clarendon Press, 1965).

29.   *Socialism* (London: Dent & Sons, 1975).

30   The germ of this contradiction has been taken from Berki's book but
its present form and terminology belong here.

31   Moreover it may not be helpful—or even possible—to classify individual
authors as belonging exclusively to the moralistic or scientific tradition.
No doubt they will favour one rather than the other, but their work
will almost certainly contain examples of both. H. G. Wells's earlier
social novels were basically moralistic in tone while much of his subsequent
work was squarely in the scientific tradition.

32   A useful introduction to such developments is to be found in, for example,
the series *The Twentieth Century Mind*, edited by C. B. Cox and A.
E. Dyson (London: Oxford University Press). Volume I deals with
1900–1918; Volume II with 1918–1945.

SECTION ONE A CRITIQUE OF CAPITALIST SOCIETY

2   *The Poverty of the Many*

1   Note Thomas Carlyle's comment: 'Recognised or not recognised, a man
has his superiors, a regular hierarchy above him; extending up, degree
above degree, to Heaven itself and God the Maker, who made his
world not for anarchy but for rule and order.' (*Chartism*) In his celebrated
novel *Fontamara*, Ignazio Silone gives a different view of the 'natural
hierarchy', the peasants' view:

'At the head of everything is God, Lord of Heaven
'After Him comes Prince Torlonia, Lord of the earth
'Then come Prince Torlonia's armed guards;
'Then come Prince Torlonia's armed guards' dogs

'Then, nothing at all. Then nothing at all. Then nothing at all. 'Then come the peasants. And that's all'.

'And the authorities, where do they come in?' asked the man from the town, more angrily than ever.

Ponzio Pilato interrupted to explain that the authorities were divided between the third and fourth categories, according to pay. The fourth category (that of the dogs) was a very large one. (London: Journeyman Press, 1975) p. 31.

2 *Boswell's Life of Johnson*, ed. Brady (Signet Classics edition, 1968) p. 297.

3 Quoted in *Shaw 'The Chucker Out'—a Biographical Exposition and Critique*, Alan Chappelow (London: George Allen & Unwin, 1969) p. 178.

4 Many novels were written about working-class life during this period, of which Arthur Morrison's *Child of the Jago* is one of the better-known examples. The novels were written by authors who were not themselves working class for an audience which was not working class. As P. J. Keating says: 'Character and environment are presented so as to contain, implicitly or explicitly, a class judgement.' We shall concentrate exclusively on Gissing here, but Keating's *The Working Classes in Victorian Fiction* (London: Routledge and Kegan Paul, 1971) provides a wide selection of these works.

5 There had been a time, however, when Gissing proclaimed himself 'a mouthpiece of the advanced Radical party' (*Letters of George Gissing to Members of his Family*, 1927, ed. A. and E. Gissing). He intended to 'bring home to people the ghastly condition . . . of our poor classes, to show the hideous injustice of our whole system of society'. (Keating, op. cit., p. 83.)

6 *Demos* (Brighton: Harvester edition, 1972) p. 382.

7 Swingewood, op. cit., p. 129.

8 *Demos*, p. 21.

9 Gissing's own passivity in the face of the injustices which he observes is not uncommon to the artist. In Durrell's *The Alexandria Quartet*, Pursewarden the novelist reflects: 'Aware of every discord, of every calamity in the nature of man, he can do nothing to warn his friends, to point, to cry out in time and to try to save them. It would be useless. *For they are the deliberate factors of their own unhappiness.* All the artist can say as an imperative is: "Reflect and weep".' (My italics.) But though he ceased to be a champion of the poor Gissing never ceased to paint poverty realistically.

10 *The Nether World* (Brighton: Harvester edition, 1974) p. 2.

11 Gissing's message is echoed in the fate of Jude in Thomas Hardy's *Jude the Obscure*. Jude also tried to 'rise above his station'. Late in the novel he says: 'I may do some good before I am dead—be a sort of success as a frightful example of what not to do . . . I was, perhaps, after all, a paltry victim to the spirit of mental and social restlessness, that makes so many unhappy in these days' (London: Macmillan, 1972) p. 337.

12 It is interesting to compare Gissing's comments on the lives of the urban

poor with another writer with first-hand experience, Arnold Bennett, who, in *A Man from the North*, tells us that his native Burslem 'thrills and reverberates with the romance of machinery and manufacture'. There is more character and individuality among its workers than a hundred Balzacs could analyse in a hundred years!

13 Preface to *Major Barbara* (Penguin edition, 1972) p. 22.

14 Before he became a playwright Shaw wrote several novels containing frequent descriptions of poverty; however they were not considered to have great merit and were not published at the time. he wrote *An Unsocial Socialist* in 1884, *Charles Byron's Profession* (1885–6), *The Irrational Knot* (1885–7) and *Love Among the Artists* (1887–8).

15 Preface to *Widowers' Houses*, in *Plays Unpleasant*, op. cit., p. 13.

16 *Mrs Warren's Profession*, op. cit., p. 24.

17 *Wife of Sir Isaac Harman* (London: Odhams, n.d.) p. 193.

18 *Major Barbara*, p. 15.

19 In *The Nether World*, John Hewett, in a similar situation, also dyes his hair and with a similar lack of success, though he speaks of others who have got employment by this means (see pp. 19, 20).

20 See Samuel Hynes, *The Edwardian Turn of Mind* (London: Oxford University Press, 1968) pp. 18–22.

21 *People of the Abyss* (London: Arco Publications, 1963) p. 47.

22 *Life in Edwardian England* (London: Batsford, 1969) p. 8.

23 *Ragged Trousered Philanthropists* (St Albans: Panther edition, 1976) p. 227.

24 See F. C. Ball, *One of the Damned* (London: Weidenfeld and Nicolson, 1973).

25 Siegfried Sassoon, though not, of course, a politician, reacted in a way typical of many of his class. In his *Memoirs of an Infantry Officer* he wrote: '... and in 1917 I was only beginning to learn that life for the majority of the population, is an unlovely struggle against unfair odds, culminating in a cheap funeral.'

26 J. B. Priestley, *The Edwardians* (London: Heinemann, 1970) p. 77.

27 *Love on the Dole* (Penguin edition, 1975) p. 50.

28 *The Road to Wigan Pier* (Penguin edition, 1963) pp. 94–5.

29 Priestley, op. cit., p. 77.

30 Hynes, op. cit., p. 54.

31 *The Road to Wigan Pier*, p. 106.

32 Despite the advent of 'social democracy', in 1977 some ten million people in Britain still live on or near the official poverty line (i.e. the qualifying level for supplementary benefit).

33 Priestley, op. cit., p. 57.

3 A Charge of Immorality

1 Marx described the alienated man as 'corrupted by the whole organisation of our society, lost to himself, sold, subjected to domination by inhuman conditions and elements—in a word, man who is *no longer* a real species being.' (*Early Texts*, quoted in D. McLellan, *Karl Marx* (Paladin, 1976) p. 99).

2 See R. Furneaux Jordan, *The Medieval Vision of William Morris* (London:

William Morris Society, 1960).

3 Quoted in L. W. Grey, *William Morris* (London: Cassell and Company, 1949) p. 138. Emphasis in the original.

4 Edward Thompson, *William Morris: Romantic to Revolutionary* (London: Lawrence and Wishart, 1955) p. 779.

5 *Art and Socialism.*

6 *Art Under Plutocracy.*

7 *Useful Work Versus Useless Toil.*

8 *First Men in the Moon* (London: Newnes, 1901) p. 24, my italics.

9 See J. Kagarlitski, *The Life and Thought of H. G. Wells* (London: Sidgwick and Jackson, 1966) esp. p. 52.

10 *Kipps, The Story of a Simple Soul* (London: Macmillan, 1926) pp. 392–3.

11 Arnold Bennett did not enthuse over Wells's treatment of the 'nace' class in general. In a letter to Wells he wrote: 'Your attitude is not that of a philosopher but of a Chelsea painter who has not 'arrived' and sits drinking at the Six Bells while cursing all Philistines and plutocrats' (9/11/1905, in *Arnold Bennett and H. G. Wells*, (ed.) H. G. Wilson (London: Hart-Davis, 1960) pp. 118–9).

12 *Kipps* p. 290.

13 *Antic Hay* (Penguin edition, 1975) p. 254.

14 Quoted in P. Bowering, *Aldous Huxley* (London: Athlone Press, 1968) p. 28.

15 Huxley's point of reference for his critique of the upper classes is Rampion's picture of a naked couple embracing at the centre of the universe—a symbol of natural harmony and love in contrast to which the characters of Huxley's world exhibit only discord and selfish frustration.

16 *Point Counter Point* (Penguin edition, 1971) p. 59.

17 *Eyeless in Gaza* (Penguin edition, 1972) p. 101.

18 *Collected Essays and Journalism*, Vol. I, pp. 235–42.

19 *Road to Wigan Pier*, pp. 141–2.

20 Raymond Williams in *Orwell* (London: Fontana Modern Masters, 1971) claims that Orwell is completely wrong and fails absolutely to understand the social and economic structures responsible for the differences he enumerates. (See p. 23.)

21 *Keep the Aspidistra Flying* (Penguin edition, 1962) p. 254.

22 As D. L. Kubal points out, Rosemary's very surname signifies defeat for Comstock: it is Waterlo(o!) (*Outside the Whale: George Orwell's Art and Politics* (London: University of Notre Dame Press, 1972) p. 18.)

23 *Coming Up For Air* (Penguin edition, 1969) p. 14.

24 In *Orwell's Fiction* (London: University of Notre Dame press, 1969), R. A. Lee argues that Bowling's attempt to rediscover his past is doomed to failure. His problems, like those of the modern world in general, have no solution!

25 Bowling does not 'rebel' to the same degree as, for example, Babbit does, in Sinclair Lewis's book of that name (Panther Books, 1974, first published in 1922). Babbit rejects his whole suburban life-style, only to return happily to the fold and take up the many symbols of that life which he had jettisoned in the name of 'freedom' and 'self-expression'.

26 *Road to Wigan Pier*, p. 31. Orwell's forceful comment may be compared

to that of Richard Mutimer in Gissing's *Demos*, when he says to his fiancée: 'Everyone who lives at ease and without a thought of changing the present state of society is tyrannising over the people. Every article of clothing you put on means a life worn out somewhere in a factory. What would your existence be without the toil of those men and women who live and die in want of every comfort which seems as natural to you as the air you breathe?' (op. cit., p. 100.)

4   Muddle and Inefficiency
  1 Quoted in W. Wagar (ed.), *H. G. Wells: Journalism and Prophecy* (London: Bodley Head, 1965) p. 277.
  2 *First and Last Things* (London: Constable, 1908).
  3 Op. cit., *Bodley Head Collected Plays with Prefaces* (London: 1973), Vol. VI, p. 597.
  4 *Cosmopolis*, III, September 1896, p. 659.
  5 Quoted in Hesketh Pearson, *Bernard Shaw—His Life and Personality* (London: Methuen and Company, 1961) p. 73.
  6 He said that Shaw had made it '. . . absolutely impossible for any British socialist . . . to talk or act like Stalin'. (See C. E. M. Joad (ed.), *Shaw and Society* (London: Odhams, 1953) p. 41.)
  7 Speech made on 26.3.1914. Quoted in Chappelow, op. cit., p. 288.
  8 *The Road to Equality*, L. Crompton (ed.) (Boston: Beacon Press, 1971) p. 183.
  9 Preface to *Heartbreak House*, (Bodley head edn) p. 14.
 10 *History of Mr Polly*, (Penguin edn), p. 158. Compare this simile with Gissing's metaphor from *Demos*, quoted in Chapter 2.
 11 *Kipps*, op. cit., p. 14.
 12 This is put tersely in another wartime novel *Boon* (1915): the Germans at least stood for something—'but what the devil do we stand for?'
 13 *Wife of Sir Isaac Harman*, op. cit., p. 63.
 14 Weybridge clearly standing for upper middle-class complacency and sobriety; Shotover, it will be remembered, uses England in the same way—as a kind of global Weybridge—when talking to Hector Hushabye about the 'coming catastrophe'.
 15 *New Worlds for Old*, (London: Constable, 1908) p. 27.
 16 Quoted in W. Wagar, op. cit., pp. 280–1.
 17 *First and Last Things*, op. cit., p. 133.
 18 *Tono Bungay* (London: Macmillan, 1909) p. 77.
 19 Ibid., p. 108. My italics.
 20 As Norman and Jean Mackenzie point out in *The Time Traveller* (London): Weidenfeld and Nicolson, 1973), Remington, like Polly—and Wells himself, for that matter—seems to believe that freedom is 'fundamentally libidinous' (p. 267).
 21 *The New Machiavelli* (Penguin edition, 1970) p. 234.
 22 *The Apple Cart* (London: Constable, 1930) Preface, p. x.
 23 Ibid., Preface, p. vi. My italics.
 24 *The Road to Equality*, op. cit., p. 23.

SECTION TWO   WHICH WAY FORWARD?
  1 Neil Harding, 'Socialism and Violence', in *The Concept of Socialism* (ed.

Parekh) (London: Croom Helm, 1975) p. 204.
2 Ibid., p. 209.
3 *Post-prison Writings and Speeches* (London: Panther Books, 1971) p. 55.
4 *Homage to Catalonia* (Penguin edition, 1966) p. 119.
5 Quoted in Chappelow, op. cit., p. 181.
6 Quoted by Leonard Woolf in C. E. M. Joad, *Shaw and Society*, op. cit., p. 44.

5 *'Revolution, Revolution Is the one correct Solution'*
1 For example, *How We Live and How We Might Live, Art and Socialism, The Hopes of Civilisation.*
2 'News From Nowhere', in *Three Works by William Morris*, ed. A. L. Morton (London: Lawrence and Wishart, 1973) p. 314.
3 As happened, in fact, during the General Strike of 1926.
4 *The Iron Heel* (London: The Journeyman Press, 1975) p. 8.
5 *The Secret Agent* (Penguin edition, 1975) chapter 3.
6 *Eyeless in Gaza* (London: Penguin edition, 1972) p. 390.
7 *Homage to Catalonia* (Penguin edition, 1966) p. 9.
8 See K. Alldritt, *The Making of George Orwell* (London: Edward Arnold, 1969) pp. 85–90.
9 'Looking Back on the Spanish War' in *Homage to Catalonia*, p. 239.
10 The allegorical symbolism of the book is generally considered to have been completely successful. Jenni Calder in *Chronicles of Conscience* (London: Secker and Warburg, 1968) claims that he achieves a rare warmth and texture, unmatched by his other work.
11 Though not Lenin, strangely enough.
12 The closeness with which the fable parodied reality is indicated by the story of the two sheep who, during one of the trials instigated by Napoleon, confess to having murdered an old ram, a particularly devoted follower of Napoleon, by 'chasing him round and round a bonfire when he was suffering from a cough'. In the trial of Bakunin, in March 1938, the accused was implicated in the death of Maxim Gorky, whose secretary claimed that on Bakunin's instructions he would take Gorky on long walks, having arranged for fires to be burning along the way, so as to damage further his already weak lungs. Jeffrey Meyers in *A Reader's Guide to George Orwell* (London: Thames and Hudson, 1975) deals in considerable detail with this and many other parallels, though he surely goes too far when he claims that Snowball was so named because Trotsky had white hair and because he 'melted' before Stalin's opposition!
13 Kubal, op. cit., p. 39.
14 Major himself, of course, was a pig, as was Marx an intellectual. But like Marx he never assumed political responsibilities in a revolution.
15 *Animal Farm* (Penguin edition, 1958) p. 15.
16 It is interesting to recall that the egalitarianism of Nowhere is buttressed by the community's not producing more than it needs so as to make trade absolutely minimal.
17 The parallel between Stalin's attempts to concentrate on industrialisation and Trotsky's to concentrate on increasing agricultural production is therefore not exact.

18 This is clearly meant to reflect the debate between Trotsky and the proponents of world-wide revolution and the Stalinist alternative of socialism in one country.

19 *Record of an Adventurous Life* (London: Macmillan, 1911) p. 432.

20 *Animal Farm*, p. 120. It is interesting to compare the obvious success of the pigs in 'self-humanisation' with the failure of Wells's Dr Moreau to humanise animals by force. The comparison suggests that self-interest is a force of no little power!

21 *Darkness at Noon* (Penguin edition, 1969) pp. 40–1.

22 A picture in many ways more chilling of the enormous powers of the post-revolution leadership and their misuse is painted by Victor Serge in *The Case of Comrade Tulayev* (1948), published by Penguin Books in 1968.

23 *Point Counter Point*, op. cit., pp. 394–5.

24 In *Man's Estate* (Penguin edition 1975), Malraux gives an example of a revolution and of revolutionaries who are really in a different category from those we have discussed here. Hemmelreich, for example, wished only: 'To requite by no matter what violence, to avenge with bombs the unspeakable horror of the existence which had poisoned him since the day of his birth, and which would poison his children in the same way' (p. 167). In despair men will act with desperation, but their real motive is revenge, not socialism.

6 *The Gradualness of Inevitability*

1 E. Wilson, *The Triple Thinkers* (London: Oxford University Press, 1939) p. 241.

2 Ibid., p. 240.

3 *Essays in Fabian Socialism* (London, 1908) pp. 235–6.

4 'New Radicalism' (1887) in L. Crompton (ed.), *The Road to Equality*, op. cit., p. 31.

5 *Fabian Election Manifesto*, 1892.

6 Preface to *The Apple Cart*.

7 A. M. Gibbs, *Shaw* (Edinburgh: Oliver and Boyd, 1969) p. 29.

8 'The Simple Truth About Socialism' (1910) in Crompton, op. cit., p. 163.

9 *Intelligent Woman's Guide to Socialism and Capitalism* (London: Constable, 1929) p. 376.

10 Shaw can be said to be guilty of the charge Hannah Arendt lays upon Plato, that he is trying to escape from politics altogether and into the concept of 'rule'—namely that some are entitled to command and others obliged to obey. Plato's influence on Shaw and Wells was acknowledged by both, though Aristotle, too, spoke of some men 'so far superior ... in virtue and political capacity' that no law could govern their action. 'Such men we take not to be part of the state but to transcend it.' *The Politics* (Penguin edition, 1969) p. 132.

11 Quoted in Chappelow, op. cit., p. 199.

12 *Time and Tide*, 10 February 1945.

13 It is set out in Chappelow, op. cit., pp. 131–61.

14 *Observer*, 24 September 1944.

15 Quoted in L. Hugo, *Bernard Shaw, Playwright and Preacher* (London: Methuen, 1971) p. 131.

16 *Man and Superman*, (Penguin edition, 1948), p. 251.

17 J. P. Smith, *Unrepentant Pilgrim* (London: Victor Gollanz, 1966) p. 151.

18 Ibid.

19 'The Simple Truth About Socialism', in Crompton, op. cit., p. 190.

20 'The Revolutionist's Handbook', in *Man and Superman*, p. 264.

21 For example, A. M. Gibbs, op. cit.

22 'Wells, Hitler and the World State', *Collected Essays and Journalism*, Vol. II, p. 139.

23 *The Discovery of the Future* (London: Fisher Unwin, 1902) p. 24.

24 R. M. Philmus and D. H. Hughes, *Early Writings by H. G. Wells* (London: University of California Press, 1975) p. 218.

25 H. G. Wells, *Boon* (London: Fisher Unwin, 1915) p. 152.

26 Quoted in N. Nicholson, *H. G. Wells* (London: Arthur Brooker, 1950) p. 43.

27 Quoted in Philmus and Hughes, op. cit., p. 185.

28 'Human Evolution' in Philmus and Hughes, p. 218.

29 In 1933 Wells set out his ideas in a polemic called *The Open Conspiracy*. He also paid personal visits to both Stalin and Roosevelt to discuss his 'open conspiracy' theories. He claimed, moreover, to have had some influence over President Wilson in the setting up of the League of Nations. His view of how international relations ought to be conducted is clear in his criticism of Grey. 'For him', said Wells, 'a League of Nations was necessarily a League of Foreign Offices.' (*Experiments in Autobiography* (London: Gollancz, 1934) p. 771.)

30 *The Shape Of Things To Come* (London: Corgi Books, 1967) p. 287.

31 Wells had always argued, though, that the central concern of 'the so-called science of sociology' ought to be what he called 'utopography'. (See P. Parrinder, *H. G. Wells* (Edinburgh: Oliver and Boyd, 1970).)

32 'Wells, Hitler and the World State', op. cit.

33 *Eyeless in Gaza*, op. cit., p. 150.

34 Ibid., p. 294, my italics.

35 Lawrence's views are expounded by Rampion in *Point Counter Point*.

36 'Sex versus Loveliness', in *Selected Essays* (Penguin edition, 1976) p. 18.

37 'Democracy', in *Selected Essays*, op. cit., p. 95.

38 George Woodcock, in *Dawn and the Darkest Hour* (London: Faber and Faber, 1972) sets out Huxley's political philosophy as advocating 'not only militant resistance to war, but also a policy of general social reorganisation aimed at replacing the institution of state . . . by a libertarian society in which . . . economics would be decentralist and Henry-Georgian and politics Kropotkinesque and cooperative' (p. 14). All the same, Huxley offered no plan of how to reach this state of affairs!

39 D. H. Lawrence 'The State of Funk', in *Selected Essays*, op. cit., p. 97.

SECTION THREE   VISIONS OF SOCIALISM

1 See Judith Shklar, 'Political Theory of Utopia: From Melancholy to

Nostalgia', *Daedalus*, Vol. 94, Spring 1965, pp. 376–81.

2 See A. L. Morton, *The English Utopia* (London: Lawrence and Wishart, 1952).

3 Chas. Walsh, *From Utopia to Nightmare* (London: Geoffrey Bles, 1952) p. 22.

4 Ibid., p. 20.

5 C. P. Snow, *A Variety of Men* (London: Macmillan, 1967) p. 58.

6 Engels, in *Socialism: Scientific and Utopian* (1892), contrasts Utopianism with scientific socialism to the former's discredit. All the same, it is true to say that most of the authors we have studied provide pictures, some optimistic some not, of societies of the future. This certainly does not make them necessarily 'unscientific' in the sense that we have used the word. Moreover even the 'scientific' socialism of Marx gains much vitality from the belief in a future 'unalienated' society.

7 *'No Masters and no Masters' Men'*

1 See *Art Under Plutocracy*. My italics. It is worth pointing out that Morris's political tracts are available in several collections, for example, in the *Complete Works of William Morris* (Longman Green and Company). A number of the more important tracts have been issued in *Political Writings of William Morris*, edited and with an introduction by A. L. Morton (London: Lawrence and Wishart, 1973). Where I refer to a tract, I have simply given its title.

2 *Art and Socialism.*

3 *Art Under Plutocracy.*

4 *The Lesser Arts*, emphasis in the original.

5 *Art and Socialism.*

6 *Useful Work versus Useless Toil.*

7 *Art and Socialism.*

8 Ibid.

9 'News From Nowhere', in *Three Works by William Morris*, edited by A. L. Morton (London: Lawrence and Wishart, 1973) p. 203.

10 *The Society Of The Future.*

11 *National Review* (London, August 1891).

12 In *Romantic to Revolutionary*, op. cit., E. P. Thompson makes the point that Morris's private life was a failure, whenever he attempted to pass '... from romantic illusion to human intimacy' (p. 187). There is reason to suppose that Morris simply did not understand people!

13 *National Review*, op. cit.

14 See S. J. Ingle, 'Socialist Man: William Morris and Bernard Shaw', in *The Concept of Socialism*, ed. B. Parekh (London: Croom, Helm, 1975) pp. 72–94.

15 Aldous Huxley, *Brave New World* (Penguin edition, 1973) p. 24.

16 It is interesting to compare the dystopian *Brave New World* with the utopian society depicted in *Island*, written nearly forty years later. Much of the technological mastery remains: 'hybridization of micro-cultures' and artificial insemination produce children, for example. Yet clearly the purpose of life for the people of Pala is to increase their knowledge of God and to live more spiritual lives.

17 It is also pertinent to consider whether, in the nature of things, society is capable of meeting the various demands the moralists make of it. Saul Bellow's Mr Sammler asks whether Western civilisation's worst enemies were not those who attacked it 'in the name of proletarian revolution, in the name of reason, in the name of irrationality, in the name of visceral depth, in the name of sex, in the name of perfect instantaneous freedom. For what it amounted to was limitless demand—insatiability, refusal of the doomed creature (death being sure and final) to go away from this earth unsatisfied. A full bill of demand and complaint was therefore presented by each individual. Non-negotiable. Recognising no scarcity of supply in any human department.' (*Mr Sammler's Planet* (Penguin edition, 1976) p. 29.)

18 G. D. H. Cole, in *William Morris as a Socialist* (London: William Morris Society, 1960) wrote: 'I became a socialist more than fifty years ago when I read *News From Nowhere* as a schoolboy and realised quite suddenly that William Morris had shown me the vision of a society in which it could be a fine and fortunate experience to live' (p. 1).

8   The Benefits of 'Regimen'

1   Don Juan, it will be remembered, leaves Hell because of its dedication to the 'tedious, vulgar pursuit of happiness'.

2   H. G. Wells, *A Modern Utopia* (London: W. Collins and Sons, n.d.) p. 5.

3   *New York Times Book Review*, November 1945.

4   'Wells, Hitler and the World State', op. cit.

5   In a letter to Wells written in 1905, Joseph Conrad makes a different judgement. 'No civilised man, in his infinite variety, need, when reading that book, feel "left" for a single moment.' (A. Fleishman, *Conrad's Politics* (Baltimore: Johns Hopkins Press, 1967).)

6   *A Modern Utopia*, p. 58.

7   In 1903 Wells actually made such a tour with the political scientist and Fabian Graham Wallas.

8   J. Baines, *Joseph Conrad* (London: Weidenfeld & Nicholson, 1960) p. 232.

9   Thus Wells was able to solve a problem which West, in *H. G. Wells* (London: Howe, 1930) claims to have been perennial (and deeply personal) for Wells: that of achieving a balanced relationship between human egotism and exceptional ability (p. 116).

10 Orwell's intention, in writing *Nineteen Eighty-Four*, is well taken by Paul O'Flynn, in *Them and Us in Literature* (London: Pluto Press, 1975) when he says: 'Either we build the socialism that Orwell believed in or they build the 1984 that Orwell was afraid of' (p. 20). Some critics have emphasised that much of the material for *Nineteen Eighty-Four* was 'borrowed' from Zamyatin's *We* (1924), Koestler's *Darkness at Noon* (1940) and James Burnham's *Managerial Revolution* (1942); others have stressed the effect Orwell's worsening illness had upon his writing. But O'Flynn is right to point out the importance of *Nineteen Eighty-Four* in Orwell's thinking, irrespective of other influences. George Woodcock in *The Crystal Spirit* (London: Jonathan Cape, 1967) wrote simply: '*Nineteen Eighty-Four*

is the culmination of twenty years of writing . . .'

11   *Nineteen Eighty-Four* (Penguin edition, 1960), pp. 62–3.

12   In 'The Road to 1984' (*Political Science Quarterly*, Vol. 81, No. 4, December 1966), George Kateb dismisses Orwell's definition of power as simply a description of sadism. Deutscher, too, felt that Orwell had succumbed to what he called the mysticism of cruelty.

13   In *The Social Crisis Of Our Time* (London: Hodge, 1950) Röpke also emphasises the importance of family life in preserving the values necessary to sustain democracy. In fact, his analysis of the 'volitional paralysis' which would lead to totalitarianism is similar to Orwell's at many points.

14   Raymond Williams, op. cit., argues otherwise. He believes that Orwell has limited the scope of his novel by showing the nature of Winston's revolt to be chiefly sexual.

15   This theme is more fully developed in S. Hynes (ed.), *Twentieth Century Interpretations of Nineteen Eighty-Four* (Englewood Cliffs: Prentice Hall, 1971).

9   *Conclusion: Socialist Thought in Imaginative Literature*

1   See K. J. W. Alexander and A. Hobbs, 'What Influences Labour MPs?', *New Society*, No. 11, 13 December 1962; a study of my own, the findings of which I discuss above, but which appears in full as 'Socialism and Literature: The Contribution of Imaginative Writers to the Development of the British Labour Party', in *Political Studies*, Vol. XXII, No. 2, June 1974, pp. 158–68. Finally, a follow-up to the Alexander and Hobbs article, with the same title, by J. Hall and J. Higgins which appeared in *New Society* on 2 December 1976. It was followed in the next issue by 'What Influences Tory MPs?', by Hall, Higgins and Rees.

2   Preface to *The Shewing Up of Blanco Posnet*.

3   Preface to *Mrs Warren's Profession*.

4   Orwell went as far as to say: 'I doubt whether anyone who was writing books between 1900 and 1920, at any rate in the English language, influenced the young so much' (*Collected Essays and Journalism*, Vol. 1, p. 164). Some MPs offered the specific example of Shaw's *The Doctor's Dilemma* (1911) as being, in the words of one, 'good spadework for the National Health Service'. Another made a similar point: 'Shaw and Wells, with Dickens, were the catalysts who made possible the welfare state'. Indeed the argument was advanced in more general terms by a number of MPs. 'Shaw and Wells made people think deeply about the whole subject of social class', said one. He went on to explain that writers gave specific form to a vague social awareness among politically uncommitted or weakly committed people. 'All three of these writers made the middle class think!' said another.

5   Many MPs, for example, referred to *Animal Farm* and its leading characters; one wrote: 'How I hated those damned pigs; and when I look around I still see them sitting there in the House of Commons.'

6   'Epistle Dedicatory', in *Man and Superman*, op. cit., pp. xxxiii, iv.

7   *Eyeless in Gaza*, op. cit., p. 293.

8   *The Discovery of the Future*, op. cit., p. 88.

9 L. W. Grey, op. cit., p. 237.
10 *Mr Sammler's Planet*, op. cit., p. 170.

Index

Alienation: Marxist view, 37, 198; Morris's view, 37–40, 136–7; portrayed in *The History of Mr Polly*, 43–4, *Kipps*, 44–5, *Point Counter Point*, 46–7, *Eyeless in Gaza*, 47–8, *Shooting an Elephant*, 49–50, *Keep the Aspidistra Flying*, 51–3, *Coming Up For Air*, 53–4

Art and Socialism, Morris's theories on, 135–7

Bellamy, Edward, 82, 83, 132; *Looking Backward*, 82

Bellow, Saul, *Mr Sammler's Planet*, 194, 205(n17)

Bennett, Arnold, 199(n11); *A Man From The North*, 198(n12)

Bergson, Henri, *L'Évolution Créatrice*, 115

Berki, R. N., contradictions within socialism, 10–11

Blake, William, 115

Bloody Sunday, 7 November 1887, 57, 83, 86, 87

Bunyan, John, 115

Burnham, James, *Managerial Revolution*, 205(n10)

Carlyle, Thomas, 4, 37, 38, 112, 196(n1); influence on Morris, 38

Charques, R. D., *Contemporary Literature and Social Revolution*, 5–6

Chartism, 110

Commitment, political, in literature, 5–9

Conrad, Joseph, 89, 169; *The Secret Agent*, 89–90; *Under Western Eyes*, 89

Conservative Party, the, Wells's analysis of, 69–70

Democracy, 60–1, 70–5, 126; 'totalitarian democracy', 112–13

'Descriptive' criticism of capitalism, 15

Dickens, Charles, 4, 7; *A Tale of Two Cities*, 82

Disraeli, Benjamin, 4, 5, 18, 70; Tory paternalism of, 18

Elites, academic, 141, 143, 145, 164–5; administrative, 144–5; political, 73, 112–14, 116–18, 121–2, 144–5, 169–75, 180, 192–4; technological, 96–8, 118, 162–3, 165–6, 173, 188–9, 194

Fabian Society, the, 56, 68, 109, 118, 159, 186; *Fabian Essay*, 108